## DATE DUE

| | |
|---|---|
| MAR - 1 1996 | |
| NOV - 9 1996 | |
| MAY 0 3 1997 | |
| FEB - 1 2000 | |
| | |
| | |
| | |
| | |
| | |
| | |
| | |
| | |
| | |
| | |
| | |
| | |
| | |
| | |
| | |
| | |

BRODART                                        Cat. No. 23-221

# Affect,
# Object,
# and
# Character
# Structure

# Affect, Object, and Character Structure

Morton Kissen, Ph.D.

International Universities Press, Inc.

Madison Connecticut

Library of Congress Cataloging-in-Publication Data

Kissen, Morton.
    Affect, object, and character structure/Morton Kissen.
      p.  cm.
    Includes bibliographical references and index.
    ISBN 0-8236-0114-5
    1. Personality and emotions. 2. Object relations (Psychoanalysis)
    3. Affect (Psychology) 4. Personality disorders. 5. Character.
    I. Title.
    RC455.4.E46K57 1994
    616.89'17—dc20
                                         94-19933
                                             CIP

Manufactured in the United States of America

To the memory of my mother
CHARLOTTE KISSEN

# CONTENTS

# ACKNOWLEDGMENTS

Many people made this book possible. During the course of my personal analysis with Herbert S. Strean, I became ever more aware of the importance of protective feelings toward internal objects as a central motivational factor underlying my own resistances to change. I have been able to apply this insight repeatedly in my work with patients. I am very grateful to the many patients who have taught me how freeing it can be to discover that they need not waste precious psychic energies on protecting me from their inner wishes and true self-strivings.

I believe that Harold Searles's creative contributions, particularly regarding the constructive use of countertransference feelings and the patient's unconscious striving to protect and heal the analyst, have deeply affected my own thinking and therapeutic work.

I am grateful to the many Derner Institute students who have taken my Object Relations Seminar over the years and helped to clarify my thinking regarding the practical therapeutic implications of the theoretical contributions of Klein, Fairbairn, Winnicott, and the more recent contributions of Ogden and Bollas.

Chapter 11 is a modified version of a paper originally published in *Techniques of Working with Resistance*, edited by D. S. Milman and G. D. Goldman, New York: Jason Aronson (1986), pp. 381–403.

Chapter 13 is a modified version of a paper originally published in *Current Issues in Psychoanalytic Practice* (1985), 2:45–63. New York: Haworth Press.

I wish to express my thanks to the editors and publishers of these two volumes for granting permission to include this material.

I wish to thank Virginia Bruchhauser, Helen Czaplinski, Joanne Arredondo, and Catherine Zayatz who have so patiently and generously provided secretarial assistance for the editorial changes required during the course of work on this book.

Finally, I wish to thank Margaret Emery for providing the skillful editing which helped me integrate my ideas into a coherent book.

# INTRODUCTION

Affects are complex experiential states that, although poorly understood and conceptualized, have central importance for psychoanalytic treatment. The psychoanalytic process, to be effective, must somehow engage the suffering patient at an emotional level. The more cognitive aspects of our analytic work, such as properly timed and formulated interpretations, are summations of affective understandings. They ultimately emanate from empathic, feeling-ful comprehensions of the patient's emotionally based dilemma. To be useful they must resonate affectively within the patient and begin to shake up the complex psychodynamic and structural configurations that are so rigidly and repetitiously enacted both internally and externally in the patient's life.

The lengthiness of contemporary psychoanalytic treatment stems in considerable part from the difficulty in affectively engaging certain pathological structures in the patient which have contributed to a seemingly endless cycle of emotionally unrewarding experiences.

Our contemporary models for conceptualizing human emotion from a psychoanalytic perspective emanate historically from Freud's struggles to conceptualize the affects primarily linked to neurotic psychopathology. Anxiety, guilt, and sadness are the three primary emotional states identified by Freud as intrinsically linked with neurotic suffering. It is not by chance that each has anhedonic characteristics. For Freud, both anxiety and guilt could be delineated as hallmark affects with anxiety, perhaps, attaining primary status in his hierarchical configuration of affects linked to neurotic disturbance. Sadness, on the other hand, although evident in certain pathological mourning and depressive reactions did not seem as significant to Freud. He viewed extended sadness as a derivative of unresolved ambivalence feeling (love and hate) toward the lost and abandoning object. Freud gave some credence to anger as a primary affect, although he needed to link both love and hate metapsychologically to the *drives* of sexuality and aggression.

Positive affects (joy, exhilaration, excitement, buoyant hopefulness, etc.) had very little place in Freud's conceptualizations with regard to the affective roots and concomitants of neurotic psychopathology. His drive theory tended to delineate most affects as complex drive derivatives, except for the hallmark affects of anxiety and guilt. Indeed, guilt could ultimately be derived from anxiety, and hence had a somewhat secondary character in Freud's conceptualizations.

From a contemporary psychoanalytic perspective, we must view Freud's contributions to affect theory as somewhat limited and limiting of a further conceptual expansion of our understanding of emotions underlying neurotic, and particularly the more severe forms of characterological pathology. Most therapists assume that Freud's early discharge view of affects, updated by his final signal theory of anxiety, provides a solid but insufficient anchoring point for a contemporary approach to understanding affects as ontogenetically and phylogenetically early forms of communication.

As the human organism matures developmentally, a complex and quite differentiated array of affects, having relatively articulated signaling attributes, is available for both intrapsychic comprehension and interpersonal communication. The broader and more articulated the range of differentiated affects available, the more effectively and autonomously is the individual able to cope with internal and external pressures.

The breadth of affective experience and communicative capacity can be at least partially comprehended via a list of phenomenologically distinct affective states. Such a list, although predominantly consisting of affects with negative hedonic tone (i.e., sadness, grief, shame, humiliation, anger, anxiety, etc.), also contains phenomenologically distinct affects possessing positive hedonic tone (i.e., happiness, exhilaration, satisfaction, joy, etc.). Each affect, from a contemporary perspective, contains a complete unit of information about the human organism's psychosomatic state of well-being. The capacity to articulate these informative values for self and others is one possibly primary indicator of the state of emotional health of the individual. The inability to establish a broad range of affective communication and experience consisting of both positively and negatively toned emotional states is, therefore, an important indicator of psychopathology.

Many of our conceptualizations about emotion have an "affect phobic" character which tends to be translated into our psychoanalytic treatment models making them inefficient and less effective than they might be. The best that most psychoanalytic therapists feel they can hope for is some greater degree of "affect tolerance" in their patients. This stems, in part, from Freud's view of anxiety as the hallmark affect. There is a need for greater emphasis upon anxiety as merely one affect among a broadly differentiated range of affects, any of which may become associated with feelings of panic or "affect storm."

Thus, any feeling state (whether it possesses a positive or negative tone) can be felt as toxic and needing to be avoided. The bulk of our affect-phobic theoretical positions explore, as Freud did, difficulties with negatively toned affects. There is a tremendous need for theoretical study of difficulties with the comprehension, signal processing, and integration of positively toned affects. The bulk of this volume will explore the issue of integrative and communicative difficulties with positive affects from a contemporary object relational and characterological perspective.

Object relations theory has been very helpful both conceptually and clinically in providing models for therapeutic work with the more difficult, characterologically impaired patient. A solid contemporary theory about the role of affect in psychopathology must, of necessity, incorporate an understanding of the object relational components underlying the particular psychopathological reactions being studied. Indeed, just as any object relational configuration has an affective component, every affective state has an object relational component. The more complex and sophisticated the affective state, the more complex are the object relational structures underlying it.

Character structures, too, from a contemporary perspective, can be analyzed in terms of the underlying affective and object relational units underlying them. A great deal of character analysis during treatment involves the exploration of these complex affect and object relational configurations. It will be argued in this volume that a considerable amount of characterological psychopathology can be illuminated, when viewed from an affective and object relational vantage point.

Difficulties with the informational processing and expressive communication of affects (both positively and negatively toned) abound in character disorders. Indeed, the predominance of difficulties in integrating hedonically toned affects in a positive fashion can be noted in more severe forms of characterological disturbance. Clinical examples abound of patients with severe character pathology who are unable to utilize positively toned affects for self-soothing, maturational, or actualizing purposes. Indeed, it may very well be the maturational potential of such affects that makes them difficult to confront in these patients. Similar difficulties with positive affects can be seen in patients across the diagnostic spectrum.

The focus of this volume, thus, will be upon affective and object relational configurations as they interface with character structure. The capacity for signal usage of negative and positive affects will be intrinsically linked to object relational and characterological structures. The relatively unexplored terrain of functional impairments in the processing of positively toned affects will be conceptually elaborated and clinically studied from an object relational and characterological perspective.

The first chapter will present a historical and conceptual framework for the functional analysis of affects, particularly positive affects, as core components in the assessment of character pathology from a maturational and object relational perspective. A treatment model focusing upon the incapacity to effectively utilize positive affects as bits of information or self signals will subsequently be outlined and clinically developed throughout the rest of the volume.

Chapters 2 through 6 present various aspects of the neglected positive affects and affective attitudes that are essential to a contemporary object relations approach to the treatment of character pathology. Chapter 2 focuses upon the absorption with unpleasant affects underlying masochistic phenomena. Chapters 3 and 4 conceptually and clinically explore the relevance of dissociated exhilarated affects and competency feelings for psychoanalytic treatment. Chapter 5 focuses upon the difficulties with positive affects, often camouflaged by various manifestations of the Oedipus complex. Chapter 6 explores the central affective attitude of courage and its implications for treatment.

Chapters 7 through 10 provide an object relations conceptual foundation for the present volume. Chapter 7 suggests that the therapist's containing task with regard to the self and object representations produced through projective identificatory interactions with patients is not a very abstract one. The therapeutically tangible and pragmatic aspects of projective identification and object usage are outlined in that chapter.

Intensive psychotherapy is anxiety provoking from both transferential and countertransferential perspectives, due to the unearthing of deeply dissociated wishes to relinquish loyally maintained and protected object attachments. Chapter 8 and 9 explore the centrality of loyally enshrined and protected object relationships in the psychoanalytic approach to diminishing treatment-destructive resistances. The wish to prematurely terminate a productive psychotherapy, in particular, is viewed from this object relational perspective. The negative oedipal conflict, a relatively neglected aspect of the complete Oedipus configuration, is explored from an object relations perspective in chapter 10. It is hypothesized that the transitional object hunger and object usage aspects of a patient's life experience offer a useful means for assessing and psychoanalytically ameliorating their negative oedipal conflicts.

Chapters 11 through 14 involve an application of the theoretical and object relational affect conceptions explored in the first two sections to treatment difficulties posed by patients manifesting characterological forms of psychopathology. Chapter 11 explores the reluctance to experience positive affects as a major resistance to the therapeutic process presented by patients manifesting character disorders. Chapter 12 explores the resistance to change manifested by character disordered patients as forms of nostalgic memorial attachment to early objects. Chapter 13 focuses upon the characterological aspects of depression and modes of resolving such tendencies from a psychoanalytic perspective. Finally, chapter 14 deals with projective identification and proxy evocation as primary mechanisms underlying the meshing character structures often noted in couples.

The primary focus of the present volume is, thus, on the essential connections between affects, internalized object and self representations, and character organization in contemporary psychoanalytic treatment.

# Part I

# Affect

# Chapter 1

# THE CENTRALITY OF AFFECTS IN CONTEMPORARY PSYCHOANALYSIS

Affects are an essential ingredient of all human actions, and thus are essential factors in the changes that are initiated during psychoanalytic treatment. Many therapists who have studied the nature of affect in the psychoanalytic situation (Novey, 1958; Dorpat, 1977; Emde, 1983) emphasize the fact that affect, conation, and cognition are all intricately interwoven in human action. Once the total functioning personality becomes our object of study, the traditional, and rather arbitrary, separation of these processes in academic psychology cannot be justified.

Gedo makes a similar point and concludes: "As I have stated before, I prefer a view of psychic functioning that makes no distinctions between thought, affectivity and volition. Hence, I stress the self-organization as a hierarchy of aims, i.e., potentials for action that implicitly include cognitive and affective aspects" (1979, p. 252).

During the course of effective psychoanalytic treatment, the patient rediscovers aims and potentials for action that had been previously dissociated and felt to be unavailable. Schafer's approach to the clinical analysis of affects during psychoanalytic treatment (1964) emphasizes that properly empathic analytic interventions may lead to the nurturing and ownership of subtle, complex affects and action potentialities that might otherwise be defensively warded off or avoided. The patient's capacity for empathic relatedness to a broader range of affects and action tendencies in herself and others is a natural byproduct of successful psychoanalytic treatment. Schafer's theoretical and clinical contributions to the evolution of an action language approach to

3

therapeutic intervention (1976) stems from the assumption that complex composites of thought, affect, and motivated action in the patient can be most effectively approached via interpretive metalanguage stressing the ownership of feelings, impulses, and dissociated action potential. In a sense, a similar broadening of the range of differentiated affect alluded to by Pine (1979) as a goal of psychoanalytic treatment is often associated with an expansion of the patient's courageous potential.

Obviously, affect is an essential ingredient in psychoanalytic treatment. The therapeutic action of psychoanalysis is often directed toward goals of enhanced expressive freedom and affective spontaneity, a broadening of the range of affects available for both introspection and empathic communication with others, and affect maturation along lines of developmental differentiation and synthesis. It is important, therefore, to review the history of psychoanalytic conceptions with regard to affect from the earliest Freudian view of affects as tension release and discharge valves, to the later view of them as "signals," and finally, to the more contemporary object relations conceptions of affect as an integral component of self and object representational configurations. During the course of this review, the historical neglect of positively toned affects will be noted and counterbalanced by a focus upon the implications of positive affects for theory and clinical practice.

A contemporary functional analysis of affects will next be provided. It will go beyond the signal affect model and offer applications to clinical observations and therapeutic issues with both negative and positively toned affects. A conceptual model will be elaborated which includes functional developmental continua for assessing a broad range of affects from an object relational and characterological perspective. Such a model has broad applicability to contemporary psychoanalytic treatment, in that it will allow for a study of the relatively unexplored terrain involving impairments in the processing of positively toned affects.

## TRANSITIONAL SHIFTS IN FREUD'S CONCEPTIONS OF AFFECT

Affect played a very central role in Freud's earliest formulations (1894, 1895, 1896). At this point in his thinking, he viewed affect as a quality of psychic energy which had become dammed up in various psychoneurotic disorders, and ultimately, was discharged through therapeutic cathartic experiences. The notion of affects as dammed up quantities of libidinal energy was associated with a further assumption with regard to their "toxicity." Anxiety was seen as the primary affect emanating from the heavy reliance upon repressive maneuvers to cope with internal libidinal energy states felt to be toxic.

This earliest conception of affect, although emphasizing its centrality, did not offer a very differentiated view of its qualitative character. Affects were vaguely delineated as experiential states of a tense, anxious, and unpleasant nature which could somehow be shifted into more pleasurable experiences via cathartic or abreactive means. A basic notion with regard to the nonhedonic character of affects was implicit in Freud's thinking at this juncture. Positive (hedonically pleasant) affects could only emanate from toxic discharge processes of tension release and did not have an independent status of their own. Anxiety, even at this early point in Freud's thinking, had become the cornerstone affect, and as a result, a view of feeling states as something to be avoided was initiated.

Freud's next position with regard to affect occurred with the joint advent of his topographic model and theory of the centrality of instinctual drives. At this next juncture, affects were understood as the nonideational components of mental representations of drive forces (1915a,b,c). His topographic model assumed the hierarchically central status of the system unconscious (Ucs) with its powerful reservoir of drives pressing toward discharge. Affects now were shunted into the secondary status of experiential drive derivatives emanating from the hierarchically secondary systems preconscious (Pcs) and conscious (Cs). Freud's conceptual interests had shifted rather markedly toward a drive theoretical position which he was never to give up, even in his later structural theoretical contributions. Greenberg and Mitchell (1983) have emphasized how central and unbending was this emphasis upon the centrality of drives in Freud's thinking and how much this led to a consequent decentralization and secondary status for affects. Once again, affects were only vaguely delineated. As drives moved topographically from the system Ucs to the systems Pcs and Cs, they were mentally represented in the form of essentially undifferentiated affective states which had an undifferentiated character that was equally hedonic. No sharpness in qualitative differentiation or articulation existed for affects at this point in Freud's theory building.

Thus, with the early advent of Freud's drive metapsychology, affect was relegated to a theoretically secondary position. Greenberg and Mitchell conclude with regard to this aspect of Freud's theorizing about affect: "The emergence of affect was seen as evidence that repression was at least partially failing, and the qualitative coloring that the discharged quantity took on was considered relatively serendipitous, and in any case inconsequential from the dynamic point of view" (1983, p. 64). Whereas Freud's earliest model offered some slight degree of differentiation of the specific qualities of affects, this second conception of affects as drive derivatives led to a virtual disregard of the specific quality of affects, except those reflecting certain aspects of the repressed instinctual impulse. Affects had almost no independent status whatsoever at this juncture in Freud's thinking.

Freud's final position with regard to affect (1926) hinged upon the cornerstone affect of anxiety, which he now viewed as being linked with an important "signal" capability of the relatively strengthened ego structures. This strengthening was a result of the evolution of a structural model (1923) which replaced the earlier topographic conception. The ego was seen as possessing some defensive and adaptive facilities and a limited degree of autonomy in struggling with preemptive drive pressures and tensions. The ego was credited with the ability to use anxiety as a signal in dangerous situations perceived as threatening abandonment or castration for fantasized actions of a drive motivated nature. Whereas in Freud's earliest model of affect it was conceived of as a byproduct of defense, this later conception viewed the anxiety affect as a "signal" in response to perceived danger situations which could evoke a variety of ego defenses. Anna Freud (1936) and the later ego psychologists (Rapaport, 1953b, 1967; Hartmann, 1964) developed a broad metapsychological base for Freud's structural model and its implications for a relatively autonomous ego possessing numerous tools and defensive, adaptive, and synthetic functions. Rapaport, in particular, explored the implications of Freud's last affect model for the conception of a relatively autonomous and active ego.

Schafer's (1976) later conceptions with regard to the importance of an action language antidote to the largely passive theoretical language implicit in Freud's drive metapsychology, owes much to Rapaport's earlier conceptual articulation of this issue. Affects could no longer be viewed as passive and undifferentiated derivatives of the drives but now were viewed as important signals for action. The stage was set for a more modern conception of affects as informative signals which enhance the individual's capabilities in terms of self-expression and social communication.

Numerous conceptual and clinical insights have evolved from Freud's signal anxiety theory. Schur (1953, 1969) generalized the theory to a variety of negative affects. Engel (1962), Dorpat (1977), and Schmale (1964) focused their theorizing upon affects such as depression, hopelessness, and helplessness as communicative signals, both inwardly for the self and outwardly for the social environment. The bulk of the contributions in the affect theory literature emanating from this rather generative conceptualization, have focused upon negatively toned affects. Only Krystal (1974, 1982b, 1988) and Isaacs (1980, 1981b, 1982b, 1983, 1984a,b, 1985, 1988, 1990) have considered the signal communicative model of affects in the context of hedonically toned affects such as joy, exhilaration, or loving feelings.

It is not surprising that what Isaacs (1990) calls an "affect phobic" theoretical bias has predominated in the literature. There was a focus upon the toxic and painful aspects of affects throughout Freud's contributions on this issue and those of theorists who have based their contributions upon

Freud's later signal model. Affects are subtly or not so subtly viewed as something to be discharged, catharted, avoided, or at best, tolerated. Although seen as a powerful signal for action or passive reactivity, they are seldom depicted in theoretical terms as having more positive informative attributes. Since the mid-1970s, psychoanalytically oriented developmental researchers (Basch, 1976; Emde, 1983; Stern, 1985) have evolved a much more sophisticated view of affects from earliest infancy on as extremely important communicative signals to the outer environment, requiring delicately attuned reactions on the parents' part. Affects are seen as exercising a guiding function on later cognitive development and as providing the motive power for both successful maturation and pathologic adaptation.

The more positive socially and maturationally guiding features of affects are clearly not central to Freud's final signal conception. A differentiated range of emotion, including more positively toned and motivationally enhancing affects, is nowhere to be found at this early stage of psychoanalytic theorizing. Indeed, the conception of affects as central communicative aspects of the inner representational world, as well as a more phenomenological and object relational perspective, would need to be introduced before any expansion and differentiation of the range of affects explored from a psychoanalytic perspective could occur.

## AFFECTS AS COMPONENTS OF THE INNER
## REPRESENTATIONAL WORLD

A solidly phenomenological perspective for the psychoanalytic study of affects was surprisingly lacking in Freud's theorizing. The earliest Freudian models and their theoretical offshoots tended to focus upon the more passive and reactive implications of a narrow range of almost totally negative affects such as anxiety, depression, helplessness, shame, and guilt. Freud's conceptions of affects were not inductively inferred on an experiential basis but rather involved hypothetical constructs deduced from the basic assumptions of drive theory. His final structural model (1923) led to a conception of affects as intrasystemic ego processes, very sensitive to intersystemic conflicts of a psychodynamic nature, between divergent pressures stemming from the id, ego, and superego. Ultimately the affects of anxiety, shame, and guilt were seen as predominantly involved in neurotic suffering and symptomatology.

The limitations of Freud's final affect theory stem from his discomfort with object relational constructs and a general lack of phenomenological and experiential focus. The narrow band of largely negative affects that he studied almost certainly stemmed from his clinging to drive theory, even as he tentatively explored more phenomenological and object relational constructs.

Greenberg and Mitchell (1983) have summarized their comprehensive review of Freud's need to "accommodate" object relational constructs involving internalization processes to more familiar drive theoretical terminology:

> There have been two major strategies for dealing with the problem of object relations. The first, employed originally by Freud, has been essentially preservative and consists of stretching and adapting his original conceptual model based on drive to accommodate later clinical emphases on object relations. Within Freud's drive theory all facets of personality and psychopathology are understood essentially as functions, or derivatives, of drive and their transformations. Thus, to solve the problem of object relations while preserving drive theory intact requires the derivation of relations with others (and of the individual's inner representations of those relations) as vicissitudes of the drives themselves. Freud and subsequent theorists employing this first strategy understand the role of objects largely in relation to the discharge of drive: they may inhibit discharge, facilitate it, or serve as its target [p. 3].

Greenberg and Mitchell proceed to differentiate object relation theorists who have offered truly divergent object relational alternatives to drive theory (Fairbairn, Winnicott, and Guntrip) from those who have articulated a construct with regard to an inner self and object representational world in the context of continuing efforts to preserve Freud's drive theoretical paradigms (Jacobson, Kernberg, and Sandler). The positions of the latter three theorists will next be briefly reviewed, particularly in terms of the object relational constructs they have articulated as being relevant to a more phenomenological conception of affects. Despite the strong allegiance of these theorists to drive theory, each of them has articulated phenomenologically based conceptions which contribute to a broadening of the differentiated range of affects that are central experiential aspects of the inner representational world. Ultimately, by struggling with the essentially phenomenological nature of affects and by articulating their intrinsically self and object representational character, they move us closer to a functional and developmental schema for analyzing affects.

### EDITH JACOBSON

In two important contributions (1953, 1971), Jacobson, although maintaining many of Freud's conceptions of drive theory, moved toward a more phenomenological, object relational, and flexible psychoanalytic theory of affect.

She suggested an interesting classification in which certain affects were seen as arising from intrasystemic tensions and some from intersystemic tensions. She understood affects such as object love, fear, and hate as arising from the ego, while affects such as sexual passion and rage arose more directly from the id. Subtler affects such as shame and disgust could be seen as emerging from tensions between the ego and the id, and guilt and aspects of depression from tensions between the ego and superego. Jacobson was quick to note the tentativeness of this classificatory scheme and the fact that there are subtler and more complex affects for which her schema cannot account such as "kindness and heartlessness, sympathy and cruelty, loving and hostility, sadness, grief and happiness, depression and elation" (1953, p. 47). This more complex list of affects, which Schafer (1964) has referred to as *compound affects*, are phenomenologically evident both in everyday life and in psychoanalytic treatment. They are some of the higher level affects that are central aspects of the experiential connectedness of the object world. Each affect has subtle attributes (pleasant vs. unpleasant), and hence is either positively or negatively valued within the experiential self and object representational world. Each of these affects, although portrayed in states of dialectical tension, involves an attitude of the self toward some representational aspect of the object world.

Although Jacobson struggled to explain these affects by drive theoretical constructs such as the pleasure and constancy principles, it was also evident that she was exploring new experiential terrain much more relevant to the phenomenological constructs of an object relations theoretical approach. What is most important about her contributions is the fact that she stretched the phenomenological range of affects beyond the toxic and largely negative affects (anxiety and guilt) seen as primary in Freud's final conceptualization of signal affect.

Jacobson (1971) applied her theoretical approach, which involved a meld of drive theory and newer object relational constructs, to the pathological continuum of depressive disorders . The range went from milder forms of neurotic depression, to more characterologically based severe depressions, to the most severe psychotic forms of depression. She explored the subtle intra- and intersystemic tensions involving id, ego, and superego, and specifically, articulated a conception of the central role of the superego in affect control. Jacobson noted that certain pathological structures within the ego and superego (largely related to self and object representations) may bring about severe distortions in the guiding mechanisms by which the superego regulates pleasurable and unpleasurable experiences. She further noted that in severe forms of characterological or psychotic depression the pleasure principle might seem to have been entirely forsaken, allowing for a highly aggressivized inner experiential world replete with sadomasochistic self and object representational interactions of a pervasive and seemingly intractable nature.

The complex interrelatedness of object relational, structural, and psychodynamic levels of inference in Jacobson's conception makes it one of the more clinically relevant contributions to the study of affective disturbance.

## OTTO KERNBERG

Kernberg extended many of the insights contained in Jacobson's rather comprehensive theoretical system to a further elucidation of the developmental sequence by which affects and object representations change in the course of maturation within the context of the inner representational world. Like Jacobson, he values both drive metapsychology (libido and aggressive drives are central to his object relational model), and the more phenomenological constructs of an inner experiential and representational world.

Kernberg chose the borderline patient as the major nosological entity for purposes of object relational theory building. His developmental contributions therefore span the first three years of life (as do those of Mahler), in which there is a progression from a state of infantile autism, to a higher level state of symbiosis, to a still higher state of separation-individuation, culminating in a state of self and object constancy. Much of this developmental progression of object relational capabilities precedes the structural conflicts typical of the later oedipal period.

Perhaps one of Kernberg's primary contributions to the interface of affect and object relations theory is his construct with regard to the ultimate object relational unit of study. He says: "Discrete units of self representation, object representation and an affect disposition linking them are the basic substructures, of these early developmental stages, and will gradually evolve into more complex substructures (such as real self and ideal-self and real-object and ideal-object representations)" (1980a, p. 17). Ultimately, Kernberg considers these affectively linked units of self and object representation to be the building blocks on which further developments of internalized object and self representations, and later on, the overall tripartite structure (ego, superego and id) rest.

For Kernberg, feelings are much more than drive derivatives. He notes:

> Feelings are more than discharge states: they represent drive investments in self and object representations as well as external objects. They constitute an obvious enrichment of mental life and should not be viewed merely as excessive or insufficient tension to be regulated. Self-esteem for example—a crucial and complex libidinal affect investment

of the self cannot be considered simply a drive-determined, affective discharge process [1980a, p. 88].

Here we note that Kernberg, like Jacobson, is struggling to expand the range of felt affects to those sophisticated, rather subtly complex feeling states, evident in mature individuals. A comprehensive theory of affect must be relevant for the highly differentiated range of positively and negatively toned affects phenomenologically discernible in adaptive and well-functioning adults. Of course, an object relations based affect theory must also be applicable to the prerepresentational affect states evident in infants and primitively organized individuals, such as those manifesting borderline personality organization.

Kernberg has much to say about the affect linked object representational units that are typical of more primitively organized borderline patients. One of his primary conceptions involves the splitting mechanisms often seen in such patients in which positively toned affective units (consisting of self and object representations) are split off from negatively toned units. He derived from these conceptions a rather useful diagnostic schema and continuum of character pathology ranging from the high-functioning neurotic characters, to the intermediate infantile and narcissistic characters, to the lowest functioning borderline personalities (1975b). He has also derived strategies and techniques involving interpretations of the primitive defensive maneuvers utilized by borderline patients (i.e., splitting, devaluation, idealization, projective identification, and denial) for effectively treating them from an object relational perspective.

Indeed, Kernberg's work contributes greatly to our capacity to therapeutically permeate a primary interface between affects and associated object relational characterological structures of a primitively organized and pathological nature. By focusing upon the mechanism of splitting, he has alerted us to the centrality of affective qualities of a pleasurable and unpleasurable nature, particularly at early and more primitive phases of psychological differentiation and development. The strongly masochistic features underlying a variety of characterological disorders and associated resistances to treatment may stem, at least partially, from a pathological splitting off of object and self representations and their associated pleasurable affective qualities. The issues of masochistic character structure, so predominantly evident during treatment, will be explored from a broadened affect theoretical perspective in chapters 2, 11, 12, and 13.

Like Jacobson, Kernberg melds object relations, structural, and drive metapsychological constructs in his study of the pathological mood states frequently evident in more primitively organized patients. Defining moods as general affective colorings of the entire experience of the self and the world of objects, he notes that they can severely distort all psychic experience. He seems comfortable with Jacobson's notions that aggressive drive derivatives and pathologically exaggerated superego structures are predominantly evident in the violent mood swings of primitively organized patients. He adds to Jacobson's notion that the superego has primary responsibility for affect and mood swing control, the fact that the superego structure itself is a composite of affect-linked self and object representational units. Under the pathological circumstances of primitive personality organization, the superego consists of highly aggressivized and sadistic object representational configurations of a pathological nature. Given the splitting mechanisms which predominate, there is an oscillation between aggressively devalued and libidinally idealized self and object representations.

Both Jacobson and Kernberg have evolved a concept of affects which focus upon their fundamental intrapsychic regulatory functions via their investments in self and object representations. Since both are loyalists with regard to drive theory, they maintain an emphasis upon the oscillations between highly libidinized and aggressivized representations. Other object relations theorists (i.e., Fairbairn and Winnicott), not quite as theoretically loyal to drive metapsychology, have evolved a conception of pathological mood states freer of drive speculations. Bollas (1987, 1989) has recently conceptualized mood states as forms of the "unthought known." He envisions these affective states, which often cannot be verbally articulated for the self or others, as subtle exemplars of internalized object relationships. Thus, an analyst's momentary, inexplicable sense of melancholy in response to an emotionally demanding but seemingly happy patient, may involve a reconnection with a preoedipal experience of the analyst with her mother struggling with her own sadness while performing nurturing duties. The analyst, sensing some unspoken demand for nurturance from the patient, gets affectively in touch with an unconscious memory of her own preoedipal mother's affective state while responding to the analysand's needs for nurturance. Bollas's conception of mood states can be effectively applied to both countertransferential and transferential experience during the course of psychotherapy.

With or without drive metapsychological speculations, a powerful conceptual paradigm for exploring affective states from an object relational perspective as internal representational states has been provided by the contributions of Jacobson and Kernberg. The notion of affects as linkages between self and object representations is a very powerful one, with generative potential for elucidating issues with regard to the etiology, diagnosis, and treatment of various psychopathological configurations.

JOSEPH SANDLER

Sandler's emphases has been upon the operationalizing of numerous structural concepts within psychoanalytic theory. His psychoanalytic index study group at the Hampstead Clinic has struggled with making more consistent, logical, and clinically useful a variety of structural constructs involving the superego and inner representational world (1987a). The representational world for Sandler is a kind of ego structure that evolves during developmental differentiation. It allows the child relatively stable ways of representing her experience to herself. Greenberg and Mitchell discuss Sandler's concepts about the representational world as:

> [O]rganized compilations of past experiences, relatively enduring impressions, constellations of perceptions and images, which the child culls from his various experiences and which, in turn, provide for the child a kind of cognitive map, a subjective landscape within which he can locate and evoke the cast of characters and events within the drama of his experience. . . . The child develops, Sandler argues, all sorts of representations, including representations of himself in various respects, his body, and his experience of drive pressure and affects [1983, p. 373].

Like McDougall who spoke of "theaters" of the mind (1982) and body (1984, 1989), Sandler depicts the inner representational world through the metaphor of a theatrical stage production in which various fantasies, feelings, wishes, drive states, bodily, self, and object representations are intermittently center stage and under the focus of the spotlight of conscious awareness. The notion of affects as components of an inner experiential and object relational drama is very useful and contributes to a broadening of the range of affects which are of psychoanalytic interest. Depending upon the focus of the spotlight, a given affect may be experienced vaguely or clearly. Affects can be informative with regard to other aspects of the inner stage production and drama (i.e., self representations, fantasies, needs, wishes, etc.), but the spotlight of consciousness must pause on them long enough for such communicative signals and information to be processed.

Isaacs has recently emphasized the potential clarity and precision of affective awareness, in the following way:

> If we are not affect blind, we have feeling awareness. We know very clearly what each emotion is. We know quite distinctly and precisely and without confusion that we are frightened, angry, ashamed, sad, surprised, lonely, joyful, guilty, hopeful, irritated, annoyed, furious,

enraged, apprehensive, remorseful, anxious, thrilled, lonesome, eager, grieving, vengeful, awed, disgusted, bitter, trustful, compassionate, despairing, delighted, suspicious, resentful, indignant, indifferent, regretful, loathing, fond, displeased, satisfied, calm, sorry, overwhelmed, ecstatic, uneasy, admiring, zestful, playful, gleeful, etc. [1985, pp. 4–5].

Such a differentiated range of feeling states, admittedly, is only a partial sampling of the affects available to conscious awareness. Nevertheless, Sandler's construct of an inner representational stage setting offers a useful metaphor for the capacity of the ego to allow for a shifting focus and scanning across a complex and broad range of differentiated affects.

Sandler argues (1976, 1987a) that the drives are not as central as more interpersonally relevant "wishes" in the stabilizing and structuralizing of the inner representational world. Thus, according to Sandler, the wishes for comfort, acceptance, and love are far more powerful than the drives as incentives for both psychopathology and ultimately for characterological shifts of a maturational nature during analytic treatment.

Using Sandler's metaphor together with Isaacs' fairly comprehensive list of affects, it can be inferred that a primary goal of psychoanalytic treatment is the expansion of the broadly differentiated range of affects that can be informatively represented on the inner stage of a patient's experience. The capacity to feel a broad range of affects and to process them as useful bits of information, rather than to merely "tolerate" or divert them defensively, is one major characteristic of emotional maturity. Pine (1979), Isaacs (1990), and Krystal (1988) have stressed the importance for personality development and mental health of the capacity to process the signal and informative characteristics of a broad range of affects. Many patients, particularly those prone to phobic or panic disorders, have a very restricted and limited inner representational capacity for emotional processing.

Thus, affects may now be viewed as significant bits of information and signals with regard to important experiential aspects of the inner world. They contain useful information with regard to the inner representational theaters of body and mind. They link the inner self and object world through essentially coherent and useful signals and bits of information with regard to valued needs, wishes, fantasies, self, object, and body representations. The "affect phobic" attitudes alluded to by Isaacs (1990) often involve a pathological dread of an "affect storm" and a consequent incapacity to allow for the continuity and "potentiation" of the affective signals. In many forms of psychopathology, particularly of a severe characterological nature, there is a great degree of intolerance for affects (both positive and negative) and consequently a severe restriction of the affective content of the inner representational world.

## THE FUNCTIONAL ANALYSIS OF AFFECTS

The complexity of affect can, at least partially, be captured by delimiting a number of its primary functions. In a rather lucid and comprehensive summary, Alexander and Isaacs (1964) list the various functions of affect. First they offer an interesting operational definition of affects via the following statement:

> Thus, all affects are related to the ego, but to regard affects only as ego functions is an inadequate view. More properly it appears to us, affects are ego experiences which, while making functional demands upon the ego, are also tamed by the ego to perform the warning function, and further to exert a motor pressure or motivation toward action appropriate to the situation [p. 232].

They proceed to note that the ego's increasing mastery and synthetic capacities with regard to affect renders it less prone to be overwhelmed by "affect storms" associated with such reactions as impulsiveness, regression, loss of poise, panic, or fainting.

They go on to list and describe the various functions of affect:

### Signal Function

Although Freud concluded that affects had signal character (1926), he restricted his exploration to the affect of anxiety. Alexander and Isaacs (1964) emphasize that affects such as shame and guilt also have important signal functions, and indeed, conclude: "Possibly all affects perform such a warning or signal service to the ego" (p. 232). This is an important early statement of the informational viewpoint with regard to affects, later more comprehensively delineated by Krystal (1988). Pathological reactions such as panic disorders and severe depression, therefore, may be viewed as aberrations of the proper psychological functions of affects such as anxiety and guilt. The normal ego informative function of the affect has been shunted into an emotional disturbance via a stormlike affective aberration. The assumption here is that a continuum exists of ego mastery over or subjugation by affects, which is correlated with a continuum of disturbed emotional functioning. The greater the disturbance, the more subjugation by affects is evident, and hence less mastery over them.

*Motivational Function*

Affects, according to Alexander and Isaacs, contribute importantly to the preparedness for action. "Persons ready to laugh, cry, flee, fight, etc., are ready for such activity by virtue of another function of affect, namely the effect affect has upon the premotor cortex and diencephalon" (1964, p. 233). There is a heroic and courageous potential for action implicit in this psychobiological connection. The brave individual is comfortably in touch with the informative aspects of affects and can easily and effortlessly translate the affect signals into decisive and courageous action. The motivational function of affects can be depicted along a continuum from the enhancement of organized effective coping strategies for action, to the creation of states of panic, disorganization, or regressive incapacity to take action.

*Integrative Function*

Affects can have a "potentiating" effect upon the ego and its functions. Hope, in particular, is a positive affect having a deeply facilitative effect upon the synthetic functions of the ego. Courage, viewed as affect, also has such a potentiating effect. Joy and exhilaration are other examples of affects having a positive impact upon both ego synthetic functions and self experience.

*Defensive Function*

The ego frequently utilizes an affect or cluster of affects (i.e., elation) as a defense against other more painful affects (i.e., depression). Sadness or mourning need not create depression if the ego can accept a loss and endure its sadness. Mourning need not create melancholia, if excessive unconscious ambivalence does not cloud the picture, as in Freud's conceptualizations on this topic (1917). What Alexander and Isaacs do not note is the fact that negative affects can often be utilized to defend against positive affects.

*Tension Reduction*

As Jacobson (1953, 1971) has noted, the pleasure–pain mechanism and tension discharge function of affects needs to be updated by the voluminous clinical and research findings indicating the importance for the ego and its competence strivings, of tension maintenance, and even tension increase. Why else ride the roller-coaster, perform the frightening action, or challenge the ego and self to some courageous forms of action (i.e., climb the mountain because it is there)? The fearful patient may very well have lost touch with the higher level sense of counterphobic bravado (which can be pathological, when taken to too extreme a point), which would facilitate the tension incremental and potentiation functions of her affects.

## The Function of Self Relation

Certain benign affects of a self-relational and potentiating nature are the result of fortunate object relation experiences during infancy and early childhood. The "good enough" parenting alluded to by Winnicott (1956) may very well facilitate the capacity for affects associated with a solid sense of self-esteem. The capacity for affects of a joyous, hopeful, and courageously self-soothing nature, as well as a relative freedom from guilt and self-doubt, are clearly related to benign early object relational encounters, above and beyond psychobiological endowment, ego autonomous characteristics, and adaptive potential.

Capacities for seriousness, dignity, poise, self-confidence, intimate loving, and commitment are all associated with maturationally high-level affects which seem related to Winnicott's formulation with regard to "true self" experience (1960).

## Reality Testing Function

In therapy, we see over and over again the fact that affects make transferential interpretations and interventions more real and effectively connect with the patient. There is a feeling of reality permeating affective experience which helps the disaffected and alienated patient to connect more fully with the therapist and make significant maturational changes in her life.

## Memory, Recall, and Communication

These are the final affect functions alluded to by Alexander and Isaacs (1964). Emde (1983) has surveyed the infant research highlighting the communicative functions of affects. He has, in the process, noted the centrality of affect to the prerepresentational aspects of self-experience. Infants are quite capable of utilizing affective expression in order to signal need states to parental caretakers. They are also capable of sensing a lack of attunement to these affective expressions of prerepresentational self-expectancies.

Certainly, memory and recall can be enhanced via affect. A purely genetic psychoanalytic model bypasses this important function of affect, in that it focuses too heavily upon cognitive memory retrieval and insufficiently upon the capacity of affects to facilitate meaningful and therapeutically powerful memory retrieval. Powerful self-potentiating actions, both in the therapeutic relationship and in significant engagements in everyday life, can occur as a result of affective experiences.

An intersubjective and self-theoretical model has recently been articulated which relates very much to the premises with regard to affect differentiation and maturity being proposed in this volume. This model also has relevance for the functional developmental conception of affects to be elaborated in the final section of this chapter.

FEATURES OF AFFECTIVE DEVELOPMENT CENTRAL TO
THE STRUCTURALIZATION OF SELF-EXPERIENCE

Stolorow, Brandchaft, and Atwood (1987) have evolved a clinical and theoretical approach to the intersubjective features of the psychoanalytic treatment process. This very functional approach to clarifying psychoanalytic theory is a solidly phenomenological distillation of the earlier development by Kohut (1971, 1977) of a model focusing upon empathic failures of attunement as the primary object relational and etiological factors underlying a variety of narcissistic injuries and psychopathology. The roots of the intersubjective model rest upon two earlier works by Stolorow and Atwood (1979) and Atwood and Stolorow (1984), which explore the implications of phenomenological philosophy and theory as a viable alternative to drive metapsychology in psychoanalytic theorizing. *Subjective* experience, both in therapist and patient, replaces the *objective* exploration of drive states, ideational and affective derivatives, and structural conflicts in the shift from a classical metapsychology to an intersubjective therapeutic paradigm.

The evolving structuralization of self-experience occurs, at least partially, via the ultimate internalization of the mother's capacity to soothe which has repeatedly been demonstrated during infancy. Tolpin (1971) explored this important aspect of self-structuralization from a Kohutian and Winnicottian theoretical perspective. She spoke of the capacity for transmuting internalization of the mother's various ministrations in the form of a transitional object as an essential developmental step. Such a developmental structuralization process allows for the beginnings of a cohesive self that can navigate difficult situations replete with signal anxiety via self-soothing capacities. Stolorow, Brandchaft, and Atwood argue that caretakers who have been highly attuned to the child's needs and who have repeatedly soothed the child during moments of powerfully negative affective experience, are an object relational requirement for this self-soothing capability to evolve. Patients whose parents were not attuned to certain painful signal affects (anxiety, depression) during childhood cannot adequately differentiate and experience those affects during adulthood.

According to Stolorow, Brandchaft, and Atwood, the capacity to utilize affects as informational signals has typically been object relationally established during childhood via effective transmuting internalization. This capacity is an essential quality of affect maturity. They emphasize this via the following statement: "Thus, some rudimentary capacity to use affects as self-signals is an important component of the capacity to tolerate disruptive feelings when they emerge. Without this self-signaling capacity, affects tend to herald traumatic states" (1987, p. 72). It should be noted that the capacity to experience a broad range of differentiated affects of both positive and negative hedonic character is implied in this statement, which only refers to negatively toned affects.

Stolorow, Brandchaft, and Atwood go on to delimit four important affective functions which are central to the structuralization of self-experience and the object relational derailments that can occur via inadequate caretaker attunement and empathic response. They will be utilized to further elaborate the central issues of this volume:

*Affect Differentiation*

The capacity for a broad range of both positively and negatively toned affects can be impaired when a child's selfobject cannot offer empathic attunement to particular affective forms of expression that conflict with the parent's own selfobject needs. Although this seems obvious and relevant for negatively toned affects, plentiful clinical examples will be offered throughout this volume of the relevance of this developmental function for positively toned affects as well.

Many children are robbed of the comfort of certain positively toned affects (i.e., joy, exhilaration, courageous self-assertion, spontaneity, and exuberance) by parents who either cannot role model such behavior via their own expressive mannerisms, or who cannot tolerate the child's natural and spontaneous expressive exhibitions of such affects, or both. Certainly, the capacity for the articulation of joyfully expansive self-boundaries is inhibited as a result of such empathic failures.

*Synthesis of Affectively Discrepant Experiences*

The child whose "good" affects meet the selfobject's needs but whose "bad" affects do not, will be required to split off and dissociate affects that do not gratify the parental selfobjects. This can lead to affect fragmentation and a lack of affect synthesis. Thus, many children are expected to express only those affects which the parents associate with the "good child" (i.e., shyness, reserve, and constraint). The child's more spontaneous, impulsive, excited, or exuberant affects are not empathically responded to, and ultimately, he or she is expected to eschew them.

Obviously, many positively toned and even maturationally high-level affects may end up being split off and derailed from the self structures as a result of such empathic failures. Characterological structures antithetical to the free expression of such affects may ensue as well as severe narrowing of the affective range.

### Affect Tolerance and the Capacity to Use Affects as Self-signals

The most important function of affects (i.e., their informative value with regard to the state of the inner representational world), is impaired as a result of the lack of empathic attunement by caretakers to strong forms of affective expression by the child. This can thoroughly inhibit the use of affects as self-signals and can lead instead to a sense of traumatic anxiety and consequent needs to disavow, dissociate, repress, or otherwise escape from potentially painful affects.

The capacity to utilize even positively toned affects as self-signals can be severely inhibited as a result of defective parental attunements. In adulthood, this may be manifested via the incapacity to tolerate a broad variety of positive affects such as joyful exhibitionism, exhilaration over personal achievements, and positive anticipation and excitement over adventurous and courageous activities.

### The Desomatization and Cognitive Articulation of Affect

The integration of affective states into "cognitive affective schemata" contributing positively to the ultimate organization and consolidation of the self, depends initially upon an articulate caregiver who verbally translates the child's somatically experienced affects. Solid affect maturation evolves via an internalized capacity for such verbal translations.

A broad and differentiated range of feelings, under conditions of a high degree of affect maturity, should be available at a verbal rather than somatic level. Both positively and negatively toned feelings should be accessible to verbalizable cognitive affective schemata.

## FUNCTIONAL–DEVELOPMENTAL SCHEMATA FOR ASSESSING AFFECTS

Any affect relevant to psychoanalytic treatment needs to be assessed in terms of its self and object representational character, topographic aspects (i.e., conscious, preconscious, or unconscious features) and structural relevance with regard to id, ego, or superego ideals. Certainly, the various functions alluded to by Alexander and Isaacs (1964) and Stolorow, Brandchaft, and Atwood (1987) need to be assessed for that particular affect. In addition, to assess more fully its object relational maturity and characterological structure, the affect would need to be assessed across the following maturationally relevant functional schemata.

*Signal Function*

An affect's available information needs to be comprehended. The capacity to translate the information contained in the affect into a clear and decisive plan of action would be associated with a high level of affect maturity, object relational, and characterological structure. A more nebulous and unclear informational quality would be associated with the helplessness, panic potential, and disorganized affect storms typical of more severely disturbed character disorders.

*Hedonic Function*

Both the positive, more pleasant quality of affects and their negative, more unpleasant aspects need to be delineated, and both should be integrated in the healthier forms of character structure and object relational maturity. An unusual weighting toward the positive affects may indicate a manic characterological orientation and toward the negative affects a masochistic–depressive characterological orientation. Neither form of hedonic loading indicates a more severe form of character pathology. Certainly, as Meehl (1975) has noted, hedonic capacity is an important indicator of personality structure.

Too great a degree of dissociation or splitting off of positively from negatively toned affects would be indicative of more severe forms of object relational and characterological disturbance.

*Activating (Energetic) Function*

Most affects vary from mild arousal (i.e., energizing and exciting affects contributing to alertness and attentiveness to real issues in both the self and objects) to a higher degree of arousal (which may be associated with hysterical excitability or affective lability), to an extremely high degree of arousal (which may be associated with explosive or severely impulsive characterological orientation).

## Expressive Function

The degree to which an affect can be spontaneously expressed in a socially communicative fashion needs to be noted. Higher levels of affect, object relational, and characterological differentiation and maturity tend to be associated with affects having a spontaneous character. Lower levels of developmental differentiation tend to be associated with more nonexpressive, hidden, and masklike communicative reactions. Schizoid character problems are frequently associated with a lack of affective expressiveness.

## Cognitive Functions

Finally, the cognitive differentiation of the affect needs to be delineated. When the idea, story line, or self and object representational character of the affect is clearly articulated and verbalizable, a higher level of affect, object relational, and characterological maturity is indicated. On the other hand, a vaguer sense of cognitive clarity and verbal articulation is associated with affect, object relational, and characterological immaturity.

Momentary pathological shifts across these four functions may be associated with an affect storm or regression of a neurotic nature (i.e., phobic, hysterical, obsessive–compulsive). More chronically structured and prolonged pathological shifts in affect differentiation, range, or articulation may be more indicative of an intermediate or more severe level of object relational or character pathology. A clinical example should help illustrate the usefulness of these functional schemata for assessing characterologically relevant aspects of affect maturation.

CLINICAL ILLUSTRATION

## Case 1

A male patient had been reviewing the various ramifications of his father's physical and emotional absence throughout the formative years of his childhood. The father's withdrawal from emotional communication with the patient was felt as having left a huge gap in his life. His masculine self-assertiveness and capacity for intimacy and loving commitment to a woman had been severely hindered as a result of this felt absence of paternal concern and love. Much of his emotional disconnectedness from women, reflected in a series of failed relationships, had seemed, at least in part, linked to a need to put his life on hold and to stay closely connected to his family of origin. In many ways, he had been unable to commit himself to a new beginning and family of his own because of an overwhelming need to play out the role of captain who must loyally go down with the "sinking ship," which was represented by his family of origin and its many problems and emotional limitations. His strong protective feelings toward his mother, who was frequently the object of the father's abuse and emotional neglect, had continued up to the present. He had also, however, tended to deny her emotional aloofness and lack of empathic attunement to his needs for loving warmth and intimacy.

The relationship between his parents was virtually bereft of emotional warmth, tenderness, or passion. They stayed married and were loyal to each other and minimally responsible with regard to child care, but almost no gratification, whatsoever, could be gleaned in observing their relationship over the years. Feelings of intimacy, trust, or loving commitment were thus quite absent from the relationship between the parents themselves and in their interactions with the children.

The patient, a warm, sensitive man with solid ego resources, intelligence, and vocational competency, emerged from the object relational milieu of his childhood virtually unscathed, except for some severe restrictions upon the spontaneity of his emotional communicativeness. His ego and superego development reflected excellent affect control, synthetic and delay capacities, despite a noticeably hypermoralistic and perfectionistic orientation. His overall characterological organization had a somewhat compulsive flavor.

With regard to affect development, the patient exhibited very solid and mature capacities for processing the *cognitive* and signal informative properties of his inner feelings. He exhibited the capacity to empathically comprehend a broad range of affects. His *expressive* range, however, was noticeably more narrow. The latter stemmed from the apparent object relational deficiencies of his childhood home milieu. Neither parent, apparently, could express affects in a spontaneous and fully engaged fashion. They could neither express feelings toward each other nor toward their children.

The activating and energetic aspects of the patient's emotional development were evidently quite normal. He exhibited almost no indication of histrionic or explosive tendencies, and if anything, tended to overmodulate and overcontrol his affects. The complaint of his various girl friends had always been that he held back his feelings too much and was uncomfortable with expressing feelings or talking about them.

Much of the patient's difficulties in communicating emotion stemmed from an identification with a father who was severely constricted emotionally and who did not have the vaguest notion either of how to communicate his own emotional needs to others around him or to empathically attune to or appreciate the emotions of other family members. The patient felt completely overlooked emotionally, and neglected by the father, but never lost the hope that one day he might obtain the father's love. His protective feelings toward his father were reflected in a need to place his life on hold, until he had obtained some form of emotional closure with the father.

This patient exhibited the extreme protectiveness and therapeutic strivings so often evident in parentified children who have been brought up in an emotionally neglectful and abusive home milieu. The continued analysis of his protectiveness and therapeutic strivings toward his parents gradually began to free him from the entrapment and enmeshment which had severely de-limited his capacity for emotional spontaneity and loving, and committed attachment to a woman in his life. At an oedipal level, this was still quite threatening for the patient, in that it would entail the discovery of loving, tender capacities in himself and in relationship to a woman that were evidently unavailable to either parent. The feeling of exhilaration and exuberance in a loving, passionate attachment to a woman, almost certainly entailed an ultimate separation and individuation from his parents and grieving over the severely crippled and emotionally deficient character of their loving attachment to each other.

This brief presentation illustrates the usefulness of the four functional continua for clinically exploring problems with affects from an object relational and characterological perspective. It is evident that the patient's difficulties predominantly involved the processing and expressive differentiation of positive affects.

# Chapter 2

# CLINGING TO NEGATIVE AFFECTS

Masochistic and masochisticlike phenomena have been studied psychoanalytically from a variety of perspectives. Intractable and seemingly pleasurable self-hurting and self-defeating tendencies have been explored from a classical (Freud, 1919, 1920, 1924b), ego psychological (Menaker, 1953; Loewenstein, 1957), object relational (Berliner, 1958; Joseph, 1982; Bollas, 1987; Rosenfeld, 1988; Kernberg 1991b), and from a self psychological viewpoint (Stolorow and Lachmann, 1980).

The affective implications of masochistic phenomena have been overlooked for the most part. The explicit clinging to negative affects and more implicit aversions to positive affects underlying masochistic behavior have not been very fully explored hitherto.

Given the basic assumption that normality involves the capacity for, receptivity to, and expression of a broad and verbally differentiated range of affect (Pine, 1979) and tolerance (Meehl, 1975) for pleasant affects, a number of patients are seen in treatment with serious limitations of their affective capabilities.

The common denominators underlying the disturbances manifested by these patients typically are weakened affective expressiveness, a clinging to diffuse negative affects, tendencies to resomatize affects in a hypochondriacal and psychosomatic fashion, and a generalized discomfort with positive affects without the artificial assistance of various sexual or chemical additions and substances. In the past these patients have been labeled masochistic (Menaker, 1953), paranoid-masochistic (Nydes, 1963), or, more recently, anhedonic (Krystal, 1988; McDougall, 1989), or alexithymic (Krystal, 1988).

Such patients utilize negative affects to defend against positive affects (Krystal, 1988; Doidge 1990); to feel alive (Giovacchini, 1984a); to establish

25

some form of intimacy and object relational connection (Bollas, 1987; Kernberg, 1991b); to establish a rather primitive sense of omnipotence (Novick and Novick, 1987, 1991); and to bolster a fragile self-structure and sense of narcissistic equilibrium (Stolorow and Lachmann, 1980). Self-defeating behaviors and a proneness toward self-attack often camouflage a sense of estrangement from affect, and, paradoxically, can be efforts to restore more positive affective connections and a sense of self-coherence and aliveness.

The Freudian concept of masochism will be briefly outlined and updated from a contemporary object relational and self psychological perspective. The linkage of such phenomena to negative affects will be particularly highlighted in Bollas' (1987) understanding of moods as a means of conserving early toxic and essentially nonverbal object relational experiences.

The anhedonic and alexithymic features of masochistic phenomena will help to highlight the essential linkages between affect and object relations underlying the proneness to cling to negative affects. Finally, case material will be presented, reflecting the object relational and affective impairments implicit in the tendency to cling to negative and unpleasant emotion.

The operational definition of masochism in this chapter will not be restricted to the classical Freudian emphasis upon a *sexualization* of self-hating modes of experience and behavior, as was recommended by Schafer (1988). His concern is that the concept of masochism will lose its meaning if broadened and applied to a general variety of clinically manifested self-defeating behavior and experience. Rather, Meyers' (1988) emphasis upon the great clinical utility of a more flexibly broadened version of the construct will be followed. The primary focus will be upon masochism as a severe restriction of self experience and ego potentialities, primarily associated with a narrowing of the range of hedonic capacity and affect tolerance to the unpleasanter end of the pleasure–pain continuum.

Although severe *characterological* issues are evidently implied by the restriction to anhedonic and/or alexithymic modes of experience, they will not be a primary focus of the present chapter. Instead it will be assumed that masochistic tendencies, particularly those associated with clinging to negative affect, can be found to a greater or lesser degree all along Kernberg's (1976a) diagnostic continuum of character pathology.

## Freudian Conceptions of Masochism

Comprehensive summaries of Freud's approach to the problem of masochism have been previously offered by Panken (1973) and more recently by Glick and Meyers (1988) and Blum (1991). Essentially, Freud's view, elaborated in a number of papers (1915a, 1919, 1920, 1923, 1924b), was that masochism involves a subtle form of camouflage and disguise of largely eroticized and unconsciously gratifying impulses, wishes, and fantasies. Some form of unconscious "beating fantasy" should be discernible in derivative form in the free associations and acting out behavior of any masochistic patient. These fantasies can be traced ultimately to oedipal wishes and drive derivatives of an incestuous nature.

Freud's gradual evolution of a structural model (1923) and dual instinct theory (1915a) culminated in his last major contribution on masochism, "The Economic Problem of Masochism" (1924b). In that work, clinical manifestations of masochism, such as "feminine masochism" (unconscious wishes in both male and females for humiliating beatings and assault at the hands of the oedipal father) and "moral masochism" (characterologically grounded unconscious wishes for punishment) were analyzed as derivatives of primary masochistic and secondary masochistic drive fusions and deflections of the aggressive drive against the ego.

The unresolved oedipal dilemma is metaphorically contained in these masochistically pleasurable pursuits of pain, humiliation, and subjugation at the hands of external authorities or fate. In Freud's final view, the unconscious and pleasurable incestuous strivings trigger signal anxiety (1926a), which culminates in an ego defensive maneuver, and ultimately, neurotically self-defeating behavior and symptoms. The defensive camouflage can be quite subtle and complexly engrained within the character structure of various disturbed individuals.

Schafer (1988) has updated Freud's (1916) thinking with regard to the character types "wrecked by success." These patients cling to negative affects and view successful ego achievements as threatening and quite dangerous. They perpetually sabotage themselves, so that accomplishments (unconsciously signifying phallic oedipal mastery of a pleasurable nature) are essentially unattainable. Earlier, Nydes (1963) offered a rather brilliant analysis of the *paranoid–masochistic* character types from a similar oedipal perspective.

Schafer concludes his essay on success-wrecking tendencies in a manner that nicely captures Freud's approach to masochism. He notes that the analysand must be made aware of the complex motives underlying his clinging to painful affects and activities

[A]nd, it must be established that the analysand engages in this wrecking action for reasons that include maintaining a sense of personal coherence, warding off the envy of others, guaranteeing a defensive security, inflicting guilty self-punishment and providing infantile wish fulfillment. This is the model that Freud established in his essay on this topic. It is a model of unconscious activity disguised manifestly as passivity, and it is a model of unconsciously gaining pleasure or security through manifest unhappiness [1988, p. 90].

The principle of "multiple function" applied to masochism by Brenman (1952) clarified some of the complexities of these phenomena. Thus, any masochistic action can be clinically understood as a complex composite of id, ego, and superego activity. Brenner (1959) goes on to amplify this point by emphasizing that a single set of masochistic fantasies and behavior may serve a variety of purposes for an individual. These fantasies may simultaneously reflect primitive unconscious sexual and aggressive wishes (id), a guilt or shame-driven wish for punishment (superego), or specific defensive processes and sublimated creative or competitive strivings (ego).

Blum (1991) recently summed up the Freudian conception of masochism rather nicely as a complex amalgam of traumatic reality experience, sadomasochistic fantasy, and behavior patterns, fixations, and regressions in psychosexual and ego development, and disturbances in object relations. Blum stresses the centrality of trauma in the genetic history of masochistic patients. They have frequently been sexually or aggressively abused or have suffered early childhood illnesses of a serious nature. This explains the prevalance of beating fantasies and self-defeating behavior in such patients.

Blum, in an earlier paper (1976), was critical of the conception of "feminine masochism," arguing that it is based upon a stereotypical and largely erroneous notion of feminine psychology. He does, however, emphasize the essentially oedipal (rather than preoedipal) roots of the beating fantasy so prevalently seen in masochistic patients. Blum further stresses the importance of aggression as a central factor in masochistic phenomena. Like Reik (1941) and others who stressed the turning of aggression against the self as a dynamic underlying depressive–masochistic character pattern, Blum views the issue of aggression as critical for an understanding of masochism. He further emphasizes the structural model, particularly the interrelationship of superego, ego, and ego ideal in the healthier masochistic sublimations (i.e., self-depriving and punitive behavior associated with competitive athletic and creative strivings and aspirations).

The bulk of psychoanalytic theorizing about masochism has stressed its theoretical complexity and clinical relevance. It is seen basically as having multiple structural causation (id, ego, and superego) and as being largely linked with fantasies and symptomatic behavior of an oedipal psychodynamic nature.

A group of post-Freudian theorists has extended the exploration to the preoedipal psychodynamic issues underlying masochism. Menaker (1953) and Berliner (1958) note that masochism can be viewed as a defensive maneuver by the ego to maintain and protect a vitally needed preoedipal love relationship. The masochistic patient yields her precious sense of willfulness, assertiveness, and ego autonomy, fearing that such behavior has, in the past, estranged the preoedipal love object and will continue to do so in the future. Menaker emphasized the submergence of ego strivings as resulting from fear of losing symbiotic object attachments, as being the primary dynamic underlying many forms of masochistic reactivity. Prince (1984) notes the deleterious impact of such ego restrictions for the sake of preoedipal attachments upon the exertion of will capacities and courageous potentialities in general.

Shapiro (1989) links masochism to a different set of problems with autonomy associated with an excessively rigid and unbending character structure. The masochist, according to Shapiro, submits and suffers visibly so as to protect a fragile but rigidly maintained sense of personal autonomy. Shapiro emphasizes the conscious, willful, and autonomy-protecting aspects paradoxically camouflaged beneath the seeming impulse-driven facade of masochistic activity.

Freudian and post-Freudian theorists have alluded to the centrality of early object relationships (both oedipal and preoedipal) as traumatic determinants underlying pain-seeking behavior. They have never, however, fully developed the implications of an object relational approach to elucidating the meaning of masochistic behavior, perhaps, in part, due to the drive theoretical assumptions that have always been so central to Freud's conceptions with regard to masochism. The British object relations theorists have evolved a number of constructs which clarify important features of masochism and its linkage with affective phenomena.

## OBJECT RELATIONAL CONCEPTIONS RELEVANT TO THE ISSUES OF MASOCHISM

Object relations theorists, according to Greenberg and Mitchell (1983), have diverged from the Freudian drive theoretical model to varying degrees. The divergence has always been in terms of a focus upon internalized object relationships rather than drive derivatives as a primary psychodynamic and structural determinant of the inner conflicts and adaptive insufficiencies typical of various pathological phenomena.

The object relational approach (particularly that of theorists such as Klein, Jacobson, Kernberg, Winnicott, and Bollas) has always discarded the view of affects as having a secondary status to drives, instead emphasizing their central significance for an understanding of a broad variety of clinical symptomatology.

The importance of object relations conceptualizations for the elucidation of masochistic phenomena cannot be underestimated. The primary contributions relevant to masochism consist of the illumination of introjective and projective identification and splitting as pervasive modes of intrapsychic and interpersonal defensiveness and communication; the clarification of the role of affects as significant aspects of internalized object relational units; the establishment of a viable diagnostic continuum of character pathology from an object relations perspective; the elucidation of the central role of externalization in characterological dysfunction; and the illumination of the object relational significance of dysphoric mood states and affective processes.

## Splitting, Projective Identification, and Masochism

Melanie Klein (1946) focused upon the primitive defense mechanisms of splitting and projective identification as intrinsic to the internalized object relations of both the paranoid–schizoid and depressive positions. Wangh (1962), Malin and Grotstein (1966), and Ogden (1982) have elaborated on the central significance of these mechanisms in a variety of therapeutic situations, but primarily with more severely disturbed patients. Kernberg (1975b), in particular, has explored these mechanisms in therapeutic work with borderline patients. Jacobson (1971) has applied these mechanisms to an elucidation of the dynamic and structural characteristics of severely depressed patients.

The common masochistic feature underlying a variety of severe forms of character pathology is, at least in part, the heavy reliance upon splitting and projective identification. Thus, in many primitive states the good objects and their associated positive affects must be split off and dissociated from bad objects and their associated negative affects. Once splitting has occurred the bad object representations are either projected into an external object so as to protect the internal good objects and affects (typical paranoid–schizoid position process), or are internalized with the good objects and associated affects being projected into an external object for safekeeping (a process that is typical of the depressive position). The latter mechanism is a primitive precursor of the maneuvers so often entrenched within the character structure of masochistic individuals. The excessive tolerance for and clinging to negative affects partially involves the need to protect good self and object representations by splitting them off and projecting them into *treasured* external object containers. The individual is, of course, then left with the split-off bad objects and ends up devaluing herself and idealizing others in her external object world.

Splitting and projective identification are essential features of a variety of character structures and styles. The phobic and paranoid patient projects dangerous bad feelings and self representations into an external object container, keeping the good and less aggressive feelings within the self. The narcissistic patient projects devalued and shameful aspects of the self into the external object container and idealizes the good aspects of the self. Depressive and masochistic patients project the valuable parts of the self and end up idealizing others in their outside world, while severely devaluing aspects of their own ego identity and self feelings.

While protectiveness is an inherent feature of most modalities of characterological dysfunction, it is particularly evident in patients with masochistic character structure. Fairbairn (1952a) has explored the significance and meaning of protectiveness as a schizoid dynamic underlying a multiple variety of defensive patterns and avoidance maneuvers. The deficient features of the early object environment (maternal and paternal) cannot be confronted assertively and angrily. Direct and assertive expressions of anger are deemed too potentially destructive of a vitally needed object bond. An abusively neglectful, depriving, rejecting, or abandoning parental object cannot be assertively confronted. This object is the only one possessed by the child during early primitive states of developmental differentiation. Indeed, during the symbiotic phases of development, destruction of the object is confused and associated with the possibility of self annihilation. Protectiveness is a severely engrained feature of the character structure, particularly in depressive and masochistic patients. It often feels far safer to attack the self and its representations than the object and its consciously or unconsciously known characteristics. The object must be protected at all costs, even at the risk of self-attack and a rigid clinging to negative affects.

Jacobson (1964) and Kernberg (1976a, 1980a) have conceptually delineated a model of ego identity differentiation that traces increasingly sophisticated integrations of self, affect, and object representation over the course of maturation and development. Self and object representations and their linking affects become increasingly more articulated, differentiated, and constantly reliable during the course of ego maturation. The shift is essentially from an outside state of ego dedifferentiation and self-isolation from the object world to a symbiotic and marginally differentiated state of selfobject fusion, and finally to a clearly differentiated sense of ego identity and object constancy.

Affects are integral to this object relational model of ego identity differentiation. At the earliest maturational phases, affects are diffuse and only primitively articulated. During the course of ego identity development, affects become increasingly more articulated, verbalizable, and constant. This agrees quite well with Krystal's (1974) theorizing regarding the developmental differentiation of affects. Patients with masochistic difficulties have become fixated at an intermediate phase of ego, object, and affect differentiation in which fusions and merger tendencies predominate. The pleasant (good) and unpleasant (bad) features of affects are frequently merged and only relatively differentiated. Similarly, the good and bad features of self and object representations tend to be frequently fused. Projective identificatory interactions abound, and affects lacking in constancy are fluidly shifted back and forth between self and object. There is a predominance of introjected bad feelings and associated negative self representations which are artificially split off from good feelings and idealized object representations. Splitting and projective identification maneuvers are utilized in the fluid context of ego identity states of selfobject fusion and symbiotic merger.

Of course, this clustering of split off and toxically negative self representation and linking affects ultimately protects the object and its idealized representational qualities at a fantasy level. Given the predominantly symbiotic mode of object relatedness, the primitive ego is meagerly nourished via a vicarious projective identificatory and empathic fusion with the idealized object and its diffuse but largely positive affective attributes. The object is protected from the toxic affects and representations felt to lie within the self, whereas the depleted self can be minimally nourished via primitively empathic connections to the idealized self representations which have been projected into the object.

Positive affects associated with an authentic sense of power, achievement, competitiveness, and self-assertion are projectively identified into the object by the masochistic patient. This leaves the patient depleted of positive affects and with diffusely articulated and differentiated negative affects.

*The Core Object Relational Unit Underlying*
*Masochistic Phenomena*

Kernberg has contributed the clearest conceptualization with regard to the affective core of object relational units underlying a diverse variety of ego identity and characterological states. He states that each and every object relations unit consists of a cluster of self representations, object representations, and specific associated affects. Kernberg notes that these affects have a *linking* or connecting function. They link the self representations to the object representations associated with the particular unit. This notion of affects goes well beyond the drive theoretical model which views affects as drive derivatives and allows for a developmental differentiation of affects across broad cognitive, ego psychological, and object relational continua. Thus, primitive and undifferentiated affects, self and object representations of a split-off nature can be distinguished from more articulated self and object constant units and their linking affects.

The highest level emotional states such as love and compassion require self, affect, and object constancy and whole object relatedness, whereas the more primitive emotions such as hate and envy involve less constancy and consist of split-off part object relations. Any qualitative emotional state, whether higher or lower level in nature, may vary along a developmental continuum of object relational articulation and differentiation. There are thus primitive and less primitive forms of hate and envy. Similarly, there are mature and more primitive forms of love and compassion. Masochistic phenomena also can be seen to vary along similar developmental continua. Thus, the affects and object relational configurations associated with the self-denial and deprivations of a young athlete grooming herself for Olympic competition are more mature and differentiated than an approximately comparable set of affects and object representational themes associated with an anorexic patient's self-deprivations. In the prior case, the self-depriving patterns and willfully determined behavior are geared toward higher level motivational goals involving ego competency and socially adaptive forms of narcissistic attainment and self-esteem enhancement. In the latter case, subtle forms of toxic introjection have led to highly self-destructive behavior and impaired ego functioning. The internalized object relational units and linking affects are much more undifferentiated and primitive in the case of the anorexic patient.

## Manifestations of Masochism Along a Continuum of Character Pathology

Kernberg (1976a, 1980a) has contributed a great deal to our understanding of the object relational units and linking affects associated with various points along a viable diagnostic continuum of characterological pathology. He distinguishes three different grades of character structure. High level character functioning involves maturely differentiated affects and affective communicative capabilities as well as object constant attachments and relationships. Most higher level neurotic characters (phobic, hysterical, compulsive) fall within this grouping. Masochistic phenomena exist but are largely associated with harsh internalized superego structures in this category of character structure.

In the intermediate category of character structure, Kernberg notes more severe forms of psychopathology and impaired object relations. A reliance upon more primitive defensive maneuvers such as splitting, projective identification, omnipotence, and self-devaluation is noticeable. Affects are more diffuse and dissociated from cognitive content in this grouping. Masochistic patterns are associated with heavy reliance upon primitive defensive maneuvers rather than with maturely internalized superego structures. Severe character problems of a passive–aggressive, higher level infantile, higher level narcissistic, and paranoid nature, as well as more severe and ego debilitating hysterical, phobic, and compulsive neuroses are typical of this intermediate range of character functioning.

The low level category of character functioning involves some of the most severe forms of masochism including anorexic–bulimic and severely addictive behavioral patterns. Ego identity and object constancy are quite impaired as are various executive adaptive ego functions. Affects are extremely split off and dissociated as a result of a sole reliance upon primitive defense mechanisms. Severe forms of anhedonia and alexithymic disorder abound in the grouping. The primary nosological categories typical of this primitive level of character structure are the low level narcissistic and infantile characters, the severe addictive disorders, and the more severe forms of borderline personality organization.

Thus, sadomasochistic behavioral manifestations have different meanings, depending upon the severity of character dysfunction. As Kernberg (1991b) has noted, there is a relatively normal integration of masochistic and sadistic fantasy in sexually passionate activity. Sadomasochism becomes more problematic and disruptive to competency and ego adaptive functioning in the context of more severely pathological forms of character structure.

*Externalization, Characterological Dysfunction, and*
*Masochism*

Giovacchini (1984a) has introduced a conception of the defense mechanism of externalization that is particularly relevant to the issue of masochism. He explores certain forms of projective identification exhibited by patients suffering from severe character disorders. He further notes that the therapist's countertransference reaction to such patients often is a response to the recreation of an environmental milieu in the consulting room similar to the toxic milieu contained in the patient's early life experiences. Thus, a patient who experienced a drab, hopeless early environmental milieu may produce a similar atmosphere in the consulting room. Giovacchini calls this process externalization.

Many therapists are unaware of this subtle projective identificatory process in their work with masochistic patients. They end up feeling hopeless about the patient's severe characterological difficulties and seemingly endless repetition of self-destructive behavior. They are unaware of the communicative function of the repetitious masochistic phenomena in the form of externalizations. Should they become aware of these externalizations, however, they can better contain the affects generated by these patients and ultimately, interpret their meaning in a fashion that is useful for the patient.

Externalizations consist of subtle forms of affective communication in which a dissociated affect (linked to an early object relations experience) is generated in the therapist. Since the bulk of such affects tend to be of a nonverbal nature, it is difficult for both patient and therapist to verbally articulate them.

## The Object Relational Significance of Dysphoric Mood States Associated with Masochistic Phenomena

The intimate connection between affect and internalized object relations is perhaps most interestingly found in mood states. Moods have seldom been explored from a psychoanalytic perspective, nor have they been clearly differentiated from other forms of affect. Isaacs (1990) has argued, somewhat controversially, that most affects are rather fleeting and do not last for an extended period. Moods clearly can last for longer periods, although they can also be of a briefer nature. Dysphoric mood states extend over time and are a pervasive personality feature in depressive, masochistic patients.

Bollas (1987) has recently noted that moods are connections to early object relational experiences that occurred during preverbal phases of an individual's psychic development. Moods can thus be analyzed from an object relations perspective. Such analyses often uncover an object which has cast its shadow preverbally on the ego and self representations of the individual. Bollas (1987) calls those early relational imagoes *conservative objects*. Thus, moods can be seen as powerful forms of object relational memory which often are difficult to shake off or to communicate to others. Dysphoric affects, so pervasively evident in depressive individuals, therefore, may be viewed as connections to early object relational experiences, and hence offer primitive forms of memorial retrieval of those experiences. Many depressive–masochistic patients remain *loyally* connected to painful experiences from their past through the affects of sadness, helplessness, futility, and despair which so often permeate their daily life experience. Therapists are often unaware that in attempting to assist a masochistic patient to shake off a dysphoric mood state, they are also asking the patient to disconnect an unconsciously maintained connection to an early object. The stubborn resistances that their ameliorative treatment efforts meet up with are, in large part, a response to the unconscious sense of disloyalty that remains essentially unanalyzed by therapist and patient.

The loyal devotion to early objects and relational experience, even those of a highly toxic nature, is a noteworthy feature of therapeutic work with patients who stubbornly cling to negative affects.

*A Self Theoretical Approach to Masochism*

Masochism, from the perspective of the self theoretical assumptions implicit in Kohut's work (1971, 1977), involves a deficiency in affective self regulation capacity. According to Kohut and a number of his followers the self system is like a thermostat which has the primary task of mood regulation. Indeed, Jacobson (1964, 1971) has alluded to similar difficulties underlying many forms of depressive disorder. The predominant character of affect states are too severely restricted and maintained at the painful end of the hedonic continuum in depressive and masochistic disorders. In such disorders there is a limited capacity to shift into lighter, more pleasant, and buoyant affective states.

Paradoxically, many narcissistically vulnerable masochistic patients end up turning their only marginally sublimated and controlled aggressive impulses against themselves, as a primitive means of bolstering their shaky self-esteem. One function of masochism, thus, is the thermostatic regulation of self-esteem. Stolorow (Stolorow and Lachmann, 1980) has articulated this position most clearly: "The inference to be drawn, then, is that masochistic activities, as *one* of their multiple functions, may serve as abortive efforts to restore, repair, buttress and sustain a self representation that had been rendered vulnerable by injurious experiences during the early preoedipal era when the self representation is most susceptible to damage" (p. 31).

In more primitively organized patients, according to Stolorow, masochism has the primarily narcissistic function of "restoring and sustaining the cohesion, stability, and positive affective coloring of a precarious, threatened, damaged, or fragmenting self representation" (p. 42). The clinging to painful affects and paradoxical pleasures seemingly obtained from self-defeating behavior are thus explainable as feeble efforts, mostly doomed to failure, at bolstering a fragile and affectively unstable self system.

The paradox implicit in this conception (that negative affects are clung to and utilized to create positive feelings and self-esteem) is not quite as paradoxical as might appear at first blush. In primitively organized patients and children, a certain sense of omnipotence and mastery can be obtained via masochistic actions. Novick and Novick (1991) recently explored masochism and omnipotent fantasies from a developmental perspective. Galenson (1988) noted a number of clinical and conceptual ramifications of *protomasochism*, a primitive and developmentally early form of masochism found in children. Sugarman (1991) offers an illuminating case example of early forms of provocative masochistic behavior in a 3-year-old child. The common denominator in early forms of masochism noted in childhood is the paradoxical sense of control obtainable from masochisticlike behavior patterns in children. Such forms of protomasochism would appear to be fueled, at least in part, by an experience of traumatic mastery attained via various forms of omnipotent fantasy. The self-hurting behavior contributes to a bolstering of the child or primitive individual's self-esteem through the omnipotent fantasies that underlie such behavior. These fantasies provide narcissistic gratification and defenses against ego vulnerability.

## Anhedonic and Alexithymic Features of Masochistic Phenomena

Clearly, above and beyond the multiple structural, dynamic, object relational, and self theoretical causes of the highly complex phenomenon of masochism, a disturbance in the expressive and receptive processing of affects is a significant feature of this disorder. Masochistic patients frequently exhibit both a discomfort with positive affects and a too great comfort with negative affects. McDougall (1989) and Krystal (1988) have conceptually and clinically elaborated the anhedonic spectrum of psychic disorder in which the informative and cognitive processing of positive affects are severely restricted or foreclosed completely, in certain individuals. Many patients with severe character problems, alcoholic or addictive personalities, and psychosomatic disorders, manifest anhedonia as peripheral or even primary features of disturbance.

Anhedonic tendencies are occasionally evident in almost every form of neurotic dysfunction and are rather pervasively evident in severe character disorders. These tendencies are frequently overlooked and camouflaged by the more dramatic aspects of neurotic symptomatology. Isaacs (1990) has noted the affect phobic aspects underlying a variety of neurotic and characterological disturbances. Positive affects, too, are feared and defended against, and a sort of reversal of the figure-ground is required to more fully explore the affect processing dysfunctions involved in many forms of psychopathology.

Krystal (1988) has reviewed the previous literature and brought the clinical concept of alexithymia up to date. This disorder, typically seen in a diverse group of severely traumatized patients, consists of an inability to process affective signals. Alexithymic patients cannot translate such signals and comprehend their meanings. They also cannot translate affective information into cognitive messages that can be verbally (or nonverbally) communicated to others. Krystal spent a great deal of time studying this disorder in Holocaust survivors, psychosomatic, and alcohol and drug addicted patients. He noted that most such patients are not amenable to traditional psychoanalytic treatment, due to lack of affective coding and decoding capabilities. Their general psychological mindedness, motivation, and ability to effectively utilize standard psychoanalytic interventions are severely hampered. These patients cannot experience and work through transference patterns, due to a severe impoverishment of their imaginative capabilities. They do not produce much analyzable fantasy material in the form of dreams or other forms of free associative psychic material.

A common object relational denominator exhibited by various alexithymic patients is their absolute incapacity to own powerful positive affects and self-soothing capabilities. Krystal (1978), in a fascinating and brilliant paper, notes the empirically demonstrated inability of drug addicted patients to successfully utilize biofeedback approaches. The fact that such an approach requires the internalization of self-soothing techniques and an ownership of the capacity to control their affects and bodily processes (without the aid of either drugs or placebo) makes it an untenable one for such patients. Krystal argues that these patients, to be cured, must reinternalize externalized object representations of a potent, self-soothing nature. By externalizing and disowning such object representational qualities, they unconsciously end up assuming that they are not entitled to the powerful soothing functions supplied by the preoedipal maternal figure of childhood. They further project and displace such soothing functions onto placebos or drugs which possess the potent properties that they feel are lacking in themselves. In the transference, they project these soothing and powerful attributes onto the therapist.

Many masochistic patients (although not completely anhedonic or alexithymic) are similarly incapable of internalizing and hence owning self-soothing functions and object representations. They project instead such powerful functions, affects, and attributes onto others in their external environment. The fact that others must be utilized as containers and repositories for potent, positive affects and self-soothing properties suggests that an anhedonic and/ or alexithymic structural feature may underlie many forms of masochistic disturbance. Treatment interventions with such patients, therefore, must take this fact into account. At least some portion of the interpretive work with these patients must be geared toward an encouragement of the reownership of potent affects and self-soothing functions. Krystal (1982a) has noted that some of the initial work with such patients must involve an educative, informative exploration of affects that have been dissociated, avoided, or eliminated.

## Case Illustrations

In each case discussed here, a clinging to negative affects is a significant thematic concern requiring some form of treatment intervention. The cases each fall at differing points along Kernberg's diagnostic continuum of character pathology. Despite the varying integrity of ego identity structures, affect differentiation, and degree of developmental deficits, each patient struggles with the need to internalize a solidly self-soothing object and is prone to an externalization of such functions via a variety of self-destructive actions which, paradoxically, maintain self-esteem.

## Case 1

The patient was a young woman who had been severely addicted to heroin and other drugs. She was also a self-mutilator, periodically cutting herself with a razor. The cuts that she made on herself tended to be of a moderately severe nature and had never been life-threatening. She also suffered from a relatively severe form of anorexia-bulimia in which she alternatingly binged on food and purged her stomach of its content.

At one point, the therapist found himself excessively involved in her treatment in terms of time. Frequent emergency telephone calls with various medical authorities and her parents were required. Out of sheer exasperation, the therapist decided to hospitalize the patient for two months at a local psychiatric facility.

Prior to accepting the patient back into individual treatment following her hospitalization, the therapist insisted on establishing a therapeutic contract with her. The terms of the agreement were that the patient not engage in any of the self-destructive actions that had led to her hospitalization. She was not to purge herself of food, abuse drugs, or cut herself. The patient agreed to these terms and was able to come back into treatment and successfully work on a more expressive and insightful level.

The structures explicitly outlined in the therapeutic contract offered the patient an externalized loving object antithetical to the toxic maternal and paternal introjects. The therapist cared for the patient in a way quite different from her distant, emotionally disengaged parents, who dealt with her in an overly intellectual and essentially disconnected fashion. The therapist cared enough to prohibit self-destructive behavior (which was the only means that the patient had to gain attention and meager attunement from her emotionally unrelated parents). Ultimately the therapist's empathic attunement paved the way for a solid therapeutic alliance allowing for work toward goals of ego maturation and affect differentiation. The therapist was available to be internalized as a transitional, "good enough," and self-soothing object, in a way that the parents never could.

## Case 2

A bulimic young woman had seldom been able to enjoy a meal without engaging in affectively unpleasant binge and purge behavior. Although her case will be described in greater detail in chapter 11, certain aspects of it relevant to the proneness to cling to negative affects will be noted here. Her natural mother had died in a painful fashion, before the patient's fifth birthday. She remembered coming back from exhilarating play one day in an excited and upbeat manner, only to be confronted with a family group of mourners. Her mother had just died and she sensed some chastisement from the mourners which quickly dampened her excited, joyful mood.

The patient proceeded to masochistically dampen her own positive moods in various ways during subsequent phases of her life. In particular, she adopted bulimic eating patterns as an effective way of doing this. She could quite easily convert a pleasant, essentially joyful activity such as eating into an extremely unpleasant one.

The object relational significance of her bulimic behavior became increasingly clear during the course of treatment. In many ways, she was preserving a relational connection to her pain-ridden natural mother through her own perseveratively unpleasant and self-punishing actions. It was as if she had vowed never again to make the mistake that she had shamefully made, upon coming home in an exhilarated mood on the day of her mother's death. She would repetitiously cling to negative affects and thereby forego any potential shame- and guilt-inducing positive affective experiences.

The loyalty implicit in her masochistic actions was a central psychodynamic which had to be interpretively explored over and over again during the course of her treatment. By foregoing identifications of a more potentially benign and affectively positive nature with other significant figures in her life (i.e., her rather competent stepmother whom she felt was a bit too eager to redecorate the family home and rid it of objects containing emotional connections to the natural mother). Her bulimic symptoms, thus, were rather characterologically entrenched and resistant to the therapist's ameliorative efforts for a lengthy period of time. Gradually she was able to give up these symptoms and substitute a more affectively positive and enjoyable attitude toward food and eating.

As in the previous case, the therapist was eventually internalized as a soothing, good enough transitional object who insisted that the patient relinquish negative affects. The object relational loyalty implied by these painful affects was productively explored and interpreted, thereby reducing the pathological symbiosis to the pain-ridden and dying mother.

*Case 3*

The patient was a creative and talented man with an extremely engaging personality. Characterological aspects of his case will be further delineated in chapter 12. His chronic patterns of drug abuse severely overshadowed and marred his considerable professional accomplishments. He could not articulate feelings verbally and tended to describe them in a concrete, thinglike fashion. He was capable, however, of producing symbolically rich and imaginative fantasy material in the form of dreams. He worked on them in an excited and engaged way, seemingly eager to please his therapist. Despite his charming and engagingly expressive exterior, he was essentially disengaged from the treatment. He defensively walled off and omitted from therapeutic discussion the fact that he had once more relapsed and had been abusing a medication prescribed for a recent physical ailment. The patient had to be hospitalized in a drug treatment facility and actively involved in a 12-step program before he could be reengaged in individual treatment of an expressive nature.

This patient clearly illustrated the fact that drug addicted patients have a great deal of difficulty, even with modified psychoanalytic treatment interventions. They have particular trouble internalizing a benign, self-soothing object. They attempt desperately to externalize the self-soothing function and repeatedly seek to flee the responsibility for such a function through a heavy reliance upon drugs of various sorts for affect maintenance purposes. It is as if they cannot experience their affects without such an artificial and external means of self-esteem regulation.

From an object relational perspective, it should be noted that the patient had a father who was sociopathic but was also very much an idealized *mister excitement*, in his eyes. His father, although an essentially absent figure, would periodically show up and take him for an exhilarating car ride and exciting day of activity. His mother, on the other hand, was seen as an emotionally constricted and affectively dead sort of person. He remembered feelings of intense sadness and loss upon being returned by the father to the hyperresponsible and emotionally constricted home environment after these brief visits.

In many way, this patient's use of drugs as a means of artificially stimulating positive, exhilarating affects involved an unconscious identification with his father who also had severe addictive problems. He attained highly idealized affective states via the internal absorption of drugs (equated with the father). Being required to give up drugs was unconsciously felt to be equivalent to a return to the emotionally dead and deadening mother.

Like the second patient, this patient was unconsciously enmeshed in a symbiotic identification to a parental figure (in this case, an artificially exciting and affectively enlivening father). Whereas the second patient's loyalty was to a dying, emotionally deadening internal object, this patient's loyalty was to an artificially enlivening object. Both patients, however, ended up self-defeatingly clinging to negative affects and needed an intepretive exploration of the affective and object relational implications of their symptoms, for a more benign internalization of self-soothing capacities to occur.

## Conclusion

The clinging to negative affects is a pervasive structural feature, underlying many forms of masochistic and self-destructive behavior. Masochistic patterns have complex characterological significance which has not been very systematically explored in the present chapter. Although the classical Freudian model has important implications for the overdetermined sexual and aggressive drives underlying many forms of self-destructive behavior, it must be updated in the context of contemporary self theoretical and object relational conceptions.

# Chapter 3

# DREAD OF "EXHILARATED" AFFECTS IN THE PHOBIC PATIENT

A great deal of emphasis has always been placed upon negative affects such as anger, guilt, anxiety, and shame in conceptualizing the etiological and dynamic factors underlying most forms of neurotic and severe character pathology. What has been almost totally overlooked is the fact that positive affects, too, have an important and perhaps even more central role in various forms of neurotic symtomatology and character disorder.

Feelings and affective attitudes of a positive, hedonically toned nature such as joy, exhilaration, enthusiasm, excitement, pride, hope, and courage are subtly involved in an important and integral fashion, in many forms of psychopathology. They are typically in the background during our efforts to comprehend and ultimately alleviate a particular patient's psychological distress. A central thesis of this chapter is that our treatment efforts can be facilitated by shifting the figure-ground focus and bringing these positive affects into more direct discussion.

The psychotherapeutic models for treating anxious and phobic patients, at least those involving a dynamically sophisticated approach, have traditionally relied upon conceptions of phobia and affect dynamics explicitly and implicitly contained in Freud's contributions relevant to this subject (1894, 1895, 1896, 1909, 1926). The phobic patient, according to these models, needs to cognitively and affectively grasp the projections, displacements, and avoidances involved in the dynamically motivated and overdetermined symbolization processes underlying their fearful symptoms. An essentially introspective, insightfully explorative and interpretive approach is assumed to be sufficient to eliminate the ego restrictive and handicapping phobic symptoms.

Rosenberg (1949) has stressed the importance of both of Freud's anxiety conceptions (i.e., the earlier "toxic discharge" [1894, 1895, 1896] and the later [1926] "signal" anxiety hypotheses) in treating neurotic disturbance. She emphasizes the significance of the patient's capacity to tolerate anxiety as being central to the ultimate success or failure of the therapeutic endeavor. The capacity to utilize anxiety as an informative signal with regard to internal affective states, rather than as a toxic and adaptively disruptive and disorganizing experience, is thus very important in psychoanalytic approaches to treating phobic symptomatology. Interpretations of dynamic, defensive, and object relational factors ultimately strengthen the phobic patient's ego and enhances her capacity to tolerate and more effectively utilize anxious affects.

The traditional psychoanalytic model for treating neurotic disorders, interestingly, has perpetuated a view of affects which Isaacs (1981a, 1983, 1987, 1990) has labeled an "affect phobic" position. Both Zetzel's contribution on depression (1965) and Rosenberg's on anxiety (1949), stress the need to assist patients in *tolerating* or *enduring* painful affects. They both assume, as did Freud (1926), that the best we can do in our work with neurotic patients is to convert a toxic and ego disruptive and restricting affect state into a more tolerable, informative affect state. Affects are ultimately depicted as unpleasant and dreaded inner states which must somehow be discharged, expressed, or endured. But what about the positive affects lurking behind these unpleasant affects in most neurotic disorders? Do they also have to be tolerated? Isaacs feels that this, indeed, is the case. Many neurotic patients are equally phobic, even about their positive affects. Patients with character disorders are particularly uncomfortable with positive affects.

Giovacchini (1956) has explored the special functional significance of anxiety for certain character disordered patients, going well beyond the signal function alluded to by Freud. Giovacchini describes a patient suffering from severe character disturbance who evidently utilized chronic feelings of anxiety as a means of feeling alive and less affectively disengaged and depersonalized. Anxiety, for such patients, may be preferable to the feelingless and vacuous state that pervades their subjective world as a result of the dissociation of a broad array of differentiated affects (both positive and negative). The extensive affect phobias and avoidances of such patients may lead to a paradoxical attachment to anxiety reactions, as a means of some form (albeit unpleasant) of affective engagement with their outer world.

It is important that we reverse the typical figure-ground implicit in the established and traditional psychoanalytic approach to treating anxious, phobic, and panic disordered patients. Whereas the traditional approach assumes that the phobic patient is avoidant solely in response to negative affects (anxiety, fear, anger, guilt, etc.), it will be argued that positive affects (i.e., joyful feelings and exhilaration) are equally avoided by these patients.

It is well known that phobic patients cannot be effectively cured without exposure to the feared object or objects. Frequently, the problem is that these patients anxiously avoid putting themselves into the very situations to which they must be exposed for purposes of symptom relief. All therapeutic approaches (i.e., psychoanalytic, behavioral, cognitive, and psychopharmacological) founder if they do not ultimately expose such patients to the primary fear-inducing situations or objects. The spider phobic patient must ultimately be exposed successfully to spiders, the agoraphobic patient to free locomotion (by foot or car) in the outer world, and the school phobic patient must be successfully exposed to being at school without mother (or father) being present.

The ultimate difficulty, frequently observed during the treatment of phobic disorder, is the unwillingness to be exposed to the phobic situation long enough to experience the informative ("signal") properties of the affects that are occurring in the here-and-now. As Krystal (1982a, 1988) has emphasized, the anticipated feelings can never be quite as overwhelming as the traumatized patient expects them to be, but she never allows herself to test out that emotional fact, and such patients require active education in this respect.

Isaacs (1990), too, argues for a cognitive restructuring and actively educative posture at an early point in the treatment of phobic patients. He notes that an educative discussion can clarify distortions about feelings associated with the *affect storms* underlying many forms of neurotic symptoms. The "affect potentiation" processes (i.e., a vicious cycle in which an anticipation of unpleasant affect triggers an even more unpleasant affect, culminating in an affect storm or anticipation of full-blown panic reactions) must be interrupted or short-circuited via educational input and cognitive clarifications. Subsequently, an exposure to the affectively stimulating and dreaded situation can occur long enough to allow for a reduction in affect expectancies of a catastrophic nature.

Most behaviorist theorists and researchers have emphasized the importance of constant exposure to affectively dreaded situations in the successful treatment of phobic and panic disorders. Marks (1987), in a rather comprehensive volume addressing etiology and treatment, reviewed a number of clinical research studies involving desensitization procedures. Marks concluded that exposure of sufficient duration to allow for habituation to the phobic stimulus or situation can quite effectively reduce subsequent anxious and panicky reactions. He further noted that, if the dissociative mechanisms utilized to deny or emotionally detach from the phobic situation are kept to a minimum, the symptom reduction will be even more effective.

Marks quotes a statement by Moshe Dayan reported in *Newsweek* (1981) to underline the fear-reducing (counterphobic) usefulness of dissociative maneuvers in everyday life:

> Everyday life is often made easier by denial or detachment. It helped Moshe Dayan, for example, weather criticism when the opposition screamed abuse at him while he was speaking in the Israeli Knesset: "Though it was not at all pleasant, I went on with my speech, and felt no psychological stress. I withdrew myself, a sensation familiar to me from the battlefield, when I would cut myself off emotionally from reality. What was happening in the Knesset was happening in a fog and was unreal to me, like the burst of shells when crossing a field of fire" [Marks, 1987, p. 477].

Marks goes on, however, to emphasize that such maneuvers diminish the potency of therapeutic interventions with phobic patients. In a subsequent section it will be stressed that a psychoanalytic theory of therapy for phobic disorders contains a developmental perspective which elevates *counterphobic* and dissociative responses to a transitional step in response to fear, a cut above the *phobic* characterological position and a cut below a more truly affectively engaged and *courageous* posture.

In a certain sense, the psychoanalytic approach to treating phobic disorder contains an unstated conception of courage as a developmentally higher level affective attitude toward which we hope our fearful patients can aspire.

Since any treatment strategy or technique that increases the willingness of phobic patients to expose themselves to anxiety producing situations can be effective in working with the symptom proper, it is important that psychoanalytic therapists at least be aware of them. Many of these procedures can be flexibly and easily incorporated into most forms of psychoanalytic treatment.

### An "Integrative" Approach to the Exposure Dilemma with Phobic Patients

All treatment approaches to the broad spectrum of anxiety disorders have struggled with the seeming intransigence of phobic symptoms. It is commonly agreed (even by psychoanalysts) that the patient must be actively encouraged to expose herself to the phobic stimulus situation for a sufficient time interval so that anxious feelings can be experienced and endured. The thesis of this chapter is that positive feelings and feeling attitudes must also be experienced for an effective cure to occur. Thus, the patient with a fear of horseback riding must somehow not only experience her fears after "getting back on the horse," but must also feel the exhilaration and joyful feelings associated with the competent performance of such an activity. The panicky affect storm which compounds painful and pleasurable affects, making both seem potentially painful and fearsome, must be short-circuited and replaced by an exposure to the gamut of differentiated affects (both positive and negative) associated with a particular activity.

Phobic patients often exhibit a dread of exhilarated affects which are not successfully differentiated from anxious and potentially panic producing affects. They must be encouraged to expose themselves to these affects, as well.

Contemporary treatment approaches of an integrative nature, which can facilitate exposure and ultimate habituation to phobic situations, were thoroughly reviewed in a 1990 issue of the *Bulletin of the Menninger Clinic* dedicated to this problem. Amongst issues discussed were psychopharmacology (Rosenbaum, 1990), hypnosis (Smith, 1990), and self-regulation and biofeedback (Fahrion and Norris, 1990) procedures for assisting phobic and anxious patients to expose themselves to severely anxiety provoking stimuli.

After providing an overview of nosological distinctions and issues with anxiety disorders, Pasnau and Bystritsky (1990) conclude that education is particularly important for patients suffering from anxiety disorders. This agrees with the recent contributions of more psychoanalytically oriented theorists such as Krystal (1988) and Isaacs (1990), who have also stressed the effectiveness of incorporating educative communications in treating anxiety disorders.

Both the contributions of Smith and those of Fahrion and Norris to the same issue of the *Bulletin* stress the central importance of self-regulation via autohypnotic (suggestive) and biofeedback procedures. Systematic desensitization exposures and associated self-regulated relaxation can be quite effective. Relaxation-induced anxiety procedures (i.e., encouraging the patient to remember anxiety producing experiences, under conditions of enhanced relaxation and meditative self-composure) can also be helpful, in the context of a psychodynamic and conflict explorative treatment intervention. Smith notes that paradoxical intentions (i.e., maximizing the exposure to fearsome stimuli, under conditions of relaxation induced by self-hypnosis) can be helpful in both encouraging exposure and ultimate habituation to anxiety producing stimuli.

Fahrion and Norris argue for an integrated approach and against the sole use of pharmacological approaches in the following statement:

Symptoms of stress can be eliminated either by pharmacological intervention or self-regulation or both, through learning opposite physiological strategies. However, pharmacological interventions alone generally skirt the issue by simply covering up the symptoms, whereas during a process of relaxation and self-regulation, related psychodynamic memories and perceptions frequently emerge. Once conflicts emerge into awareness, the therapist can help the patient gradually resolve them. Ideally, self-regulation treatment for anxiety eventually focuses on understanding how unconscious and unrecognized motives and fears affect symptoms and behavior. Focus is most easily accomplished when the patient learns to relax deeply, bringing the unconscious closer to the surface. Without the usual defensive operations of the ego, the patient then begins to confront—first in imagination and later in actuality—the anxiety-producing stimulus while maintaining psychophysiological control of associated anxiety and symptoms [1990, p. 225].

While a bit too optimistic about the potency of relaxed states in uncovering previously repressed and unconscious conflicts for therapeutic exploration, these authors provide a nice summary of the usefulness of an integrative approach.

Thus, various approaches flexibly integrating hypnosis, biofeedback, and educational communications of a clarifying nature have been flexibly and effectively utilized within the context of a psychodynamic treatment intervention with anxiety disorders. Hoffert and Martinsen (1990), in a recent Scandinavian study, were successfully able to treat agoraphobic symptoms by an integrative approach combining cognitive (educative) interventions with psychodynamic conflict exploration and interpretive work. They were able to do this effectively within a controlled hospital environment. They emphasize the central importance of bypassing the typical avoidances of agoraphobic patients via a directive, educative, and ultimately self-directed confrontation with previously frightening experiences outside the home. Their patients were actively encouraged and expected to be increasingly active outdoors.

All patients in this study were taken off medication because of a primary premise (which agrees with psychodynamic models) that the patient must reduce her "fear of fear" and avoidant response to a sense of potentially catastrophic anxiety. The patient must feel the sense of dread and impending panic, noting the psychophysiological fear reactions in her body. Such patients can be offered some cognitive and educative reassurances that their anxiety symptoms will diminish after a relatively brief period of time. This dovetails nicely with Isaacs' (1990) notion that affects are relatively time-limited experiences of an informative nature. His somewhat controversial emphasis upon the fact that they cannot be stored over long periods of time is also quite relevant here. This also agrees with Krystal's educative reassurances to his affectively traumatized patients that they need not worry because they can never relive a traumatic experience at the intense level of affect felt in childhood.

Thus, the main goal of contemporary integrative approaches is to get the anxious patient to feel her feelings, reduce her "fear of fear" and consequent avoidant maneuvers, and ultimately, confront the diverse gamut of inner feelings (both positive and negative) appreciating them for their informative (signal anxiety) rather than phobic value.

The bulk of such integrative approaches, however, cannot fully do the job in treating phobic patients, because they neglect the "secondary gain" value of anxious symptomatology within the overall character organization of a particular patient. The addictive dependency gratifications obtainable via phobic symptoms ultimately must be addressed along with other ego syntonic and character resistive aspects of this form of psychopathology. In addition, some of the complex object relational implications of the phobic symptoms need to be interpretively worked with for effective affect and character maturation to occur. Finally, the positive affects dissociated via phobic avoidances need to be experientially confronted.

## Reversing the Figure-Ground in the Psychoanalytic Treatment of Anxiety Disorders

Psychoanalytic approaches to treating anxiety disorders stress the strengthening of the patient's ego via a patient interpretive exploration of unconscious conflicts. The ultimate affective goals of such exploration include an enhanced capacity to bear anxiety (Rosenberg, 1949), a reduction in "affect storms" (Isaacs, 1990) in coping with a differentiated array of affects (both positive and negative), and a greater capacity for self-monitoring, regulating, and soothing responses (Kohut 1971, 1977; Stolorow and Lachmann, 1980).

Historically, psychoanalytic conceptions of anxiety and treatment goals for phobic disorders have subtly implied a characterological and developmental paradigm in which the patient is assisted toward a more counterphobic attitude. This attitude has been delineated by Fenichel (1939) and involves a capacity for seemingly courageous feelings, in response to previously fear-provoking stimuli. As Fenichel has noted, however, a great deal of denial and dissociative defensiveness props up these outwardly courageous forms of action.

A counterphobic attitude, certainly preferable to and developmentally higher than a phobic attitude, must be viewed, however, as a transitional characterological position. A truly courageous attitude involves maturationally higher character structures and assumes a fuller, richer exposure to a broad range of affects (positive and negative). The capacity for positive affects and affective attitudes is particularly relevant. Thus, the joyful exhilaration and feelings of excitement in reaching toward new developmental ego attainments and accomplishments are sure signs that a truly courageous characterological position has been attained.

From a contemporary object relational perspective, a projective identificatory container model has evolved asserting that the therapist's capacity to tolerate and contain painful affects interactively stirred up during the course of treatment will ultimately be positively internalized by the patient (Malin and Grotstein, 1966; Ogden, 1979). Giovacchini (1984a) has specifically noted with regard to character disorders, that these difficult patients internalize a benign *analytic introject* by identifying with the analyst's mode of containing projective identifications during treatment. Zerbe (1990) has formulated object relational principles relevant for therapeutic work with anxiety disorders. Positive affects, in particular, need to be contained by the therapist for many such patients.

The intersubjective viewpoint, which has evolved out of Kohut's object relational and self psychological conceptions, has been most cogently articulated by Stolorow, Brandchaft, and Atwood (1987). Their affect theoretical model is a very functional one. It stresses the need for an empathic response from the therapist to a variety of affects such as anxiety and depression to which the patient's parents frequently failed to be attuned. The therapist's more empathic affective attunements assist the patient's tolerance and self-soothing capabilities in response to these affects. Ultimately, a broadening of the patient's range of affects and a diminishment of the need to split off and dissociate unpleasant affects occurs via such intersubjective attunements.

Both the contemporary object relational and intersubjective conceptions neglect, as did the earlier classical paradigms, more positive and pleasant hedonically toned affects and affective attitudes. Such patients have frequently not been empathically responded to during childhood. They need to be effectively contained and require empathic attunements on the part of the therapist. A kind of figure–ground reversal is required in our thinking with regard to this issue. We must focus our empathy more in the direction of the positive affects which for too long have been overshadowed and camouflaged by the more visible negative affects during the treatment of phobic disorders.

The case material highlights the ways in which this figure–ground reversal can be implemented in the psychotherapy of phobic patients.

CASE ILLUSTRATIONS

*Case 1*

A woman complained to her therapist that she was experiencing intense feelings of panic about a recent relationship that she had begun. Interestingly, her complaints seemed to center about this man's many attractive attributes which apparently were triggering an intensely passionate reaction. This was not the first time that she had experienced such a reaction. In the past, intense anxiety and a sense of potential disorganization had always been felt whenever a relationship was initiated involving the potential for passionate, loving, and attachment feelings. Without going into the various psychodynamics underlying this affect-avoidant pattern, it can be noted that the feelings of exhilaration typically felt during the initial stages of a passionate relationship were deeply threatening to this woman. They were sufficiently frightening to provoke a phobic inhibitory response. She had often in the past sabotaged potentially passionate and loving attachments so as not to have to be exposed to feelings of exhilaration.

The ultimate focus of therapy for this woman involved a thorough exploration of the dread of exhilarated affects which underlay her anxious reactions. She must first note that she was cutting off potentially exhilarated affects in her repeated avoidance of passionate attachments. Eventually, she needed to better understand the reasons for such a reluctance to experience positive affects. She also, of course, had to expose herself to these positive affects via risking a passionate relationship with a man.

*Case 2*

A young woman with a chronic history of acne developed a number of diffuse psychosomatic reactions following a brief sexual contact. Subsequent to this event, she began progressively to avoid sexual contacts or passionate relationships of any sort. This avoidance pattern continued to exacerbate over the course of many years. She became more and more obsessed with her skin, spending hour upon hour fussing and compulsively cleaning and applying various ointments. She was unable to work or become involved in relationships with men for these many years.

Recently, she had met an attractive man and initiated a relationship with him. As the relationship became more passionate and loving, she began to raise serious doubts about her acceptability to this man. She was increasingly convinced that he was bound to reject her for various reasons. The therapist repeatedly reversed the affective figure and ground and focused upon the greater risks inherent in the possibility that the man might accept her.

Should she be acceptable to this man, she would have to shift out of her "Rip Van Winkle"-like withdrawal from life and confront the risks inherent in a budding intimate relationship. Her fear of unpleasant affects of rejection camouflaged her even more intense dread and avoidance of exciting feelings and exhilaration. Passionate relationships stirred up a host of body image and separation–individuation concerns in this patient. Ultimately, a loving attachment stirred up anxieties with regard to separating from her parents with whom she was severely enmeshed in a symbiotic and mutually protective relationship. She felt very protective toward her parents, unconsciously wondering whether they could avoid a life pervaded by despair were she not to have these severe difficulties. Were she to move on with her life, she sensed that their life would be even emptier and less gratifying than was already the case.

The reversal of figure and ground with regard to affects opened up unconscious protectiveness and separation concerns underlying the phobic avoidance of relationships for this patient. She, therefore, ultimately exposed herself to a relationship and the feelings (both positive and negative) aroused during the course of it. She particularly needed to be sensitized to the positive feelings that were being bypassed via her phobic avoidance maneuvers.

*Case 3*

A man had reacted with intense anxiety feelings of dread and almost paniclike anxiety whenever an impending event requiring travel was about to occur. Consciously, he reported feelings of dread with regard to most forms of travel and locomotion. He ruminated obsessively about the physical risks to himself and about the tragic consequences for his wife and children, should he become involved in a travel related accident and die.

The therapist found it useful to reverse figure and ground and focus upon this patient's unconscious dread of exhilarated affects associated with travel or vacations. Rather than focus solely upon the consciously dreaded anxiety reactions and fear of locomotion and travel, it was important to spend much time exploring the meaning of exhilarating experiences of a relatively adventurous nature. Historically, his risk-taking and joyful locomotion within the world in an independent fashion were not empathically responded to by his parents. They responded instead in a fearful, overprotective manner, making the patient feel that joyful, explorative ventures out into the world were dangerous and hence need to be dreaded and avoided.

The patient became generally less fearful and timid about travel as a result of such a reversal of affective figure and ground. He became increasingly open to the positive affects associated with adventurous activities.

*Case 4*

A patient suffering from a severe agoraphobic disorder was treated from a psychoanalytic perspective. During his treatment, considerable character analytic exploration took place with regard to the multiple motives and conflicts that underlay his phobic symptomatology. His dependency gratifications in childhood were severely restricted by an emotionally cold, controlling, and rejecting mother and a harshly dominating and physically abusive father.

His younger brother responded to the father's physical abusiveness via explosive outbursts and direct confrontations and was free of phobic symptoms. The patient, on the other hand, responded in a far more timid and outwardly compliant fashion. He had memories of urinating in his pants in response to direct physical attacks by the father. The patient had acted out some of his anger in a displaced fashion by physically abusing and torturing the family dog and by some fire-setting behavior, but basically he never felt able to take on the father.

After high school, the father suggested that he join the navy and he did so. After a period of marriage subsequent to his military service, he abandoned his wife and two children having become involved in a rather passionate and tempestuous extramarital affair. The father, hearing of this, told him that he was doing "irreparable damage" to his family through such actions and insisted that he return to them. He returned home to his wife and children as ordered. Shortly thereafter, he developed his first panic attack and had to give up a quite successful business that he had been able to establish. His activities outside of his home became progressively limited. He needed his wife to be with him at all times, in order to travel anywhere in the outside world and to forestall a panic attack.

His wife had to accompany him to therapy sessions, although the therapist's office was only a few miles from his home. She also had to accompany him to his new place of employment or else he could not get there. As much as possible, he preferred to perform work assignments by telephone from his home, so that he did not need to leave the home. Fortunately (or, perhaps, unfortunately), his particular line of business allowed for a great deal of work being completed by telephone.

The patient's agoraphobic symptoms became more and more entrenched and were, initially, resistant to character analytic interpretations. The manipulative, sadistic control that the patient was able to exert over his wife (and transferentially over the therapist and therapy process) were repeatedly explored and insight gained. The patient was able to comprehend that he was unconsciously attacking his wife and therapist via subtle but stubbornly intractable resistances to a letting go of the agoraphobic avoidance patterns that were pervasively restricting his capacity to freely locomote in the world. He also became aware of the historical antecedents of his symptoms in the traumatic physical abuse and cold emotional rejection that he experienced at the hands of his parents. Thus, he was manipulating and controlling his wife in an unconsciously aggressive fashion, much as his father had treated him (identification with the aggressor).

He was doing to his wife what he could never do to his emotionally cold and uncaring mother (who used to keep him locked out of the house whenever she was not at home, so that the house would stay impeccably neat and clean). His wife, on the other hand, was seen as a warm and caring person who would either remain imprisoned with him in the home, when his agoraphobic symptoms were at their height, or allow him to stay imprisoned in the home, as his symptoms began to be resolved and subside somewhat through therapy. At this point, he allowed his wife to go on errands and shopping trips without him.

The wife's apparently martyred character structure was, unfortunately, well meshed with the patient's phobic character structure. She was a bit too eager to comfort the patient by driving him wherever he needed to go, including the therapy sessions. Her own probable masochistic tendencies were evident in statements made by the patient, but neither she nor the patient seemed interested in her becoming involved in treatment. The pathological interdependency and symbiosis inherent in their relationship was collusively maintained and could only be unilaterally worked on (in a relatively ineffective fashion) through the husband's treatment.

A primary emphasis during treatment involved having the patient drive himself to the therapy sessions, so that he could experience the feelings of fear and survive them. Much time was spent on educating him about how avoidance maneuvers work (i.e., his insistence that his wife drive him) to perpetuate the phobic symptoms. He was also alerted to the fact that the high level of panic anxiety which he dreaded was unlikely to recur and that his anxiety feelings had important informative, communicative, and "signal" value of a psychosomatic nature. They did not automatically mean that an impending danger situation was realistically present, since he had already survived his father's physical assaults. The "shriveled" pathetic old man whom he now saw whenever he was in his father's presence was unlikely to hurt him anymore. Indeed, the unconscious danger that he might physically strike out and assault his father, and transferentially, the therapist and others in his external work and social world, was unlikely to occur as well.

Finally, a great deal of therapeutic work was done on helping the patient differentiate his negative feelings (anxiety, fear of impending panic) from his more positive feelings (joy, exhilaration, and intense excitement over beginning to move about freely in his outer world). This was perhaps the most important clarifying effort for the patient and allowed him eventually to risk driving to therapy sessions alone, leaving his wife at home.

Every time the patient even imagined coming to sessions alone his heart began to race wildly. He said to the therapist, "My heart is pounding," and the therapist responded, "Yes, that's because you are beginning to feel the exhilaration." These exchanges occurred repeatedly and over the course of a number of months. Gradually, the patient was able to gear up his courage to imagine coming to the sessions by himself, and eventually, to risk actually driving to sessions by himself. Once he was able to do this, he was encouraged to extend his brave and adventurous forays alone into the outer world by stopping for desired and pleasurable items such as a newspaper or bakery items, prior to rushing back home. He resisted such suggestions and chose to rush back to the safety of his home rather than attempt such side excursions.

This portion of the therapeutic work was tedious, with many regressions and relapses back to the seeming safety of the patient's avoidant agoraphobic patterns. A tenacious focus, however, upon the broad range of feelings (both positive and negative) and, especially, upon the dreaded feelings of exhilaration and joy short-circuited and derailed via his phobic avoidance maneuvers, helped the patient to eventually risk exposing himself to the phobic stimulus situation. He began to drive to therapy by himself, admittedly, in a very hesitant and fearful fashion.

## IMPLICATIONS OF THE CLINICAL MATERIAL

The last patient posed formidable treatment difficulties, given the tremendous secondary gain value of his symptoms (i.e., dependency gratifications from a seemingly compassionate, warm, and excessively supportive wife–mother figure; gratifications from displaced sadistic attacks against the traumatizing parents of his childhood, camouflaged by his own martyred masochistic and phobic self-imprisonment). The symbiotic enmeshment and collusive sabotaging of his treatment by the wife was difficult to approach via individual psychotherapy. The wife ultimately needed to be involved in treatment herself for a more effective diminishment of the pathologically symbiotic couple system to be facilitated.

Extensive character analysis work had to be done with the patient to facilitate a more permanent diminishment of his regressive affect storms and panic stricken reactions. His phobic symptoms were ego syntonically ensconced within a passive dependent character structure that was far too comfortable with the phobic avoidance patterns quickly evoked by signal anxiety. He had also to be constantly exposed to the joyful, exhilarating, and positive excitement feelings lurking beneath his frequent sense of affect dread.

## CONCLUSIONS

All four of the patients mentioned have experienced what Isaacs (1990) calls "affect phobic" reactions. None of them was aware that positive affects such as joy and exhilaration were being short-circuited by the avoidant maneuvers. Thus, in addition to the encouragement of greater fear tolerance and counterphobic attitudes from the patient, a considerable emphasis needed to be placed upon the exposure to positive affects camouflaged and submerged beneath the patient's fearful affects.

Ultimately, a systematic character analytic approach was required to thoroughly explore the dynamic, object relational, and structural underpinnings of the patient's secondary gain resistances and ego syntonic phobic character patterns. The patient can most effectively attain truly courageous rather than merely counterphobic attitudes, through such intensive psychoanalytic work.

# Chapter 4

# DIFFICULTIES WITH COMPETENT, POTENT AFFECTS

Historically, psychoanalytic theorists have been interested in unconscious conflicts, impulses, and defensive maneuvers which interfere with smooth, adaptive coping capacities and competent actions. Robert White (1959, 1960, 1963) has been one of the few theorists to utilize insights obtainable from Freud's structural model and the subsequent ego psychological contributions of Hartmann (1939) and Erikson (1950, 1959), to develop a maturational grid tracking the evolution of competency motives alongside of the psychosexual and psychosocial passages alluded to by both Freud and Erikson. White questioned the validity of Freud's drive reduction conceptions and gathered plentiful clinical and experimental data indicating the existence of competency and explorative needs which, although associated with *tension* incremental tendencies and preferences, seem nevertheless to have a strong drive and motivational character. White found useful the contributions of theorists such as Mittelman (1954) with regard to the reality testing enhancements stemming from "motility" activities, and of Hendrick (1942, 1943) with regard to the drive toward "mastery," but felt they begged the basic theoretical questions posed by Freud's drive reduction model of motivation.

White argued that these conceptualizations did not go far enough toward eliminating Freud's drive model and replacing it with a more defensible competency model of motivation that is easier to validate. He spoke of the sense of "effectance" as the ultimate motivational and affective state associated with the various strivings to effectively contact and interactively explore and master the environment: "Such activities in the ultimate service of competence must, therefore, be conceived to be motivated in their own right. It is proposed to designate this motivation by the term effectance [sic], and to characterize the experience produced as a feeling of efficacy'' (1959, p. 329).[1]

White's allusion to the affective implications of competent, motivated action is central to the thesis of the present chapter. Since all forms of motivated activity have affective states associated with them, the inhibition of such motivated actions will lead to the simultaneous dissociation or unavailability for conscious experience of these associated affects. Emotions such as joy, exhilaration, pride, and exuberance are those typically associated with the sense of effectiveness. Competent performances are evidently associated with such affective states. Successful and competent performers in diverse spheres of endeavor can be observed to openly exhibit such emotions. The television cameras are frequently present during the champagne dousings and exuberant and joyous victory celebrations of professional or amateur athletes who have attained the pinnacles of achievement in their particular sport. A similar range of positive affects is evident in successful musicians or other artists whose attainments are honored by their audiences.

Although talent is a significant factor, it is not the only one underlying the various inhibitions interfering with the smooth and adaptive expression of competent actions and motivated patterns. Many truly talented individuals are unable to utilize their talents in a competent and motivated fashion. The reasons for this are quite complex and typically involve a variety of psychodynamic, structural, object relational, and characterological factors. The primary focus of the present chapter, however, will be upon the *affective* impairments associated with the psychological interferences and impediments to competence motivation and a sense of effectiveness.

A primary thesis of the present volume is that the broad range of affects available for experience, particularly those of a *positive* hedonically toned nature, is severely inhibited in certain forms of psychopathology.

Both simpler affects and more complex *affective attitudes* (i.e., determination, courage, commitment, hope, optimism, etc.) of a positive nature are inhibited in various forms of neurotic, characterological, and psychotic psychopathology. Thus, patients who exhibit an impaired capacity for affective competency manifest inhibitions in their ability to appropriately experience and express emotions such as joy, exhilaration, pride, exuberance, and excitement, and also in their overall sense of effectiveness, confidence, and self-esteem. Their optimism with regard to the future rewards obtainable through competent, motivated action is severely impoverished.

---

[1]White apparently felt the need to create a word to capture motivational aspects associated with feelings of efficacy and mastery.

Throughout the subsequent text of this chapter, the simpler term *effectiveness* rather than *effectance* will be used.

A Developmental Ladder for Competency Motivation
and Its Associated Affects and Affective Attitudes

White (1960) has very little difficulty with Freud's (1905a) image of the suckling infant at the breast as an important metaphor for depicting central psychodynamic issues surrounding the earliest *oral* psychosexual stage of development. Issues of passivity, receptivity (sucking), and oral aggressiveness (biting) can be nicely linked to subsequent personality tendencies and characterological issues typically found in clinical practice.

White begins his critique of the adequacy and comprehensiveness of such a conception of the earliest developmental phase in the following way:

> The thesis of this paper can be set forth at this point in the form of two propositions. I shall contend, first, that the *child's emotional development cannot be adequately conceptualized by an exclusive libido model*, no matter how liberally we interpret this concept. Second, I shall try to show that *when the prototypes derived from libido theory are translated into interpersonal terms they still do not constitute adequate models for development.* The best of those prototypes is undoubtedly the feeding child of the oral stage, who cuts a prominent figure even in Sullivan's revision, but from then on the models simply miss part of the significant problems of growth. In particular they fail to embody the development of competence, and they tend to direct attention away from certain crises in the growth of the child's sense of competence [1960, p. 99].

White proceeds to argue that the pleasurable drive characteristics of the feeding change subtly and gradually over the course of the first 8 months of life. Soon, the infant begins to investigate its external environment during feedings and even requires playful and interesting distractions in order to continue with a given feeding. The exploration of toys and other objects becomes very important for the rapidly developing infant. Although White does not explicitly note this, there is an increasingly excited, joyful, and even exuberant affective quality to the infant's constant sensorimotor and cognitive learning during the first year of life. Gesell and Ilg (1943) and Piaget (1936) stress the *explorative* zest and determination to incorporate new sensorimotor schemata evident in the child's play during the first year. They imply, but largely overlook, the affective components of the explorative play and locomotion, and sense of discovery which takes place during the first year of infancy.

A sense of effectiveness ("I can do it and it feels great") is the firm affective core deriving from sensorimotor accomplishments during the first

year of life. The oral receptive and oral aggressive activities, accomplishments, and associated affects (i.e., the more passive pleasures of receptivity
and sucking or the more aggressive or sadistic gratifications of biting), obviously do not tell the whole tale of this developmental period.

White, by highlighting the importance of the actively curious and playful
or socially explorative infant, and the sense of effectiveness derivable from
the competent negotiation of such actions, has opened up the possibility for a
more thorough analysis of the affects typically associated with such competent
behavior. Clearly, early forerunners of positive affects such as joy, exhilaration, and excitement, and affective attitudes such as trust, optimism, determination, confidence, and a sense of self-esteem are central to the sense of
effectiveness and accomplishment here.

The weaning process, too, according to White, involves important ele-
ments of competence motivation and a sense of effectiveness. The *depriving*
aspects which have been highlighted in the Freudian conception need to be
augmented by an appreciation of the sense of effectiveness the infant feels
upon successfully mastering the cup and giving up the bottle. A rewarding
maturational attainment, in this regard, is probably associated with the capacity for the affective attitude of *developmental courage* (see chapter 6).

The applause and celebratory reactions on the part of parental caretakers
are certainly central for a positive maturational experience here. The *mirroring* reactions of a joyous and celebratory nature on the part of the parents
can be assumed to assure a maximally positive affective experience in the
infant following such early demonstrations of competence. White suggests,
however, and this is much later validated in the developmental research
summarized by Emde (1988), that the competent attainments of this developmental period can lead to positive affects of effectiveness even without the
celebratory reactions of parental caretakers.

There is a natural emergence of curious, explorative engagements with
the external environment which occurs simultaneously with interactions domi-
nated by more passive, receptive, and oral needs. These active and explorative
actions give the infant (and parental caretakers) a great deal of pleasure and
have an extremely energizing affective impact on the family social system.

The anal phase which follows next involves much more, according to
White, than the battle over bowel training which the infant is doomed to
lose. The battle for autonomy during this phase is permeated by the risks of
experiencing shame and doubt, as noted in Erikson's (1950, 1959) psychosocial translation of Freud's psychosexual schema.

At the ages of 2 to 3, we almost always see a child engage in an emerging
sense of self-mastery and willfulness which pits her in what appears to be a
control battle with her parents. The toilet is only one place in which the
struggle for mastery and autonomy is engaged. Essentially, the negativism

and oppositionalism so prevalent during the "terrible two's" reflects, in accordance with the competence model, an increased struggle for personal habituation, order, and control. The wish not to be pushed around leads to an inevitable struggle with the parents who seem to want things their way. The parents are always severely tested during this difficult phase. Their own sense of competence (and, almost certainly, their capacity for flexibility coupled with firmness) are tested to the limit. White finds it helpful if the parents can sense the struggle for competency lurking beneath their child's defiant, stubbornly willful and oppositional behavior. A focus upon the issue of competency and the wish for a sense of effectiveness will almost always facilitate the potential for a joyous, celebratory outcome to the toilet crisis. Such open, empathic, and yet firmly expectant parental attitudes will need to be exhibited over and over again during the various struggles for control and personal autonomy typical of this age.

A character structure free of compulsive rigidity and excessive idealization of control and mastery is the ideal resolution of the competency conflicts during this phase. A sense of personal autonomy and pride in one's accomplishments and personal attainments is still another desirable result. A capacity for joyous and exuberant affects at moments of personal triumph, control over the environment, and effectiveness, as well as an ability to yield control and "let go" in a productive, flexible, and enjoyable fashion would be still other examples of the sense of effectiveness emanating from a successful resolution of the core conflicts during this developmental phase.

During the *phallic* stage, according to White, the 4- or 5-year-old child experiences an increased sense of potency in spheres well beyond the unconscious wish to supplant the same sex parent in a libidinal relationship to the opposite sex parent. An increased sense of power in three spheres of competence (locomotion, language, and imagination) leads the female child to compare herself with her mother, using a variety of competitive yardsticks. The male child does the same with his father.

White argues rather cogently that, depending upon the sensitivity and empathic nature of the parental response, the child will end up feeling either negative affects of anxiety, guilt, and shame or more positive affects of joyful, exuberant self-confidence.

The child's intrusive, arrogant thrusts out into the world, if met with a sensitive, nonthreatened, and even joyful and celebratory reaction on the part of the parents (particularly the parent of the opposite sex), may very well lead to the solidifying of a competent and assertive character structure in adulthood. The capacity for exuberant, energetic, and competitive encounters of a potentially joyful nature is a natural result of the establishment of a sense of effectiveness and competence during this phase.

The parents, according to White, must not puncture the child's illusions of competence too harshly because the child will be left with feelings of shame, guilt, and a deep sense of inferiority. Excessive fearfulness on the parents' part with regard to risk-taking actions of various sorts would be another negative outcome of parental insensitivity to the child's competency needs during this phase. An impairment of the child's potential for courageousness, self-confidence, initiative, and joyful feelings regarding assertive and competitive aspirations are dangers here as well.

Finally, while White is greatly interested in the *latency* period in terms of competence testing, this period apparently held only minimal interest for Freud. Paradoxically, Freud underestimated the degree of sexual fantasies and energy level during this phase. Also, Freud's apparent disinterest in the extensive competency strivings in fantasy, play, and learning activities led to a disregard for the powerful evolution of mastery, self-confidence, and ego development during this highly significant maturational period.

Competence is repeatedly tested during this developmental period by success or failure experiences in social relationships with peers, competitive games and sports, learning experiences at school, and work experiences such as taking on a newspaper delivery route, or going door to door collecting for charity.

An adequate sense of effectiveness is strongly consolidated during this developmental phase. Feelings and attitudes of self-confidence, mastery, and a willingness to compete and take risks will permeate the central core of the self structure of children who successfully navigate this competency testing phase.

A sense of zestful enthusiasm and joyfulness in competitive work and play situations are definite results of the successful navigation of this phase. On the other hand, fears of both success and failure and a reluctance to take risks in school and work situations are the result of severe difficulties during this phase.

Overall, the successful navigation of the competency struggles during these four developmental phases can lead to a broadly differentiated range of affect with a predominance of positive affects and affective attitudes such as joy, excitement, enthusiasm, self-confidence, courage, determination, pride, and optimism. Failures in competency struggles during these phases, on the other hand, are associated with negative affects and affective attitudes such as sadness, anxiety, depression, shame, guilt, inferiority feelings, and a pessimistic outlook.

Although White believes he is sketching a model for the development of competency motivation, he has also presented a model delineating the evolution of a sense of effectiveness and the affects typically associated with such an inner sense of masterfulness and self-confidence.

### A More Contemporary Position Regarding the Sense of Effectiveness and the "Affective Core of the Self"

The sense of competence and effectiveness is intrinsically associated with positive affects. The developmental scaffolding for this sense of effectiveness and associated positive affects needs to be established quite early, considerably earlier than White assumed was the case. Developmental research, summarized in the work of Stern (1985), has emphasized the *interpersonal* aspects of the infant's experiential world. In many ways, Winnicott's (1965) statement that "there is no such thing as a baby" has been empirically validated by the developmental research referred to in Stern's important volume.

Emde (1988) has been one of the more creative recent developmental theorists and empirical researchers. His current work emphasizes the intrinsic relationships between positive affect and competency motivation and the sense of effectiveness. He argues rather forcefully that the infant is primed biologically to express a diverse series of affects (positive and negative) which are *signals* both for the infant's self-regulatory capacities (also biologically primed) and for the external caretaker environment. He argues further that there is a biological propensity in the normative parental environment to respond in an empathically attuned and *positive* affective fashion to those signals from their infant.

In summarizing basic infant motivational patterns, Emde classifies four distinctively different types (i.e., activity, self-regulation, social fittedness, and affective monitoring). The "activity" pattern subsumes much of what White (1959, 1960, 1963) classified as competency behavior and Mittelman (1954) as "motility" behavior. Thus, the need of the infant to be active is linked to an expressive cueing interaction with the parent which has the natural, biologically given potential to trigger a positive affective mirroring response from the parent. Emde states:

> Nowhere is the affective core of self more salient than in infancy. Emotional signalling between infant and caregiver provides the basis for communicating needs, intentions and satisfaction. It communicates meaning and motivates. It provides a guide not only for need satisfaction but for learning, loving and exploring. Indeed it is the emotional availability of the caregiver in infancy which seems to be the most central growth-promoting feature of the early rearing experience [1988, p. 32].

The motivational principle of *self-regulation* is linked by Emde to Bertalanffy's (1968) principle of "equifinality." Development is depicted as a goal-oriented process with multiple ways of reaching species-important goals.

Congenitally blind and paraplegic children are, thus, able to establish a cognitive sense of object permanence, although they clearly reach this attainment from sharply different sensorimotor pathways. This is a rather optimistic motivational principle that may be linked to the "self-soothing" behavior noted by the self theorists (Kohut, 1977; Stolorow and Lachmann, 1980).

Emde views *social fittedness* as a preferable term to the biologically based motivational system of *attachment* behavior studied by Bowlby (1969). The universal tendency for "baby talk" in parents is perhaps the most dramatic example of an intuitive response of socially connected parents to early communicative activity in the infant.

The fourth basic motive of *affective monitoring* indicates a biologically innate propensity to monitor experience according to what is pleasurable and unpleasurable:

> From the mother's point of view, infant affective expressions are predominant in guiding caregiving. Mother hears a cry and acts to relieve the cause of distress; she sees a smile and hears cooing and cannot resist maintaining a playful interaction. From the infant's point of view, research such as we will review below documents an increasing use of affective monitoring for guiding one's behavior whether a mother intervenes or not [1988, p. 31].

According to Emde, these four motivational principles are inborn, universal, and operate throughout life. They are intrinsically linked to the enhancement of competency motivation, a sense of effectiveness, and the essential scaffolding of the self and its affective core. Emde argues rather convincingly that affects (particularly *positive* affects) provide a coherent, continuous sense of self and ego identity.

Positive emotions (such as joy, surprise, and interest) are extremely important and can maximize the natural developmental thrust in the infant in motoric, cognitive, and social spheres of activity. Competency and a sense of effectiveness are enhanced in an interpersonal context of such positive affective states. Emde stresses that pleasure and interest are major indicators of *affect attunement* and concludes: "we have found the most sensitive clinical indicator of emotional availability in infancy to be the presence or absence of positive affects" (1988, p. 33).

Moral development occurs quite early in Emde's developmental schema. The child is able to make important moral distinctions between 2 and 3 years of age. The internalization of parental "do's" and "don't's" can occur and be utilized in their absence at this relatively early maturational phase. Although Emde does not state this directly, it can be inferred that the *loving and beloved* aspects of the parental superegos alluded to by Schafer (1960) are initially introjected at this early phase, as are the more prohibitive and critical aspects.

Emde notes the fact that he is studying a *normative* sample of middle-class parents and infants. He further emphasizes the fact that parents suffering from various forms of psychopathology (i.e., depressed mothers, unwed teenage mothers, addicted or abusive parents, etc.) cannot always provide the *average expectable environment* stressed as being maturationally necessary in the work of Hartmann (1939). Instead, they provide unpredictable empathic attunements. The *feed cycle* depicted in the work of Winnicott (1965) and Giovacchini (1984a) impinges upon the infant in either an excessively depriving or indulgent manner.

Although Emde does not analyze this issue very fully, it can be assumed that the self-regulation motivational structures are insufficient in coping with a continuously dysfunctional parental caregiving environment. The ultimate result of such environmental impingements and failures are the *false self* disturbances noted by Winnicott (1965) and the various forms of character-ological impairment described by Giovacchini (1984). The conception of introjects offers a conceptual tool with considerable clinical utility in the study of the adaptive and competency impairments frequently seen in parents who are themselves the products of dysfunctional and unempathic parenting.

Emde does note, however, the *repetitious* and continuous self structures of a pathological nature that often may emanate from parents who permeate the early interpersonal world of their infant with negative rather than positive affects. He does not use the word *introject*, although Stern (1985) does in delineating a similar pathological internalization process during infancy. The restriction of the range of affect to largely negative rather than positive affects, in light of contemporary developmental research, leads to a diminished capacity for competency motivation, a sense of effectiveness, and ultimately, self-coherence and ego identity. Self structures are permeated, instead, by affects such as shame, guilt, anxiety, and depression. The capacity to experience affects and affective attitudes such as pride, self-esteem, optimism, and joy are severely diminished.

### Dysfunctional Parenting, Nonfunctional Introjects, and Competence Disturbance

Emde's seeming optimism with regard to the biological predisposition for *self-regulation* in infants, which he associates to the systems idea of equifinal-ity, may be restricted to areas of sensorimotor cognition and intellectual competencies. In the social sphere, average expectable interpersonal at-tunement competencies and empathic responses are clearly required from parental caretakers.

In a public place the present author once observed a parent responding to her approximately 1½-year-old child in a highly unattuned fashion. The child, perched on her lap, had a toy which she held for a brief period and then repeatedly let fall to the ground. The mother, looking more and more exasperated and preoccupied, went along with the game for a while, but then became increasingly impatient. She was obviously in no mood for this game. Finally, the infant dropped the toy one time too many. The mother proceeded to step on the toy and break it. The infant began to cry uncontrollably and the mother made little effort to comfort or console her.

Many children who grow up in dysfunctional family environments have repeatedly experienced similar failures of empathic attunement. Their competency strivings, which initially emerge in a joyful and playful fashion, are repeatedly extinguished by the mirroring failures and negative affects that permeate the parental response. The positive affects required to nurture and reinforce joyful explorative activity are almost totally lacking in the parental environment. The deficiencies in appropriate *affective monitoring* lead to a prevalance of negative over positive affects associated with a diverse variety of competence strivings and actions.

Clinical experience with patients who manifest characterological disturbance has repeatedly demonstrated the noxious impact of dysfunctional parenting upon self-esteem and adaptive coping capacity. Giovacchini (1984a) has comprehensively delineated the structural and object relational factors involved in therapeutic work with patients who have experienced a dysfunctional parental environment. He stresses that, although plentiful clinical indications exist of the deleterious psychodynamic impact of such pathological parenting, the bulk of the psychopathology emanating from these encounters is of a structural nature. Executive ego adaptive functions allowing for a competent and active approach to the outer physical and social environment become severely delimited and inhibited.

Giovacchini stresses that the dysfunctional parent produces a character disorder in their child through a process of social learning and internalization. Projective identificatory interactions repeatedly occur in which the parent places a sense of adaptational incompetence (which they have internalized from their own parents) into their child. Giovacchini gives the example of two young boys playing in a forbidden and dangerous pond area on the home property of one of the boys. The parents of that boy overheard them playing and approached them screaming that the children should not be playing near the pond. The son proceeded to wade into the pond and was in water well above his head. He began thrashing around as though he were drowning. The friend had run off into the nearby bushes to hide from the approaching parents.

As the parents neared the pond and spotted their son thrashing helplessly in the water, both of them became paralyzed with fright. The friend, feeling that he had to do something, forgot his own fear of discovery by the parents and ran into the pond. He swam over to his friend and pulled him to safety. It is not surprising that the boy who was drowning developed serious characterological difficulties. His sense of competence, adaptive capabilities, and self-esteem were severely marred as a result of dysfunctional parenting. He internalized the tendency to ego paralysis repeatedly exhibited by his parents and manifested similar tendencies at various stress points of his later adult life.

Giovacchini (1984a) describes another example of a young mother who became convinced that she was unable to comprehend or perform the basics of mothering with her newborn infant child. She felt unable to perform basic chores such as diapering or feeding her infant. She also felt that she could not recognize or decipher the baby's affective signals and hence was convinced that she could not meet her baby's needs in even the most rudimentary fashion.

Upon further analysis, it became evident that the patient's mother had been extremely inadequate and emotionally unavailable during the patient's infancy and childhood. The mother, like the patient, had felt unable to master in a competent manner the basics of maternal functioning. Giovacchini helped the patient to become aware of the deleterious impact of the introjects internalized from the relationship with her own mother. During the course of the symbiotic attachment to her mother, she had identified with the mother's dysfunctional behavior and affective attitudes. Her own sense of competency, particularly in the sphere of maternal adaptational functioning, had been seriously marred as a result of these early encounters with her mother.

Giovacchini's use of the *nonfunctional introject* construct has broad clinical utility, particularly in work with competency disturbances stemming from experiences with dysfunctional parents. Many perceived competency insufficiencies and consequent self-critical reactions involve an unconscious attack against an internalized parental object representation. As Freud delineated in his work, ''Mourning and Melancholia'' (1917), the greater the unconscious ambivalence toward the object, the greater the internalized aggression implicit in the melancholic self-attacks following the loss of that object. The individual attacks her own ego and self representation, unconsciously shielding the original object and its deficiencies from more direct confrontation and attack.

Many patients brought up in homes with dysfunctional parents become extremely critical of perceived competence deficiencies in themselves, and in many cases this masks a dreaded and more direct assault against the incompetent parent from childhood. Thus, a woman following a period of successes in certain other spheres of endeavor began to mercilessly attack her own professional work competency. She felt unable to communicate effectively with fellow employees and to instruct them in skill areas related to her own expertise. She was doing to herself something that her mother had often done to her during childhood. While instructing her on a musical instrument (which the mother was herself adept at playing) the mother was extremely critical of the patient's response to her training efforts. Interestingly, the patient felt that her mother was a very poor instructor. Her attack against her own instructional and communicative capabilities camouflaged the unconsciously felt criticism of her mother's deficiencies as an instructor.

The perception of inadequacy or personal incompetency, thus, in many cases, involves a veiled critical attack against an internalized object who has exhibited similar forms of nonfunctional behavior in the past. Giovacchini's therapeutic model, which derived from extensive experience with character disordered patients, allows for an effective surfacing of these nonfunctional introjects for purposes of interpretive exploration. Ultimately, the therapist's competent use of interpretations is internalized by the patient in the form of a new *analytic introject*. This new introject has a much more functional and effectiveness-promoting character, and eventually replaces the original less functional introjects within the patient's ego and character structure. The patient begins to reown dissociated competency actions and the joyous, prideful affects linked to them.

CASE ILLUSTRATIONS

A young man attained a considerable degree of proficiency and evident competency in his professional career. Nevertheless he insisted upon continually heaping abuse upon himself, noting various deficiencies in the quality of his work. At one point he screamed out defiantly at the therapist (who had been noting the evidence of his competency in his professional work) that he should never have chosen such a career and would have been much better off working as a construction worker. In such a line of work, he emphasized, he could at least utilize his considerable physical strength and mechanical dexterity, and would not need to work on complex problems of a more abstract nature.

His feelings of being an undeserving imposter who was fooling both peers and authorities at his place of employment were insistently repeated throughout much of the treatment. He insisted that he probably did not deserve to be paid for such shoddy work efforts and accomplishments.

As the patient's confidence, self-esteem and sense of effectiveness began to improve during the course of therapy, he expressed more openly critical reactions to the therapist's various foibles and incompetencies in conducting the treatment. (During that period the therapist felt incompetent, as if he did not deserve to be paid for such shoddy and ineffective work efforts, but he did not verbalize these feelings.) The patient often found the therapist's interpretations or observations to be long-winded and noted that they frequently missed the basic point of what the patient had been saying. He felt that there was no need to bring in further dreams for analysis, since the therapist only made him analyze them by himself anyway. His criticism of the therapist in many ways resembled the critical way his mother had approached him and his father throughout his childhood.

Both the patient and his father felt a strong need to protect the mother from their angry reactions to her critical assaults on their feelings of competency and sense of effectiveness. He followed the lead of the father who would avoid any angry confrontations with the mother in order to maintain a peaceful household.

The transferential expression of confrontational and angry critical feelings toward the therapist assisted the patient in working through the angry feelings toward his mother. The fact that the therapist did not retaliate by cruelly criticizing him (or even worse, become saddened, depressed, or keel over and die), offered him a valuable containing experience, one which had not been afforded him during his early developmental years.

Feelings of competency and self-expression for this particular patient had always been associated with a sense of danger and fearfulness. Both of his parents tended to hover overprotectively, shielding him from the natural risks inherent in any form of risk-taking activity. Any form of autonomous or self-directive activity was fearfully reacted to by both parents who had never, themselves, been able to fully attain a sense of competency and autonomy.

His parents, by reacting with anxiety and tension to his explorations, tended to place a shroud of danger and fearfulness about them. Much of the therapeutic task for this patient involved the creation of a totally different affective context for his competency strivings. The therapist, on the other hand, frequently applauded competency activities, an adventurous exploration of the world, and any form of reasonable risk-taking activity.

Another patient, a successful man in a profession hand-chosen by his parents, could never extract much satisfaction from his various professional activities which, evidently, were performed quite well. He would consistently underestimate the degree of competency he exhibited on various work assignments. On one occasion he took over a difficult assignment including many employees who were not performing their duties in an efficient or cooperative fashion. He implemented a new managerial system and utilized his own authority to completely turn the project around, making a successful work unit out of a highly unsuccessful one.

The modesty of this man, in recounting this accomplishment, was quite noticeable. He seemed surprised and uncomfortable by any reference to this achievement at later points in the treatment. He preferred to view himself as an unsuccessful person who was merely plodding along at work. At least a part of his incapacity to own a sense of competency, potency, or effectiveness was linked to a need to unconsciously castigate himself for having submitted to the career chosen for him by his parents. He was forever expressing regrets and mourning over the past vocational choice points in his life and the "roads not taken." His sense of inferiority and feeling of impotence could be directly linked to the inability to assert himself and differ with his parents.

His parents were both willful individuals who, although not capable of a warm, loving relationship with each other, always were able to establish a united front in response to any form of defiant behavior on the part of their children. Indeed, they could not tolerate any assertiveness from their children and quickly united to squelch the merest hint of confrontational reactions on their children's part.

Associated with this man's lack of a solid sense of effectiveness were strong feelings of sexual inadequacy with his wife and a sense that he could never passionately arouse or please her. It was interesting to note that, although having sufficient motoric skills to be an excellent tennis player, he would become very clumsy during the course of lovemaking with his wife.

Thus, both in the spheres of work and love, this man was not capable of feeling powerful, competent, or effective. He always seemed too squelched by his internalized, more powerful parental introjects and, hence, was perpetually unable to express his competency, either at work or in a sexually assertive fashion with his wife. He did succeed, however, in temporarily pervading the atmosphere of the therapy room with a sense of impotence and helplessness. The therapist often felt in dealing with this man that he was actually dealing with the powerful "bulldozer" parents who stubbornly refused to be budged toward taking the perspective of anyone else but themselves. It was quite helpful for this patient, when the therapist repeatedly shared with him his sense of being constantly beaten down by two stubborn, unbudging parents. This feeling would often occur in the therapist, following an interpretation that clearly made absolutely no sense at all to the patient. It would particularly occur whenever the patient made it clear that he needed to stubbornly persist in disowning his more potent, competent affects and strivings for effectiveness (this aspect of the treatment will be more extensively discussed in chapter 12).

It is, of course, not surprising that this man's sexual and work competency increased as he became more in touch with angry feelings toward both parents, which were transferentially expressed toward both the therapist and the patient's wife. His awareness of his latent, much more confrontational true self began to come to the fore in his treatment.

He increasingly became aware that he was perpetually beating himself down and hitting himself "below the belt" in the same manner as his parents had done to him at the slightest sign of competent or assertive activity. It was surprising for this man to discover the possibility that his competency might have made him a threat to his father. His need to constantly keep his competency strivings under check was thus linked to an unconscious need to protect his father from them.

### Conclusions

Both cases involve individuals whose competency strivings were severely inhibited due to nonfunctional introjects stemming from early object relational encounters with parents who could not joyfully celebrate their children's strivings toward effectiveness and competence, and indeed were threatened by them. Although the dynamics and motives for the unreceptive response on the part of the parents may very well have been different in these two cases, the fact remains that neither set of parents responded with positive affective attunement and empathy to their children's explorative and competence strivings. In the first case, the parents created a phobic reaction toward explorative activity by overprotectively hovering over their child. In the second case, the parents stubbornly shot down any confrontational or assertive actions that did not agree with their own viewpoints.

In both cases, the budding potential for activities relating to explorative competency and a sense of effectiveness was weakened by parents who gave ample evidence of their lack of comfort with such activities. They could not provide the positive affects alluded to by Emde (1988) as necessary for the nurturing of a sense of effectiveness in their children.

In the present chapter, stress has been placed on an aspect of the issue of competency disturbance that has not been emphasized in previous studies of this problem. The notion of the linkage of a sense of effectiveness with a process of pathological introjection consisting of the pervasive dissociation and disownership of positive affects and affective attitudes has been neglected in the literature.

Two lines of study of competency difficulties have been previously pursued. The first involves the "he can but he won't" disorders typically seen in various forms of learning disorder and underachievement patterns. The second involves the work inhibitory and *imposter* feelings associated with individuals exhibiting the *catastrophe of success*[2] syndrome.

---

[2]The title of a recent biography of Frank Capra by Joseph McBride. The title is derived from a statement by Tennessee Williams regarding the pain he felt following the success of *The Glass Menagerie.*

The bulk of the academic underachievement literature (Halpern, 1964; Newman, Dember, and Krug, 1973) has focused upon clinical case material consisting of male patients. Almost all of the imposter studies, on the other hand, have involved clinical studies of female patients (Horner, 1970; Horner and Walsh, 1974; Moulton, 1986; Ruderman, 1986). Despite this gender discrepancy in the literature, it should be evident that the dissociated affective disturbances linked with impaired effectiveness can occur equally in both males and females who have been unfortunate enough to have their strivings for competency in early childhood greeted by parental reactions reflecting negative rather than positive affects.

# Chapter 5

# POSITIVE AFFECT AND OEDIPAL CONFLICT

The attainment and resolution of some form of oedipal phase struggle has always been a central issue underlying psychoanalytic treatment. It has typically been depicted as a triangular constellation in which the child's budding self strivings and ego capacities are brought into hostile confrontation with the parallel strivings and capacities of the parent of the same sex. The object of this highly competitive struggle is the affection and sexualized attentions of the beloved parent of the opposite sex.

In the classic view, the dangers of castration (particularly in the male child, but also in the female) somehow lead to a resolution involving a renunciation of the original libidinal strivings for the parent of the opposite sex and of the hostile antagonism toward the same sex parent. An ego and superego enhancing identification with the same sex parent is the internalized structural end product of this renunciation which ultimately contributes to broad maturational advancement in the child's ego, self, characterological, and affective structures.

The oedipal struggle has typically been delineated in negative affective terms. Affects such as shame, envy, guilt, anger, anxiety, and fear have always predominated in clinical examples of the oedipal crisis and have become central conceptual underpinnings of the Oedipus dynamic. An essentially "shock" theory of affect is typically utilized to delineate the motivations for renunciation of libidinal strivings and angry, rageful, and even murderous fantasies and impulsive action tendencies. The risky oedipal strivings are given up due to unconsciously perceived danger signals and fantasies of somatic injury, particularly in the form of castration. A very anxious, fearful child submits to a threatening and dangerous adult authority due to the shocking recognition of potentially dangerous consequences to the self and its

73

body integrity. This admittedly oversimplified version of the resolution of the oedipal struggle has typically given a negative affective cast to the classical triangular metaphor. Positive affects and affective attitudes such as love, courage, joy, and an exhilarated sense of effectiveness have often been neglected in this traditional version of the oedipal conflict.

## THE IMPACT OF FREUD'S VIEWS ABOUT AFFECT UPON HIS CONCEPTUALIZATION OF THE OEDIPAL CONFLICT

As was noted in more detail in chapter 1, Freud shifted from a view of affects as toxic discharge phenomena (1894, 1895, 1896) to his ultimate conception of them as having *signal* properties which alert the ego to dangers requiring defensive action. He never viewed affects as mental phenomena in their own right but rather saw them as derivatives of the much more central drives. In his later theorizing (1915a,b,c), Freud became increasingly locked into a theoretical orientation of *drive reduction* in which drives (and their affective derivatives) were potentially noxious, toxic, and dangerous impulse-generating states requiring active efforts by the ego to cope with, curtail, or, at best, sublimate and neutralize them, so that they might be diverted to more socially constructive and useful purposes.

Freud's cornerstone conception with regard to the centrality of the oedipal conflicts at the root of all neuroses (1905a) was ultimately enmeshed and intimately linked with his theoretical biases toward drive and affect reduction. Thus, the oedipal child is depicted as angry, murderously rageful (at least in fantasy), competitively envious and jealous, and highly vulnerable to feelings of shame and guilt. All of these negative affects, although having adaptive signal functions, are experienced as painful internal states. Once appraised, they motivate various forms of action geared toward reducing the inner discomfort emanating from them. The oedipal male child ends up identifying with the father and internalizing a more solid ego and superego in the process. He does this in order to extinguish or diminish painful feelings of shame, guilt, and anxiety stemming from the unconsciously felt dangers of castration.

Freud's "shock" viewpoint with regard to affects associated with oedipal triangular strivings are particularly evident in his conception of the motivations for the ultimate dissolution of the oedipal dilemma in both boys and girls (1924a). The little boy views the vagina with shock, dreading that a similar punishment might befall him (i.e., castration), were he to further seek gratification of his oedipal impulses, fantasies, and wishes. The little girl, on the other hand, is shocked and disappointed by her mother's failure to provide her with a much desired penis. Whereas the male child turns away from libidinized aspirations and fantasies with regard to the mother out of the perceived threat of castration, the female oedipal child turns away in disappointment from the mother and substitutes a wish for a baby from father. The unpleasantness and dangers of hostile and retaliatory confrontations from a jealous, angry mother ultimately lead to a dissolution of her conflict and a displacement of her wishes for father's love to a more suitable male figure. The little boy must ultimately repress his oedipal strivings toward mother and ultimately will more adaptively displace these feelings and wishes to a suitable female figure. The successful resolution of the Oedipus conflict is thereby linked for both males and females to an eventual capacity for intimacy and feelings of loving tenderness and commitment in adulthood. The capacity for loving, object constant attachments is severely inhibited, however, in those who have not successfully resolved their oedipal conflicts. Kernberg (1980b, 1991a) has developed a number of Freud's original ideas with regard to successful loving and coupling capacity from both an oedipal and an object relations perspective.

Ogden (1989) has further differentiated the oedipal issues relevant for men from those for women, elaborating upon certain *transitional* oedipal states for each gender that Freud had overlooked. Working from an object relational theoretical paradigm, he questions the shock theory of affect that underlies much of Freud's theorizing about the Oedipus conflict. He particularly questions the affect shock theories implicit in Freud's (1925, 1931, 1933) views of castration anxiety, shameful penis envy, and disappointment and contempt for the mother, as being the basic affects underlying the little girl's turning away from the mother to the father.

For Ogden, it doesn't make good object relational sense that the little girl would turn away from her preoedipal love of her mother to a maturationally higher level and oedipal triangular love for her father, out of disappointment over the fact that both the mother and she lack a penis. A traumatically shocking affective experience of disappointment should rather, according to Ogden, lead to a more regressed state of narcissistic withdrawal and omnipotent fantasies. He, thus, states:

A love relationship entered into as a result of a flight from shame and narcissistic injury is almost certain to be constructed for the purpose of narcissistic defense, and is unlikely to involve genuine object love. It is only a foundation of healthy narcissism, generating feelings of hope and of openness to the unknown, that prepares the way for the little girl's taking the risk of falling in love with the external object father—a person outside her omnipotent control. The picture of the little girl shamefully, defeatedly and angrily turning away from the mother to the father is at odds with one of the most fundamental psychoanalytic propositions: the concept of the Oedipus complex as the cornerstone of the development of mature object love [1989, pp. 113–114].

Ogden further notes that the mother must prepare her daughter for the transition to oedipal love attachments via certain object relational experiences of a lovingly, caretaking, nurturing and sexually accepting and receptive nature. The mother reacts appreciatively to the daughter's various aesthetic attributes on an unconcious fantasy level, as the mother's own father might have done with her. The mother's capacity for empathic attunement to her daughter at this critical point paves the way for a successful entrance into and ultimate resolution of the actual oedipal process. Ogden concludes: "It is the success of the early oedipal transitional relationship that paves the way for the little girl's act of courage in allowing herself to fall in love with the actual father" (1989, p. 122). Ogden argues that a similar transitional experience from a somewhat different object relational perspective must be provided for the boy to successfully navigate his oedipal conflicts.

Freud's clinging to a drive metapsychology in which affects (particularly positive affects) are of secondary importance, is responsible for the conceptual and clinical limitations of his oedipal conflict theory. The shocking and potentially traumatic impact of negative affects such as envy, shame, humiliation, jealousy, anxiety, rage, fear, and disappointment are insufficient to fully explain the maturationally sophisticated loving, object constant attachment capacities that result from a successful dissolution and resolution of the oedipal crisis.

Freud was severely hindered in this regard by his reluctance to give a functionally autonomous status to affects, particularly positive affects, in his conceptualization of the Oedipus conflict and its resolution. By viewing affects as secondary to the drives, he ended up with a focus upon the more shocking and largely negative affects in his depiction of the oedipal dilemma. Freud was also restricted by his tendency to give primary status to biological factors such as *constitutional bisexuality* (1924a), in his explanations of the sexual identifications resulting after the dissolution of the Oedipus complex. His concordant tendency to give secondary status to object relational conceptualizations, well documented in the scholarly summary of his work by Greenberg and Mitchell (1983), also handicapped Freud's theorizing with regard to the Oedipus complex. Freud tended to neglect certain features of the complete Oedipus complex, as a result of his loyally held assumptions about the metapsychology of drive theory.

## THE CLASSICAL VIEWPOINT WITH REGARD TO THE "COMPLETE" OEDIPUS COMPLEX

The classical conception of the complete Oedipus complex assumes that three distinct developmental phases can be noted: a *preoedipal* phase of a largely dyadic nature in which both the boy and girl are involved in a relatively comfortable, largely narcissistic, and symbiotic attachment to the mother. This is followed by a transitional *negative oedipal* phase in which there is an envious and identificatory attitude toward the mother's sexual experience with the father on the part of the boy and of the father's sexual experience with mother on the part of the girl. Finally, there is a clearly and truly *oedipal* phase in which the envious identificatory attitudes are reversed for the boy and the girl. The boy envies the father and wishes to replace him with the mother, and the girl envies the mother, wishing to replace her with the father.

Ogden (1989) makes it clear that his *transitional* oedipal phase is not synonymous with the negative oedipal phase which is classically depicted as an interlude of a largely triangular and homoerotic nature in which both the boy and girl envy and wish to replace the opposite sex parent in their intimate sexual relationship to the same sex parent. Ogden's transitional phase is an essentially dyadic transaction between the boy or girl and the mother. On an object relational and essentially fantasy level, a transitional experience of attunement is provided by the mother who contains the *father-in-mother* (via her fantasized object attachments to her own father) and prepares both the boy and girl for entrance into a more fully triangular relationship with both herself and her husband.

Although Freud explores the negative oedipal conflict in "The Ego and the Id" (1923), Frankiel (1991) is surprised by his lack of attention to the passive feminine loving attitude toward the father in his analysis of little Hans (1909), and links this to the limitations of his own self-analysis.

Freud was most comfortable in linking a strongly homoerotic negative oedipal orientation in both the boy and girl to biologically determined variations in their constitutional bisexuality. He did not feel it necessary to explore either the object relational characteristics of such attachment tendencies or the positive affects that underlie them. As with the positive oedipal attachments, Freud envisioned an ambivalent, essentially conflictual attitude which either was a regressive and passive–feminine defense against more threatening and dangerous incestuous impulses on the part of the boy toward the mother, or was linked to a weakened and biologically based sense of masculinity.

Freud barely delineated at all the homoerotic and negative oedipal issues involved in the girl's triangular relationship to her parents. His rather limited and unsystematic explorations of negative oedipal issues in general, but particularly in relationship to girls and women, may partially be explainable in terms of empathic deficiencies stemming from the limitations of his self-analysis. It may also stem from his paternalism and lack of comfort with women or a conceptualization of their psychodynamics. Additionally, his limited conceptualizations of negative oedipal dynamics almost certainly stems from his drive theoretical orientation and lack of a view of affects as autonomous experiential states in their own right. His lack of formulations with regard to a broad range of differentiated affects (including positive ones) excluded the joyful, exhilarating, risk-taking, and courageous affects associated with attachment and bonding needs toward the parent of the same sex. The girl envies, for many reasons, the intimacy available to the father in his sexual relationship with the mother. The boy, similarly, envies the intimacy provided the mother in her sexual relationship with the father.

Strong bonding needs (perhaps of a partly sexual character) exist between the boy and his father and between the boy's father and his own father and men in general. Bly (1991) has recently explored the joyful affects associated with strong male bonding attachments. Similarly strong bonding needs of a potentially joyful, risk-taking, and courageous nature exist between the girl and her mother and between the girl's mother and her own mother and women in general. Women seem generally more courageous than men in their comfort with joyful bonding attachments with members of the same sex (perhaps of an unconsciously sexualized nature).

Whereas Freud's view of the negative oedipal phase is highly biologized and largely focused upon the same negative affects involved in his exploration of the positive oedipal phase, it is much easier from a contemporary perspective to delineate the positive affects involved in such psychological struggles. The advances in both object relations and affect theory alluded to in chapter 1 are largely responsible for this greater ease in formulating the positive affects of a joyful and exhilarated nature associated with negative oedipal fantasies and interpersonal relationships. Blos (1985) has elaborated on some of the strong positive affects associated with early same sex bonding in adolescent males.

Freud did not spend much time or energy in explicating preoedipal attachments, other than in his few writings on women and female sexuality (1925, 1931, 1933). It was largely left to subsequent writers such as Mahler (1967) and McDougall (1982), and object relations theorists such as Klein (1946), Fairbairn (1952b), and Winnicott (1965) to elaborate conceptualizations with regard to preoedipal phases of development and their psychodynamics. From a contemporary perspective, it is evidently not very easy to neatly differentiate oedipal from preoedipal psychodynamics. A good example of this clinical and conceptual blurring of boundaries was evident in Tyson's (1991) interpretive emphasis upon preoedipal rather than oedipal factors in reaction to an extensive psychoanalytic case summary by Feldman (1990) focusing upon what he considered the essentially oedipal issues in that case. Simon (1991) recently emphasized the blurring of conceptual and clinical boundaries between these two forms of oedipal terrain and seems to agree with Ogden (1989) who emphasizes the essentially dialectical nature of all forms of psychic experience emanating from both preoedipal and oedipal sources.

A simultaneously present dialectical tension exists across a broad range of experiential data and modes of relatedness at any given moment of time. Almost any clinical data manifesting oedipal conflictual material can also be assumed to reflect preoedipal, negative oedipal, and transitional oedipal modes of psychic experience and relatedness.

Freud almost completely neglected the actual behavioral impact of the parents in their *counteroedipal* reactions to the child's preoedipal, negative oedipal, transitional, and oedipal action tendencies. A contemporary approach to the centrality of oedipal psychodynamics, however, cannot do the same. We must, rather, assume that it *does* make a difference how the idiosyncratic parental character structure tendencies, affective reactions, and object relational orientations, interface with a child's oedipal fantasies, feelings, and aspirations.

## COUNTEROEDIPAL REACTIONS OF THE PARENTS

The classical conception of the oedipal conflict is largely focused upon assumptions with regard to intrapsychic dynamics within the mind of the child. There is almost no focus, however, on what is going on within the minds of the parents. Simon notes that the "counteroedipal" aspects of the parents' response must also be carefully studied, defining this form of reactivity in the following way: "That term [counteroedipal] is shorthand for the parental wishes, desires, and behavior toward the child, such as oedipal conflicts the parent experiences vis-à-vis the child" (1991, p. 655). Although Freud briefly flirted with a counteroedipal focus in his interest in tendencies toward "seductive" attitudes and actions on the part of parents, he soon decided that *fantasies* of seduction were more critical determinants of neurotic pathology than actual seduction experiences. In his paper on female sexuality (1931), he emphasized the more general and universal role of the mother as seducer in exercising her ordinary bodily care of the young child. In contemporary psychoanalytic thinking, we are much more aware of the actual exposure of children to physical and sexual forms of abuse as one aspect of the interactive matrix in dysfunctional families.

Family and couple dynamics are now seen as extremely important factors in determining oedipal conflicts and neurotic and characterological dysfuntion. Simon, summarizing the contributions of Scharff and Scharff (1987) in the sphere of family therapy, states that:

[They] offer a particularly lucid framework, emphasizing the complementary roles of how the parents create the child, including creating the child's complex, and of how the child creates the parents. Within this "field theory" (or, in their terms, an object-relations theory), one can see how it might be difficult to determine exactly where, or inside of whom a particular Oedipus complex is located. It exists in a field of forces, both within the child and within the family system as it were. Any one person's (or any one family member's) Oedipus complex is a somewhat arbitrary construct, a localization of iron filings within a magnetic field. If you shift the relative positions of the magnets or distances of the magnet from the iron filings, or the strength of the magnetic field, you get corresponding rearrangements of the iron filings. Their characterization of oedipal development as experienced by the child emphasizes the stabilizing role of the parental couple, in the face of the child's "genital sexualization of triangular relationships" [1991, p. 658].

Thus, the nature of the sexual relationship between the parents is a quite important family systemic factor in determining their child's oedipal conflicts. The oedipal child who can too easily "divide and conquer" her parents, due to the weakness of their loving, joyful, and passionate attachments and effective experiences together, is severely underdeveloped, cramped, and restricted as a result of the pathological nature of the parental counteroedipal response.

The capacity to experience loving feelings, which Krystal (1988) has argued are the most maturationally differentiated form of affect in adults, is severely hindered and impeded by pathological responses on the part of the parents during the oedipal phase. The capacity for positive affective experience in general may be severely inhibited as a result of a pathological parental response to the child's noticeably sexualized and aggressivized oedipal motivations.

The classical psychoanalytic model, for various reasons, has overlooked counteroedipal aspects of the parental response. It has particularly overlooked the positive affects that may be more normatively prevalent in both parent and child during the oedipal period than has been assumed on the basis of that theoretical position.

### POSITIVE AFFECT IN THE PARENTAL RESPONSE TO THE CHILD'S OEDIPAL STRIVINGS

Kohut's self theoretical explorations with patients exhibiting narcissistic disorders (1971, 1977) led him to emphasize the positive affective features of the oedipal period. He repeatedly noticed that, as such patients began to move into an oedipal phase, the analytic ambience typically had a joyful quality:

"a joy that has all the earmarks of an emotionality that accompanies a maturational or a developmental achievement" (1977, p. 229).

Kohut went on to argue that the child who enters the oedipal phase with a firm, cohesive, and continuous sense of self will experience assertive–possessive and affectionate–sexual desires for the parent of the opposite sex and assertive, self-confident, competitive feelings for the parent of the same sex. Kohut argues that the normal counteroedipal response should be as follows:

> The affectionate desire and the assertive–competitive rivalry of the oedipal child will be responded to by normally empathic parents in two ways. The parents will react to the sexual desires and to the competitive rivalry of the child by becoming sexually stimulated and counteraggressive, and, at the same time, they will react with joy and pride to the child's developmental achievement, to his vigor and assertiveness [1977, pp. 230–231].

The positive affects alluded to by Kohut are at the heart of the oedipal interaction between parent and child. They are noteworthy omissions in the classical description, according to Kohut, because of the *disintegration products* often emanating from parental empathic failures during the child's oedipal phase of development. Parents who respond defensively to their child's newfound sense of sexuality, assertiveness, and competitiveness will inhibit and distort such strivings and their associated positive affects. Thus, a joyful, sexually curious, and actively explorative child can be diverted into becoming a joyless, ambivalent, and symptom-ridden adult.

For Kohut, it is the parental incapacity to mirror the positive affects in the child at moments of oedipal experimentation that is disastrous for the ultimate expansion of the child's self-confidence. Stolorow, Brandchaft, and Atwood make a similar point in their elaboration of intersubjective aspects of Kohut's work:

> His discovery of the developmental importance of phase-appropriate mirroring of grandiose, exhibitionistic experiences points, from our perspective, to the critical role of attuned responsiveness in the integration of affect states involving pride, expansiveness, efficacy and pleasureable excitement. As Kohut has shown, the integration of such affect states is crucial for the combination of self-esteem and self-confident ambition [1987, pp. 67–68].

The natural joy and exhilaration inherent in the child's assertive, active, explorative thrusts outward toward the world during the "phallic oedipal" period, under ideal circumstances, is met with an equally joyful, proud, and empathic mirroring response from the parents. The father is not threatened by the latent sexual competitiveness and aggressiveness of his son and does not feel the need to respond in an excessively counteraggressive and competitive fashion. Neither does the father respond in an excessively passive or idealizing fashion, implying that the child's assertiveness and active thrust is greater and hence more valued than his own capacity. In either case, the oedipal male child would pick up unconscious signals of a need to parent and protect the father. The child's natural spontaneity and *true self* potential (Winnicott, 1965) would subsequently be discouraged and diverted toward an excessively protective and essentially false characterological organization.

A similarly joyful thrust outward toward the world by the oedipal female child needs to be met by an equally positive and joyfully excited response from her mother. The empathically attuned mother will be neither threatened nor excessively idealizing in response to the child's assertive, competitive, and active probes of the outer environment. She will experience, as does the father with the boy, the counteraggressive and sexual feelings, but will not respond in a manner indicating a need for protection from her daughter. She will not exhibit any form of intolerance of the positive affects and affective attitudes generated via these new oedipal level interactions. The little girl's courage in exhibiting an assertive sexual move toward the father will be responded to proudly and with some generative joy, rather than via competitiveness or some form of idealizing proxy evocation.

Erikson's (1950) conception of the *generativity* implicit in the emotionally mature parent's response to their child's creative aspirations, which may very well outdistance their own attainments, is relevant to the present discussion. The parents who can accept their powers are more capable of empowering their child toward greater and greater self-confidence, assertiveness, and competitive self-actualizing forms of creativity and achievement. Providing that the parent is not too narcissistically engaged with the child's attainments as a proxy extension for their own fantasized accomplishments (Elkind, 1991), the child's self-confidence and breadth of affect range (especially in the sphere of positive affect tolerance) will be propelled forward.

A critical factor, as Scharff and Scharff (1987) and Kernberg (1991a,b) have noted, is the solidity of the sexual, passionate, and loving attachment between the parents. The child (whether male or female) attains an awareness of the intimate sexual bonding and loving connectedness of the parents. Both can shift comfortably back and forth between lovingly attentive reactions to the child and to their mate. "Divide and conquer" scenarios cannot very easily be enacted. Neither mother nor father is so needy and deprived vis-à-vis their mate that they must turn to the child for protection, symbiotic merger, or excessively seductive exchanges. Despite or because of the puncturing of narcissistic fantasies and illusions, the child ultimately feels supported and protected against preoedipal, negative oedipal, or oedipal (incestuous) danger situations.

As Ogden (1989) has emphasized, the mother who has had a positive sexual, affective, and identificatory experience with her own father can provide a solid transitional oedipal experience for both her male and female child. She will be similarly available, of course, on a passionate and loving level with her husband. Such a mother can provide a celebratory and joyful matrix for her son's (or daughter's) oedipal experimentation and playfulness. The father, too, if he has been fortunate enough to have been provided with joyful and free access to his mother in the oedipal sphere, can provide his male or female child with similarly joyful access to either the mother within himself or to his wife, the mother of his children. He should be able to be passionate and loving with his wife as well.

Bollas (1989) has emphasized the importance of celebratory affects as a central ingredient in the psychotherapy process. He argues that too often we tend to focus upon constructs such as resistance and negative transference and exclude more positive affectual experience from our survey of the treatment process. The therapist often feels uncomfortable with positive affects, particularly the wish to applaud or celebrate the patient's accomplishments. Worrying a bit too much about the seductive potential of such applause or appreciative reactions, the therapist tends to eschew them. Given the fact that the bulk of our patients have had parents who could not provide freedom of access to the expression and experience of positive affects, it is frequently important that the therapist be allowed to experience such affects together with the patient.

Ogden (1989) provides a rather poignant example of a female therapist brought to the verge of joyful tears by her drab, sexually undifferentiated young female patient's tentative experimental efforts to wear more feminine clothing. The patient's mother had been abandoned by the father and had had a series of relationships with men whom the daughter was never allowed to confront or get to know. The daughter, it seemed, had the need to protect her mother against her own feminine sexuality (as the mother seemed to need to do for her). She felt similarly in the transference, but gradually allowed herself to experiment with a different scenario vis-à-vis her therapist. She hesitantly exposed her feminine sexuality to the therapist, and was met with a joyful and celebratory response. The patient's joyful oedipal feelings could now be experienced more freely and without the need to protect the therapist (mother) from them.

Many patients currently seen in treatment have felt the need to shield parents from their positive affects associated with oedipal fantasies and aspirations. Their parents seemed either unreceptive to such positive affects or potentially damaged or destroyed by them. These patients have proceeded in many ways to obliterate their oedipal aspirations and the positive affects associated with them. Their intense unconscious need to protect the parents from their oedipal self representations and associated affects, forms the heart of the resistance analysis during the course of treatment.

A few clinical examples will next be provided illustrating the potentially debilitating impact of parental incapacities for joyful oedipal encounters with their children. Parents who have not experienced such encounters with their own parents cannot provide celebratory experiences at highly significant oedipal moments for their own children. As Ogden (1989) has noted, they cannot provide the father-in-mother or the mother-in-father transitional experiences for the child, since they are largely lacking as internalized object relational structures within themselves. A range of character difficulties and oedipal inhibitions ensue in the children of such parents.

Perhaps, one of the most common spheres of dysfunction stemming from such oedipal interferences is reflected in the incapacity to establish committed long-term relationships. These patients seem unable to experience the "oedipal victories" implicit in successful object constant attachments. When they do allow themselves the luxury of such victories, they experience extreme discomfort over the joyous affects suddenly made available to them. The unconscious loyalty to their oedipally deficient parents leads to a need to protect the parent from the joyous affects implicit in their potential or actual victories. These patients unconsciously view joyous oedipal experiences as having a potentially destructive impact upon their supposedly fragile and vulnerable parents. Such fears do not merely stem from unconscious death wishes toward the parents, but rather are natural end products of the counteroedipal attitudes of the parents that have been repetitiously evident throughout their lives.

## CASE ILLUSTRATIONS

### Case 1

The patient represented a catastrophic example of counteroedipal failure on the part of the parents. She was a 60-year-old woman who had never been able to marry or to successfully become involved in a long-term intimate relationship. Her parents' disastrously unsuccessful relationship had been a major traumatic factor for her. The parents became involved with each other as a result of an arranged marriage and maintained a bitter, combative, and essentially nonsexual relationship throughout her childhood. The mother literally used the patient as a "chastity belt" by sleeping with her rather than the father until the patient's fourteenth birthday.

The patient recalls the father imploring the mother for sexual intimacy, to no avail. The mother, a helpless and fearful woman, had established a viciously symbiotic enmeshment with her daughter throughout her childhood. The mother made it clear that sexuality or passion were unessential aspects of life. The father, on the other hand, became increasingly bitter toward the patient whom he recognized was being hopelessly enmeshed and identified with the mother. Throughout her early adolescence he disparaged and devalued her sexuality and frequently called her a "whore" when she exhibited any passionate interests or behavior. He used a similarly disparaging term for the mother, despite her failure to manifest passionate interest of any sort.

The patient gradually developed a sense of herself as the "ugly duckling" who could never successfully engage in an intimate or passionate relationship with a man. She felt doomed to the role of "oedipal loser." Even in her dreams, she could not envision herself in successful oedipal terms. In one dream in particular, she pictured herself at her wedding. She began to walk down the aisle, but diagonally rather than straight ahead toward the priest awaiting her on a stage. She never successfully reached the front platform and awoke with a feeling of deep dissatisfaction and unhappiness.

The object relational significance of her felt oedipal insufficiencies had to be intensively explored throughout the treatment. Her loyalty to the symbiotically devouring mother and furiously rejecting and devaluing father introjects needed to be repeatedly confronted and interpretively explored. Opportunities for joyous or celebratory oedipal transferential experience were few and far between during the course of treatment, but were preciously savored when they did occur.

## Case 2

The patient was a rather intense and conscientious young man who carried around within him the unhappy and emotionally uncommunicative relationship between his parents. He became involved in a protective relationship with his mother who frequently seemed in danger of physical abuse at the hands of his father. His wishes for warm emotional contact and identificatory bonding with the father were perpetually frustrated via the father's workaholic tendencies and emotional unavailability.

His relationships with women had never been completely satisfactory and had often ended prematurely. His capacity for a joyous and victorious oedipal experience had been dulled and inhibited as a result of the lack of joyous responsiveness of the parents either with each other or in relationship with their children. He had recently become involved in a fairly serious relationship that had progressed longer and more deeply than any of his previous intimate attachments. His anxiety with regard to the dangers of commitment to this woman in certain ways camouflaged his unconscious dilemma with regard to the meaning of oedipal victory. Since his parents had never exhibited any form of oedipal success, and nevertheless had become embroiled in a not very satisfactory marital relationship, he dreaded that he too would repeat such an imprisoning attachment pattern, should the current woman not truly be the right one for him.

Since there was absolutely no way that he could ever know in advance whether the current woman was right for him, he remained somewhat paralyzed and unable to make a courageously decisive commitment. The patient was plagued by the parents' lack of courage for the decisive action required to extricate themselves from their unhappy relationship, and this led him to incessant worries with regard to his own capacity to extricate himself, once he was fully committed. Such anxieties and worrisome concerns, however, were the negative affects which camouflaged his more deeply embedded dreads with regard to the joyous affects integrally connected to oedipal success. After all, a marriage is typically a joyous event in which parents and friends celebrate the intimate bonding of the couple. For this patient to commit himself to the initiation of such an intimate bonding, he had to allow himself to experience the joyous celebration and toasting of his oedipal success. He was unable to do this, however, due to an unconscious sense of disloyalty, were he to successfully integrate into his life a loving attachment to a woman.

Whereas his father was always a vocational and financial underachiever, the patient had succeeded quite well and was highly respected in his professional endeavors. Although unable to fully experience feelings of exhilaration and pride in regard to his professional accomplishments, he had, at least, allowed himself such attainments. He could not, however, very easily allow himself the oedipal victory of a successful marriage.

The primary focus with this patient was on the positive affects that were felt as dangerous and essentially disloyal to his unhappily married parents. His intense identificatory attachment with the unsuccessful parents had to be given up and mourned, if he was to allow himself an oedipally successful sexual relationship. He had begun to appreciate the dread of positive affects implicit in his oedipal conflicts. This had helped him to move even closer toward a more courageous oedipal position.

## Case 3

The patient allowed herself an oedipal victory in that, after many years of struggle and self-doubt, she was able to successfully marry just prior to her fiftieth birthday. Having been involved in an intense, hostile, and ambivalent enmeshment with a tenaciously and symbiotically attached mother, her successful attainment of an intimate object constant commitment could be seen as a highly courageous oedipal act.

She was an only child whose father died when she was still an infant. She had very few memories of him and had not been assisted by her narcissistically ungiving mother who only grudgingly shared memorabilia or anecdotes about him with the patient. The mother's incapacity to joyously share oedipal experience with her daughter stemmed, at least in part, from the gaps in her object relational history with her own severely rejecting and abandoning father. The mother's incapacities for joyous sharing and nurturing of maturational potentials in the patient, of course, pervaded her preoedipal period of development, as well. As a result of the mother's incapacity and unwillingness to nurture her separation–individuation and assertive sexual identity strivings, she struggled with severe dependency conflicts.

The mother's reactions to her daughter's recent wedding were examples of her lack of capacity for grace or generativity which had been repeated throughout the patient's life. The patient took the mother on a shopping expedition to buy her a dress to wear to the wedding. The mother's lack of zest or positive excitement for the task was quite evident throughout the day. After vetoing dress after dress as too expensive, finally she grudgingly agreed to the purchase of a dress which cost $35. The patient ended up with an exceedingly bitter taste from the experience. She was enraged about the mother's inability to generate celebratory enthusiasm for her daughter's joyful impending experience. Her therapeutic self-explorations had made it exceedingly clear that this lack of joyousness, in response to oedipal victories, had been characteristic of the mother's reactions throughout the patient's life.

Her loyalty and need to protect her mother from the positive affects generated by oedipal achievement had diminished sufficiently to allow her to successfully marry. The joyful affects typical for such an accomplishment, however, were not to be her due. This largely stemmed from her unrealistic expectations that the mother would, somehow, be able to break through her characterological rigidity and respond differently than she had always done in the past. She still wished that her mother could join her in an exhilarated, joyful celebration of her impending accomplishment. The mother, of course, had no capacity whatsoever for such a generative, graceful, and joyous reaction to her daughter's success.

The patient courageously proceeded with the wedding and worked through in her treatment some of the bitter resentment of her mother's lack of happiness for her. She needed to continuously explore, however, her frustrated expectations for positive affective reactivity from the mother. The possibility that she might be able to have a joyous oedipal experience, while her mother remained embedded in her sad and ungiving inner world, was difficult for her to accept. This would involve a separation–individuation experience which, unconsciously, would be felt as equivalent to disloyalty toward the mother. Her naturally protective instincts, well honed over the course of her lengthy hostile–dependent bonding with the mother, made her potentially joyful experience an exceedingly difficult one.

She continued to struggle in treatment with her bitterness and resentment of the mother's incapacity for joyful or generous reactivity of any sort. Periodic crises in her marital relationship to her husband, often allowed her the opportunity to suppress and inhibit her happiness. She unconsciously struggled at such moments with self-destructive fantasies and wishes directed against her oedipal success. Her unconscious expectations for intimate bonding and merger with the mother are also underlying dynamics during these crises.

The patient's optimism and zest for life somehow prevented her from taking a truly self-defeating or destructive course of action against her marriage. She was able to successfully mourn the separation from and loss of her mother which she had been propelled ever more toward, as a result of her oedipal victory.

### CONCLUSIONS

All three cases reflect the tremendous difficulties with positive affects that can be associated with oedipal accomplishment, particularly when the parents have exhibited markedly impaired counteroedipal responsiveness. In each case, the parents were historically unable to joyfully celebrate preoedipal, negative oedipal, or oedipal accomplishment, and hence could not provide a solid transitional substructure for subsequent maturational attainments of an oedipal nature. As Ogden has noted (1989), such transitional oedipal object provisions are essential building blocks for the later negative oedipal and oedipal conflictual struggles of both child and adult. Ultimately, it may be assumed that either father or mother can provide such a transitional oedipal maturational experience for their child.

Whereas traditionally, the mother has provided the nurturant and lovingly celebratory mirroring and the father the sense of combative and competitive otherness, that need not always be the case. In many contemporary families, the father may provide the nurturant bonding and joyful receptivity and the mother the sense of heroic assertiveness and counteraggressivity. Kaftal (1991) recently discussed this issue in the context of difficulties with intimate bonding between fathers and sons. Either mother or father (depending upon the nurturant capacity of their own mother or father) may be able to provide such a transitional function for their male or female child. Similarly, either mother or father may be able to provide the competitive and combative sense of otherness for their child of either gender.

Also, even more essentially, either mother or father may be able to provide a celebratory and joyous mirroring for their male or female child's oedipal ambitions and maturational accomplishments. Under the most favorable circumstances, ideally, both parents are able to provide such a positive, affective context for oedipal achievements. In the three cases briefly described, neither parent was able to provide very much of a semblance of such joyous reactivity. The dire consequences for oedipal conflict resolution of such counteroedipal parental insufficiencies are evident in the struggles of each of these patients.

The classical oedipal theory, with its emphasis upon largely negative affects, has led to an overlooking of the characterological difficulties and resistances to positive affective experience which are so important in the therapeutic resolution of oedipal difficulties. In contemporary psychoanalytic work with oedipal difficulties, the reluctance to experience positive affects needs to be continually explored. The loyalties and protectiveness toward parents is a central object relational issue which also needs to be thoroughly addressed in the treatment. A greater focus upon positive affects linked with oedipal conflicts needs to be incorporated into the treatment both from a conceptual and practical therapeutic perspective.

# Chapter 6

# COURAGEOUS ATTITUDES AND THE
# THERAPEUTIC PROCESS

Much of the success of psychoanalytic treatment hinges upon the enhancement of affect differentiation and tolerance capacities. Most therapeutic strategies are geared toward an expansion of the range of affects (both positive and negative) that can be verbally articulated and adaptively utilized as informative signals by the patient. A number of authors have explored the importance of affect educative aspects of the treatment process from a psychoanalytic perspective (Krystal, 1988; Isaacs, 1990).

Patients are encouraged to become aware of the important signal aspects of affects and to thereby expand their affect tolerance and differentiation capabilities. It is becoming more and more obvious that many patients have only a limited tolerance for both positive and negative affects. Many patients have as much difficulty and intolerance for affects such as joy and exhilaration as they do for painful affects such as sadness, anger, and anxiety.

Patients not only have difficulty in experientially tolerating a broad range of basic affects but also in tolerating and expressively exhibiting the more complex ego autonomous affective attitudes noted by Alexander and Isaacs (1963), such as determination, hope, commitment, and courage. These generally positive and largely preconscious affective attitudes are difficult to attain and maintain during the course of treatment. The therapeutic implications of these attitudinal factors have seldom been explored in a comprehensive fashion.

As has been noted in chapter 3, the issue of courage is indirectly implicated from an unpleasant affective perspective in the psychoanalytic approaches to the treatment of patients suffering from various anxiety and phobic

91

disorders. Many patients can be propelled during the course of therapy from a phobic to a developmentally higher counterphobic attitudinal position. Nevertheless, they may still move further along to a developmentally still higher courageous position. Before reviewing some strategies for assisting patients with such developmental shifts, the complex affective attitude we call courage needs to be more clearly defined and phenomenologically classified. Just as Krystal (1988) has classified love as the purest example of a highly desomatized, verbalizable, and cognitively (thematically) differentiated affect, courage may similarly be considered an example of a highly differentiated emotional attitude in affective and cognitive terms. This high-level affective attitude is, paradoxically, both a necessary requirement for an effective therapeutic intervention and an enhanced attainment of such an intervention.

## A DICTIONARY DEFINITION OF COURAGE

Two quite similar definitions of courage are offered by the Random House and Webster dictionaries. The Random House definition is as follows: "The quality of mind or spirit that enables one to face difficulty, danger, pain, etc., with firmness and without fear" (Stein and Urdang, 1967). Webster defines courage thus: "Mental or moral strength enabling one to venture, persevere and withstand danger, fear or difficulty firmly and resolutely" (Babcock, 1976). Both definitions emphasize the ability to face up to dangerous, fearful, or painful circumstances resolutely, one without and one in spite of fear. Perhaps the famous Franklin Delano Roosevelt speech in which he stated, "There is nothing to fear except fear itself," best captures that everyday view of courage (Jacobs, 1980).

Of course, dangers, in the mental health sphere, stem from a variety of sources. Typically, they involve perceptions and expectations with regard to potentially dangerous circumstances. Such apprehension may or may not be able to be consensually validated by an objective observer or psychotherapist. They are certainly very real, however, to the individual whose functioning can be severely restricted, inhibited, or handicapped as a result of inner feelings of anxiety and dreaded expectations of potentially dangerous outcomes. The bulk of our therapeutic practice, it can be argued, involves work with individual patients who cannot behave in an adaptively courageous fashion as a result of a broad array of crippling anxieties and fears. The normal capacity for courageous resolve is limited to varying degrees in the variety of psychopathological conditions we see in treatment. One obvious goal of our therapeutic endeavor, therefore, is the freeing of the hidden courageous potential in our patients that have been blocked off as a result of varying forms of crippling psychopathology.

## ASPECTS OF COURAGE IN EVERYDAY LIFE

We have no difficulty whatsoever in identifying courageous individuals and actions in everyday life. From a phenomenological perspective, courage is transparent in anecdotes and news reports depicting various heroic actions. The man who, with little or no concern for his own safety, bolts into a burning house or icy river to rescue trapped or drowning individuals obviously has a courageous nature. The soldier who places himself in the line of fire, and thereby shields a close buddy, similarly can be seen as manifesting valor under stressful and dangerous circumstances. Most of these instances involve a physical form of bravery and courageous action. Interestingly, the media have repeatedly presented us with images of courageous behavior that contribute to a rather simplified sociopsychological portrait of courage. Some of our most popular imagoes for physically courageous individuals are captured in the *Rocky* and *Rambo* film series.

The folk heroes depicted in those films allow for a projection of the more adolescent, macho, and essentially phallic ego ideals of courage. They thrive on a fearless and courageous plane of physical action not unlike the early portrayals of the James Bond character in the film versions of Ian Fleming's novels. There is seemingly no room for passivity, indecision, or fearfulness in these very popular folk heroes. The appeal is to the adolescent need for cockiness, recklessness, and bravado in the face of outwardly frightening physical danger. The James Bond character highlights a form of physical courage that, paradoxically, flies in the face of social courage (intimacy capabilities) in that the character has fleeting sexual contacts with a bevy of beautiful and sensual women without becoming even slightly intimate or attached to any of them. This courageous image captures the adolescent male's need to flee in fear from intimate enmeshment with females, while harboring a macho and phallic bravado and sense of prideful self-idealization.

Thus, it is quite possible to be courageous in one sense and extremely uncourageous in another. The limitations of our contemporary sociopsychological fixation on physically brave and charismatic icons is thus reflected in the undifferentiated nature of these ego ideals and the overly simplified view of their courageousness.

From a phenomenological perspective, we prefer the physical aspects in our imagoes and definitions of courage. A great football player is automatically assumed to be courageous because of his willingness to risk his body in the dangerous arena of physical action on the football field. Our own unwillingness or incapacity to do the same makes for a rather natural tendency to idealize and even iconicize the heroes of contact sports. The gender biases implicit in these idealization processes are quite subtle but nevertheless present. Masculine ego ideals of courage permeate the media and considerably oversimplify our notions with regard to courage. The capacity for intimacy, mature interdependence, and socially adaptive cooperativeness are seldom similarly idealized, although they form major components of our psychological and psychiatric definitions of the developmentally evolved and generative personality structure.

Moral attributes such as the tenacious maintenance of ethical values and ideals in the face of oppressive social forces are seldom implicated in those oversimplified courageous imagoes. The sort of courage exhibited by Alexander Solzhenitsyn or Nelson Mandela reflects a developmentally higher level of heroic behavior and makes it obvious that we need to differentiate our definitions and phenomenology of courage.

Examples of courage abound in the psychotherapy field within a paradoxical and playful context of unlikely heroes and acts of heroism. Thus, fear-ridden patients whose conscious and unconscious belief systems initially preclude certain more courageous forms of action, upon gradually gaining insight into the true psychic scars underlying their phobic behavioral patterns, hesitantly begin to risk some new and truly frightening form of behavioral action. Such a person, by temporarily dropping a characterologically favored defensive maneuver (i.e., phobic projections and displacements) and risking a more direct confrontation with the phobic object, is exhibiting a form of characterological and maturational stretching that is no less courageous than is the gifted contact sports figure, the macho soldier of fortune, or the "Rocky Balboa" sorts of determined and physically brave heroes. The capacity to flexibly shift away from some favored characterological style or phobic defensive maneuver involves a seldom noted form of developmental courage quite familiar to psychotherapists.

*Types of Courage*

Rollo May (1975) has written an important treatise that delineates four types of courage, physical, moral, social, and creative, all of which stem from an inner sensitivity, awareness, and sense of responsibility for others. For May, the capacity to face an unknown future in a responsible, ethical, and socially intimate and committed fashion is the central characteristic of courage, which he considered to be the opposite of apathy and social uninvolvement. He states rather pointedly, "A chief characteristic of this courage is that it requires a centeredness within our own being, without which we would feel ourselves to be a vacuum. The 'emptiness' within corresponds to an apathy without; and apathy adds up, in the long run, to cowardice" (1975, p. 13).

*Physical Courage.* In its extreme form, physical courage dovetails quite nicely with the phallic and macho forms of bravado so often idealized in Western society. In its less extreme form, it is exemplified by heroic and altruistic forms of action, which take place under potentially dangerous circumstances in a physical sense.

*Moral Courage.* Moral courage involves the capacity to let oneself empathically perceive and feel the suffering of fellow human beings. This may lead to heroic acts of moral resistance in the face of powerful political and social pressures to ignore and relinquish the identification with oppressed and suffering individuals. Gandhi, Solzhenitsyn, and Mandela come to mind as heroic figures who have exhibited this form of morally courageous action.

*Social Courage.* Social courage is even more clearly the opposite of apathy, according to May. It consists of a successful resolution of the conflictual dialectic between the fear of self-absorption and enmeshment with an intimately cared for other and an equally pervasive fear of separation from the loss of that intimate other. Social courage is exhibited by individuals capable of life-long intimate attachments to a mate. The unwavering object-constant intimate attachment that over time weathers the ambivalences, narcissistic injuries, and ultimate separation and loss that is depicted in the movie *On Golden Pond*, captures this form of courage quite nicely. Obviously, apathetic, loveless, and immaturely symbiotic enmeshments do not qualify as exemplars of this form of courage. It is that rarer form of object constant attachment exemplified in successful, long-term loving relationships that is being alluded to here. Such mature forms of object attachment, between two relatively individuated persons, reflect a willingness to risk loving enmeshment and partial self-boundary merger in the context of potential separations, narcissistic injury, and the ultimate danger of loss of that relationship through abandonment or death.

Given the developmental sophistication and object relational maturity required for the successful maintenance of such forms of loving object constant attachment, it is no surprise that persons who manifest the gamut of narcissistic difficulties—from the mild neurotic to the severe psychotic end of the psychopathologic continuum—cannot successfully experience or exhibit this form of social courage. Most forms of characterologic difficulty are linked to relatively severe ego and self restrictions upon the socially desirable and normative capacity to relate in a loving and empathic manner to another human being over the long term. That is probably related to the often noted observation that, lacking courage, the most characterologically and narcissistically damaged individuals are least likely to seek out long-term therapeutic relationships for assistance with their personal problems. The ego syntonic nature of most forms of character pathology, alluded to by psychoanalytic therapists such as Wilhelm Reich (1933) and Peter Giovacchini (1984a) is linked to a certain sensitivity to narcissistic injury that severely inhibits and restricts the dissociated true self strivings and capacities for more mature object constant and loving relatedness elaborated in the contributions of Winnicott (1965).

In the most severe character disorders, individuals are "bumped" into treatment against their will by a friend, lover, or mate. Such persons dread coming to terms with the emptiness, lack of true self-development, and bankruptcy in social courage that is permeating their existence. The idea of a relatively long-term relationship to an empathic therapist is as unconsciously dreaded as is the latent striving to relate in an individuated and maturely loving attachment to a life-long mate.

*Creative Courage.* Creative courage is the final type of courage delineated by May. It involves the tolerance for ambiguity and lack of knowledge that allows an individual to create new forms and give up older, far more familiar forms. This very special quality of energetic commitment to the creation of new forms involves a kind of risk taking and courageous "leap of faith" in which a person risks the public exposure of self-created new forms with no certainty as to the reception awaiting such self-exposure. Many potentially creative individuals who dread the risk of narcissistic injury cannot energetically commit themselves to creative or generative projects. Some forms of "writer's block" are linked to a failure in this form of courage.

The courageous capacity to risk separateness and a lovingly dedicated commitment to a creative project is clearly both similar to and different from the ability to risk a loving attachment implicit in social courage. The common denominators are the capacities to risk loss and narcissistic injury via an energetic commitment of the self to a beloved object.

Most forms of psychopathology seen in our everyday therapeutic practice reflect inhibitions and restrictions of the four forms of courage. It is most obvious in the phobic patient whose symptomatic fears become focal points for treatment. Not quite as obvious, but nevertheless discernible, is the impulsive, action-oriented patient who tends to mask underlying fears and anxieties beneath counterphobic action tendencies and defensive maneuvers. It can be argued that ultimately every form of psychopathology is intrinsically linked to some form of phobic tendency, unconscious signal anxiety (expectancy), or belief with regard to the danger implicit in various forms of courageous action. Therefore, the essential therapeutic task is a developmental one in which the patient is encouraged to give up favored but immature characterological styles and defensive maneuvers for maturationally higher adaptive techniques and competencies.

Thus, the very heart of the therapeutic process consists of subtle and not-so-subtle prods and encouragements to risk characterological shifts of a maturationally higher nature. The capacity to risk such characterological evolution is linked to a fifth form of courage that is intrinsic to the therapeutic relationship.

*Developmental Courage.* Bill Russell, the great Boston Celtic center, describes in his autobiography (1980) his feelings of fright as a young player upon discovering that he could jump high above the basket. Why should a discovery with regard to newfound physical talents lead to a fearful reaction? It must be noted that it occurred when no player had ever demonstrated the "dunking" capacity so effortlessly exhibited by Michael Jordan and many other current basketball superstars. Russell's fearful reaction is much like that exhibited by patients in psychotherapy who suddenly discover some newfound physical, moral, social, or creative capacity. Paradoxically, such self-discoveries of new talents and competencies can lead to the regressive behavior often noted in infants just beginning to walk or talk. The capacity to locomote involves complex body image shifts that can be frightening at the earliest stages of such attainments. A similar anxiety often accompanies the developmental shifts during the course of treatment described by Michael Balint (1968) as "new beginnings" from an object-relational perspective.

The courage exhibited by Balint's patient, who for the first time in her life successfully turned a somersault in one of her psychotherapy sessions, is a good example of the maturational attainments that occasionally occur during the course of treatment. One of my patients, an extremely fearful man, once proudly began a therapy session with a spontaneous demonstration of his ability to juggle three balls simultaneously. Interestingly, this motoric demonstration occurred just prior to his decision to embark on a much feared serious relationship of a more intimate nature than he had ever risked before. New beginnings occur at moments in treatment when there is an expansion in the patient's capacity for physical, moral, social, or creative courage and risk taking. The overall capacity for such new beginnings and risk taking can be described as developmental courage. It is a natural, ego autonomous, and largely preconscious courageous attribute in many healthy personalities and a secondarily acquired derivative of the successful therapeutic experience.

Much of the therapist's inquiry, confrontation, and interpretive work involves subtle goads toward ego and self development. The maturational expectations implicit in the treatment interaction occasionally pay off in the form of defensive and characterological shifts that free the patient to rediscover talents and competencies that had to be defensively dissociated, denied, or avoided because of pathological signal anxiety expectations and belief systems. That special form of developmental courage expands incrementally during the course of good therapeutic experiences, and ultimately unlocks the hidden characterological, creative, and maturational potential latent in each individual patient. Perhaps, in addition to the ego-strength factor used to assess the readiness of various patients to profit from therapy experience, it might also be useful to assess their capacity for developmental courage at points of new beginnings during the course of psychotherapy.

Developmental courage is perhaps the most central aspect of courage relevant to the psychotherapy process. It can touch upon any of the other four forms of courage as they evolve during successful therapeutic experiences.

### OBJECT RELATIONAL IMPEDIMENTS TO DEVELOPMENTAL COURAGE DURING TREATMENT

Freud's contribution (1926) with regard to the signal anxiety (anticipations and expectancies of danger) that instigates specific ego defense, neurotic character styles, ego, and self-restrictions, has had vast implications for the psychoanalytic study of courage and its inhibitions. According to Freud's final position on anxiety, it has certain signal and expectancy attributes that motivate a defensive retrenchment from any course of action that might place the individual in a danger situation. Of course, the potential danger is very much in the eye of the beholder. Most phobic reactions lead to restrictions of spontaneous expressive and courageous functions of the ego. For example, I had a phobic patient who could perform as a highly competitive and successful businessman as long as his wife was nearby as a protector against the unconsciously felt dangerous implications of his business activities.

Weiss, Sampson, and the Mount Zion Psychotherapy Research Group (1986) have updated Freud's signal anxiety theory from an object relational and control mastery perspective. They note that a pathological belief system is ultimately responsible for the ego inhibitions and restrictions of most patients. Thus, my phobic patient (discussed in chapter 3) believed that dangerously aggressive consequences could arise if his wife were not around to protect him in his business environment. His agoraphobic dependency upon his wife stemmed from a belief, rooted in early childhood interactions with his parents, that danger would befall him and those about him if he successfully asserted himself and competed in the business world. The true danger, however, was that he would hurt others as he had fantasized hurting his mother and father who were cruel and rejecting toward him during early childhood. This man's potential courageousness had been severely inhibited along with his ability to assertively compete and independently locomote in the world. Even though his 15-year-old son felt free enough of anxiety to travel alone to Europe, the patient was unable to travel the few miles to his place of business without his wife. Pathological belief systems stemming from early childhood interactions with his parents had led to a crippling of his developmental, courageous capacities.

From an object relations perspective, this man's true self and courageous capacity to risk new beginnings had been severely hindered. He had a pathological need to protect others from hostile projective identifications and fantasies of attack stemming from within himself. He had always felt a need to protect his parents from his hostile impulses. Occasional lapses in his control over hostile impulses during childhood led to fire-setting episodes and sadistic–aggressive behavior toward the family dog.

He had always experienced his aggressive feelings as potentially harmful to those around him. His experience with the family dog had reinforced this impression. More and more, he began to inhibit angry feelings, fearing that were he to express them (much like his physically abusive and assaultive father), he might do additional harm to those around him. His phobic characterological armor allowed for a fantasized protection of others, at the expense of his own capacity to assert himself and move freely within his environment.

## An "Encouraging" Therapeutic Model

Our ultimate therapeutic model, therefore, must incorporate strategies for diminishing the potency of pathological beliefs of a protective nature that obstruct the natural unfolding of the patient's developmental courage and self-assertive potential. The primary goals involve a clarification through repeatedly playful and active use of inquiry, confrontation, and interpretation of the protective feelings and beliefs underlying the patient's failure of courage. These feelings and beliefs need to be explored in the here-and-now of the transference relationship to the therapist as well as in its earlier antecedents in the childhood relationship to the parents. The therapist offers an encouraging milieu, quite in contrast to the highly discouraging environment provided in the patient's early childhood interactions with parental figures. The encouragement does not stem, however, from direct exhortations like those issued by a successful basketball coach to his players but rather from subtle forms of playful enactment of an understanding and containing nature that are highly dissimilar to those that led to the patient's pathological expectations and belief systems during childhood.

The therapist repeatedly demonstrates that he or she cannot be destroyed or overwhelmed by the patient's angry or self-assertive actions. The encouragement involves a subtle but constant expectation that developmentally courageous behavior is highly desirable and not dangerous to others, especially the therapist.

## Conclusions

Courage has largely been studied from a phenomenological and existential, rather than a psychoanalytic perspective. Four types of courage have been delineated and differentiated. A fifth form (developmental) needs to be included from a more object relational psychoanalytic perspective. Developmental aspects of courage are severely inhibited and restricted in a broad variety of psychopathological configurations. Pathological belief systems involving danger to significant figures and objects in the patient's world (including the therapist) are a primary psychodynamic underlying the patient's crippling failures of courage. The patient feels the need to protect others from his or her self-assertive and courageous action potential. Continuously active clarifications by the therapist can enhance and encourage the patient's willingness to risk more courageous forms of action and positive affect tolerance. Just as Krystal (1988) has delineated love as an example of the most highly differentiated form of affect, courage may similarly be delineated as an example of one of the most differentiated preconscious and ego autonomous affective attitudes. The capacities for both love and courage can be heightened via an effective psychoanalytic treatment intervention.

# PART II
# OBJECT

# Chapter 7

# THE THERAPEUTIC USE OF SELF AND OBJECT REPRESENTATIONS

An object relational approach to the therapy process consists of a sensitivity to self and object representations repeatedly generated in the interpersonal interaction between patient and therapist. As Kernberg (1976a) has noted, these inner representational states and identity fragments are frequently conveyed in an *affective* context. These "linking affects" may have a positive or negative quality. The therapist's primary task, according to theorists such as Winnicott (1965), Kernberg (1975b), Langs (1976), and Giovacchini (1984a), is to somehow contain and provide a holding environment for these affectively toned representational processes so that they can eventually be metabolized and communicated back to the patient in a therapeutically useful fashion.

Although much of the early object relations literature, as particularly evident in the contributions of Balint (1968), stressed the special need for a dyadic object relations experience of a curative nature in more primitively organized patients, many contemporary theorists such as Langs (1976), Ogden (1982, 1986, 1989), and Bollas (1987), have emphasized the importance of such a bipersonal container model in work with patients exhibiting a diverse spectrum of psychopathology.

Members of the *paradigmatic* school of psychotherapy (Nelson, 1962b,c; Spotnitz, 1969; Strean, 1970a) have pursued Balint's (1968) emphasis on the need for an active object relational encounter in certain difficult patients and have developed a number of role-playing techniques. These techniques allow for a *playful*, ironic, and humorous exploration of self and object representations with more primitively organized patients. Searles

(1979) has, similarly, stressed a provocative, playful playback of intimate countertransference feelings in his work with schizophrenic patients.

An object relations approach to treatment, however, need not involve an active, psychodramatic playback of self and object representations generated during the course of the interaction with patients. Recently, Bollas (1989) stressed concern over the potentially manipulative character of more active object relational approaches. He emphasized instead the importance of authenticity in object relational communications with patients.

From a contemporary perspective, there is no need to artificially and actively play back for the patient self and object representational images generated in the therapist during the course of the treatment interaction. The therapist can more naturally utilize her curiosity regarding inner representational states and role enactment expectancies evoked in her via an explorative and preinterpretive attitude of inquiry with the patient.

The therapist, to do this effectively, must first experience and contain what Winnicott (1965) and Bollas (1987, 1989) have termed the *object usage* demands emanating from the patient. The therapist, from the Winnicottian perspective, developed in the recent writings of Bollas, must allow herself to be used, while holding firmly to the ground rules and systems boundaries of a maturationally facilitating object relational encounter. Just as the child therapist, working within a play therapy format, allows herself to be manipulated and used by the child within certain bounded limits (e.g., no hitting, punching, destruction of play materials or the therapist's other possessions), the object relational approach with adults allows for similar forms of object usage experience.

Before listing a number of the typical self and object representational encounters that naturally occur during the course of treatment, and offering clinical illustrations of some of them, the therapeutic significance and usefulness of the concept of projective identification needs to be reviewed and updated.

## The Therapeutically Useful Conception of Projective Identification

The concept of projective identification was originally introduced by Melanie Klein (1946) and linked to the splitting off of good from bad object representations typically seen in the paranoid–schizoid and depressive positions. Since the projection of split-off part objects typically has its inception in the highly aggressivized paranoid–schizoid phase, it frequently has a highly manipulative, controlling, exploitative, and sadistic character. Many subsequent theorists influenced by Klein's thinking (Heimann, 1952; Joseph, 1987; Kernberg,

1987) have tended to stress the exploitative and assaultive aspects of projective identificatory interactions and defensive processes. The container is utilized in a highly sadistic and controlling fashion. Some aspect of the self representation (typically a malevolent, unpleasant, and hateful portion) is intrusively and aggressively pushed into an external object container.

Verbs such as "pushed," "prodded," or "provoked" are used to capture the nature of the interpersonal experience in which unpleasant feelings, impulses, and action tendencies are actively shifted from one individual to another. Whereas pure projection can be sufficiently described via the preposition "onto," the concept of projective identification from a Kleinian perspective requires the preposition "into." Unacceptable feelings and action tendencies are pushed into the unconsciously chosen object container by the projector.

It is important to note that these feelings and associated role enactments may have both a positive and negative hedonic character. Thus, during the depressive position, the object needs to be protected against the projector's angry, assaultive impulses and may be provoked to hold dissociated positive feelings instead. The depressive individual holds onto the angry, aggressive feelings and turns them against herself, while protectively idealizing an external good object. The idealized good object, of course, ends up possessing the positive traits disowned and denied by the projector. The projector has depleted herself of her good parts and placed them for safekeeping in a highly idealized external container.

Much of Klein's thinking and writing (1946) have stressed the largely *intrapsychic* and extremely pathological aspects of projective identification. Kernberg (1987), while much more aware of the *interactive* nature of this defensive maneuver, nevertheless stresses its pathological features. He emphasizes that it is much more typically found in severely disturbed borderline patients prone toward the use of splitting mechanisms, while simpler forms of projection are much more prevalent in better organized neurotic patients who are also capable of utilizing higher level repressive defenses.

The history of projective identification as a *systems* concept actually began with Freud whose original work on group psychology (1921) distinguished between groups such as the church in which ego ideals are internalized via an introjection of the powerful positive qualities of a martyred figure (i.e., symbolized in the communion ceremony by the taking in of Christ's body through the wafer and wine) and the army, in which all of the individual soldiers project their ego ideals onto the commanding officer. The church group dynamic may be seen as parallel to a more contemporary conception of introjective identification. The army group dynamic, on the other hand, is parallel to the contemporary conception of projective identification.

Bennis (1976) has extended Freud's group dynamic conceptions of projective identification to the study of defenses against depressive anxiety that typically occur in groups whose leader is called away and must be absent for a period of time. Such groups typically illustrate projective identificatory mechanisms by splitting into rival camps and idealizing substitute leaders and experiences in the group process. They also often scapegoat and severely victimize particular members who are too individuated and do not follow along with group themes or action predilections. The present author, in a series of group dynamic writings (1976, 1980a, 1992), has further specified some of the group systems implications of the concepts of splitting and projective identification.

Although Malin and Grotstein (1966) have essentially stayed within a Kleinian theoretical frame of reference, they have amplified the therapeutic usefulness of the concept of projective identification. They note the importance of a *validational* posture on the part of the therapist who is asked to contain certain projective identifications for the patient. They view projective identifications also as contributing to the establishment of a protective scaffolding for the ego development and characterological maturation which is to unfold during the subsequent course of the psychotherapy process. The bulk of therapeutic action during the course of psychoanalytic treatment, according to Malin and Grotstein, hinges upon the successful management of projective identificatory interactions.

The containing process is most effective, they say, when the therapist takes the patient's primitive projections seriously and seeks to validate their objectivity via various forms of inquiry. The therapist's curiosity about their potential validity diminishes the negative transferences linked to the projective identifications. The therapist comes across as a less judgmental or emotionally threatened and defensive figure, by assuming such a validating posture and attitude of curiosity.

The essentially interactive nature of projective identifications has been further specified in the writings of Sandler (1976, 1987b) on this topic. Sandler's conception of transference as a role evocative process specified, both conceptually and clinically, the enactment demands implicit in many transference interactions with patients. Sandler gives the example of a woman patient being seen by a therapist who, somehow, repeatedly found himself offering her a tissue at emotionally intense and painful points in the analysis. While such an enactment might ordinarily not be considered unusual in itself, it was an atypical one for this particular therapist.

In another example the therapist repeatedly found himself helping a female patient on with her coat at the end of her therapy sessions. Once again, this therapist did not do this with any of his other patients. Momentarily, neglecting the *countertransferential* meanings of these enactments, they may be viewed as examples of what Grinberg (1962) has labeled *projective counteridentification*. The therapist, rather than remaining curious and attempting to objectively validate the role enactment expectancies (projective identifications) emanating from the patient, responds to them in a more real fashion and consequently becomes involved in concrete enactments that remain essentially unanalyzed.

Ogden (1982) has contributed perhaps the most comprehensive analysis of projective identification. He offers as close to an operational definition of this complex phenomenon as is possible by breaking it up into three stages. The first stage involves a fantasy process of a largely intrapsychic nature in which, as in the Kleinian conception, certain fantasies occur of eliminating undesirable feelings and impulses by aggressively putting them into another person. In the second stage, a variety of enactment demands and actual interactions ensue by which the external container object is provoked to experience feelings and action tendencies that have been dissociated and projected into her. The third and final step consists of an internal processing, validating, and metabolizing of these projected psychic contents so that they can be projectively relayed back to the projector in a *useful* way.

Ogden's very trenchant analysis of this phenomenon specifies quite clearly its interactive nature. It also articulates the important communicative value of projective identifications. They cannot be viewed solely as pathological processes that inhibit and primarily distract the communication process between two individuals. They also need to be viewed as important forms of object relational communication within various bipersonal fields and systems such as couple relationships, the family, and other larger group systems. Indeed, the *systems* nature of this construct is, perhaps, one of its most essential attributes.

Scharff (1992) has produced a creative volume which expands upon the earlier important contributions of Scharff and Scharff (1987) regarding an object relations approach to couple and family treatment. In this recent work, she offers many clinical illustrations of the importance of projective identification as a primary form of communication across individual, couple, and family systems boundaries. The intergenerational structures underlying many forms of projective identificatory communication in couple and family systems are nicely articulated by Scharff. Thus, as is implicit in Bollas' (1987) constructs regarding the shadow of the object cast during various forms of therapeutic interaction, most couple relationships typically involve complex composites of projective identificatory interaction. In these interactions internalized parental objects and associated self representations are repeatedly projected and contained in either a pathological or maturationally constructive and useful fashion across the boundaries of the two partners.

Similarly, static and inhibiting or flexible and maturationally useful forms of projective identificatory communication occur across the systems boundaries of a family grouping. Scharff offers many examples which clarify the object relational implications of projective identificatory transactions for individuals as well as the couple and family systems as a whole.

In many ways, a contemporary and therapeutically useful conception of projective identification takes us far beyond the original Kleinian notions with regard to the primitive sadistic and controlling features of projective identification. We now tend to view these processes as potentially quite constructive and maturationally helpful role-enactment expectancies whose latent object relational significance needs to be explored with considerable curiosity and efforts toward objective validation of their inner meaning.

We can now tentatively list some of the ways in which these object relational processes reveal themselves during the course of an ordinary therapeutic interaction.

### THERAPEUTIC ENCOUNTERS WITH PROJECTED SELF AND OBJECT REPRESENTATIONS

We are confronted repeatedly with the patient's significant self and object representations. The sources for these confrontations can be quite varied, but at least some of them may be listed. A partial listing might include representational data linked to the patient's character structure, particular mood states, and communications regarding a mate. There might also be an unconsciously conveyed sense of significant early objects (parents, grandparents, etc.), and an externalized sense of a significant early familial or environmental milieu which begins to pervade the therapist's office, and invitations for self and object representational role enactments.

A brief sketch of each of these six forms of therapeutic encounters with significant self and object representations can now be presented.

### *"Character Structure" as a Representational Form of Communication*

Our traditional models for explaining character structure (Reich, 1933; A. Freud, 1936) stress ego syntonic defensive maneuvers and coping styles which are frequently enacted as resistances to the psychotherapy process. The representational qualities of these character structures, however, have seldom been noted.

Bollas (1974) is a significant exception. He views character from a representational perspective and emphasizes the significant object relational memories contained in a given individual's character structures. During repeated encounters with characterological aspects of our patients' functioning, we also become acquainted with their early object relationships.

The beaten down quality conveyed in the way a given individual stoops over or carries his shoulders, thus, may suggest an oppressive early relationship to an authoritarian and controlling father or mother. The extreme disinterest in financial matters seen in a particular patient may suggest either an acceptance and internalization of similar traits in her mother or a rejection of the mother's much more miserly and controlling qualities with regard to money.

Character traits, viewed from an object relational perspective, capture significant aspects of the object world and their impact upon the self representation. As a result, we obtain an experiential feel for a given individual's self and object representations through their character organization.

*Mood States*

Moods may convey object relational encounters that occurred at a developmental phase in which words were largely unavailable. Thus, a tendency to shift into sad, dysphoric states may be related to early infantile encounters with an unhappy mother. A constantly ebullient, excited, and energetic mood may be linked to a need to cheer up and energize an unhappy mother or father.

Bollas (1987) has described certain moods as *conservative object* states, in that they may reveal a loyal affective connection to a beloved or ambivalent object from the past. He alludes to the fact that moods have a conservative character which, during the course of psychoanalytic treatment, may be traced to their object relational roots. The self and object representations underlying them may become a bit clearer through analysis.

Certainly, a therapist's own affective states can offer clues to important self and object representations in the patient. Occasionally, an avoidant attitude at a point of initial contact with a patient may reflect an unconscious premonition and sense of unpleasant affects and mood states (and their attendant object relationships) that will be prevalent factors in subsequent interactions with this patient. Some therapists, sensing sad, wrenchingly painful, or dysphoric mood states in a new patient (and the empathic need to attune to their patient by getting in touch with similar moods in themselves) become anxious and unconsciously seek to avoid these aspects of the patient's affective experience. Such manic defenses in the therapist, of course, have a particular connection to the therapist's unique object relational history. They may lead to a bypassing of the important object relational roots of these mood states for the patient.

Mood states, thus, offer a fertile and frequently neglected field for object relational study in our work with a diverse variety of patients.

## Impressions of the Mate

During the course of individual treatment with a patient engaged in a brief or relatively long-term relationship, we often gain a fairly definitive sense of the object relational characteristics of the patient's mate.

Occasionally, we are invited by the patient to meet their mate in person to assist in solving some current dilemma in the couple's relationship. At such times, it is essential that we become aware of the *proxy evocation* and other projective identificatory issues implicit in such invitations to meet a real object in the patient's life. Couple and family therapists work directly with such object relational encounters and are probably most aware of both the difficulties and opportunities implicit in such encounters.

It is important to note that we are repeatedly confronted with object representational images of the mates of our patients during the course of individual psychoanalytic treatment. Linking affects and self representations with regard to the mate are also projected into us. Thus, we occasionally may find ourselves feeling angry toward the mate, while our patient manifests a seemingly discrepant attitude of indifference, comfortable acceptance, or even an idealizing and loving attitude toward the mate. At such times, we need to ask ourselves why we are having these seemingly discrepant feelings. Often, a proxy evocation maneuver (Wangh, 1962) can be discerned following such self-assessments. It may become evident that the patient has subtly provoked feelings of anger toward the mate in us that they themselves have been unable to own or assertively express with the mate.

Similar feelings, of course, may be provoked in the therapist toward other family members such as the patient's mother or father, during their narrative recounting of various events from either the past or present. Self analysis will often uncover the object and self representations linked to these induced affects which, subsequently, can be fruitfully inquired about and explored with the patient.

Indeed, all of the patient's significant object relations are affectively and interactively shared with the therapist via her narrative. Emotionally noteworthy impressions and role enactment tendencies are produced in the therapist toward all of the significant persons described by the patient. These evoked affects and action tendencies all have important communicative values which are maximized the more the therapist is able to contain and metabolize them via her own synthetic ego functions and empathic capacities.

## The Sense that More than Two People Are in the Room

Bollas (1987) has made an interesting use of two questions frequently asked by Paula Heimann regarding a patient's free associations. She would ask, "Who is speaking?" and "To whom is this person speaking?" A number of possibilities exist in response to these two questions. Thus, the patient may be speaking in the voice of her easily defeated mother succumbing to the seemingly overwhelming powerfulness of the patient's father or the mother's own father. On the other hand, the patient may be speaking in the voice of her weak and fearful child self responding to her seemingly overpowering and intimidating father. Numerous other possibilities, of course, exist in response to the question about who is speaking.

With regard to Paula Heimann's question about whom the patient is speaking to, she may be speaking to her unhappy father and trying to cheer him up, or frustratedly, to an insatiably demanding and difficult to satisfy mother. The important point for Bollas (1987) is that we cannot assume that the therapeutic dyadic system always consists of a patient speaking to a therapist. Typically, many more than two people, in an object relational sense, are in the room and are speaking during the course of the therapeutic dialogue. This becomes even more complicated as the countertransference availability of the therapist's inner objects is taken into account. Thus, the therapist's defensively provocative inner mother or fearful father may be stirred into responding to aspects of the patient's object representations that seem particularly important at a particular moment in the therapeutic interaction.

From an object relations perspective, Bollas argues that the therapist must continuously monitor any discussion with the patient for both her own and the patient's inner self and object representations. The affects linking these two forms of representational states need to be carefully and continuously monitored as well. The fact that both the patient and therapist speak with multiple voices needs to be understood and directly applied during treatment.

## The Externalization of an Early Environmental Experience

Giovacchini (1984a) has made the interesting observation that the consultation room, in work with certain difficult patients, becomes permeated by representations and associated affects linked to early environmental experiences from the patient's life. He gives the example of a patient who succeeded in making his office feel like the shabby and hopeless ghetto environment that the patient had lived in during his childhood. Giovacchini was invited to feel the sense of helplessness and impotence regarding the future that the patient had experienced continually during childhood.

Giovacchini describes this form of countertransference experience as resulting from *externalizations* rather than projective identificatory interactions. The subtle distinction introduced by Giovacchini is a useful one, in that it allows for a description of a sharing with the therapist of early defensive adaptations and associated affects in response to an environmental milieu rather than to persons from the patient's early life history.

One patient described her early family environment as being like the one depicted in the play *The Glass Menagerie*. She and her older sister lived together with their mother in a household of women with no loving male anywhere in sight. Her father had emotionally abandoned the family, and eventually abandoned it in actuality by dying. The mother persisted in the dreamlike belief that one day her two fragile daughters, neither of whom could establish even a semblance of a relationship to a man, would meet men and marry. This patient repeatedly succeeded in permeating the therapist's office with a similarly sad and despairing environment. The therapist often felt the need to maintain a frail sense of hope that one day the patient would meet a man and happily marry. As it became evident that this was not to be, the office became suffused more and more with the sense of empty hopefulness (at least with regard to the marriage issue) that the patient had described with regard to her early home environment.

As Giovacchini (1984a) has noted, the therapist often must experience early milieux permeated by a sense of helplessness, hopelessness, or pessimism in work with difficult patients. To some degree, however, all patients succeed in externalizing subtle aspects of their early environment during treatment. The degree to which the therapist is able to contain these externalizations while maintaining a positive affect and an affective attitude of optimism may have important implications for the success or failure of the treatment.

Schafer (1983) has alluded to the patient's tendency to externalize an inner sense of imprisonment during the course of psychoanalytic treatment. Thus, despite the analyst's strong wish to create a consultative environment permeated by the sense of freedom for new forms of risk taking and courageous action, the patient may need to have both herself and the analyst experience a prisonlike environment with limited possibilities for change or new forms of experimental action.

How well the therapist handles such attempts at externalization on the part of the patient, will have important implications for the success or failure of the treatment.

Healthy externalization processes can occur, too, but seldom are confronted during psychotherapy. Thus, individuals who grow up in a more positive and reinforcing environment in which problems are opportunities for effective coping and competent problem solving, tend to externalize that environment via an air of confidence and optimism. They also reproduce that environment throughout their interpersonal relationships. Some patients have not allowed the more benign and optimistic aspects of their early childhood environment to impact upon them so that they can be internalized.

Unconscious choices, thus, need to be explored in dealing with externalization processes during treatment. A continuous monitoring of and inquiry into the identificatory potential of various aspects of the early childhood environment may, therefore, open the patient to the more positive aspects of the therapist's personality and the environment which she hopes to provide.

## Self and Object Representational Aspects of "Role Responsiveness"

Sandler (1976) has refined our conception of transference to include those interactions in which the therapist is expected to enact particular roles for the patient. The paradigmatic theorists (Nelson, 1962b,c; Spotnitz, 1969; Strean, 1970a), on the other hand, have attempted to actively enact particular unconscious role paradigms and object representations as a means of alleviating narcissistic defenses and resistances in difficult patients. Sandler's position is that these paradigms occur naturally during transference interactions.

The transference and countertransference relationship, from a contemporary object relational perspective, involves mutual role enactment expectations and responsiveness. Both therapist and patient periodically make role enactment demands upon each other. These mutual role expectations have a communicative character, although they occur via projective identificatory and counteridentificatory processes of interaction.

The representational aspects of these mutual demands for role responsiveness need to be assessed, and ultimately explored via interpretation during treatment. It may occasionally be noted that the therapist has been invited to enact an object representation, while the patient enacts a self representation. An example would be the typical eroticized transference interactions in which the therapist is idealized and subtly invited to act out seductive or sexually competitive behavior while the patient enacts the self representations of a charming, flirtatious, and very attractive child.

A different form of role enactment expectation consists of the transference demand that the therapist play out the role of helpless, intimidated child while the patient enacts the role of a cruelly critical and assaultive father figure. Such enactments involve the projective identification of a self representation into the therapist while the patient acts out the traumatically assaultive object representation. Of course, the reverse can occur and the therapist can be invited to enact the critical and sadistic father role while the patient enacts the vulnerable and intimidated child self representation.

Given the Winnicottian (1965) notions of object usage mentioned earlier, that have been updated by Bollas (1987, 1989), it would appear essential that therapists be receptive to such role enactment demands and expectations. They need not always be seen as demands for pathological regression, acting out, or acting in the transference. Occasionally they convey early demands placed upon the patient by significant parental figures or typical responses by these figures to the patient's needs and demands.

The dramatic enactments of these early childhood object relations paradigms in the transference eventually can be inquired about and interpretively explored in a maturationally useful fashion. The therapist's task, however, may be to contain these object relational expectations for an extensive period of time, until they can be satisfactorily metabolized and played back for the patient in an interpretively useful and growth enhancing manner. The readiness for such communicative and therapeutic utilization of these role enactment paradigms should become more evident over time in a given treatment relationship. A great deal of patience, courageous countertransference, and optimism, however, may be required upon the part of the therapist during the containing and largely preinterpretive period of mutual role enactment demands and responsiveness.

CASE ILLUSTRATIONS

The therapeutic use of self and object representations may be explored through a set of examples involving representational encounters with the self and a different set of examples involving encounters with the object.

*Encounters with the Self Representation*

*Case 1.* The therapist began to feel more and more helpless and thwarted in attempting to convince a male patient of the need to change certain patterns by which he related to his wife. The patient was successful in his professional career but unable to give satisfaction in his relationship with his wife. After many months of frustrating dialogue with this patient, it dawned upon the therapist that this patient had invited his parents into the consultation room, perhaps to see how the therapist was able to handle them. (This particular patient's case was more extensively discussed in chapter 4 and briefly in chapter 5.)

The patient had experienced a "united front" in his two bull-headed parents during childhood, both of whom became extraordinarily negative and resistant to any suggestions he attempted to make for changes in the way things were being done in the family. The therapist, thus, was being given the delightful opportunity of meeting the parents through the stubbornly negative and oppositional quality of the patient's responses to the therapist's efforts at convincing him of a need for change in his own interactive behavior.

The stubborn, oppositional core of the patient's character structure allowed for an introduction to his parents. Unbeknownst to the patient, he was taking the parts of his parents that he found most offensive during childhood and replaying them for others in his external environment. Anyone wishing for an intimate relationship with him received the rather definite impression of what the patient felt like as a child when he wished something from the parents that required a change in their usual way of doing things.

*Case 2.* Invitations from the patient for the therapist to actually meet a mate or parent often have potentials for encounters with dissociated self representations in the patient. A young woman, whose case is further described in chapter 14, was hesitantly beginning to reinitiate relationships with men after a long period of abstinence due to an incapacitating skin condition. Upon meeting a young man whom she felt herself attracted to, she decided that she wanted to bring him into the office so that the therapist could meet him. This wish was not agreed to by the therapist. Subsequent analysis revealed a fear of the intimate wishes and feelings that were beginning to surface in the patient. The unconscious hope was that the therapist might be able to enact them for the patient. The danger of such an enactment, of course, was that the patient might passively and vicariously enjoy the therapist's enactments without having to act on them herself.

It is not surprising that this particular patient had a rather passive mother who felt extremely ineffectual in the area of intimacy with men. The patient had spent considerable periods of time in her earlier life identifying with her mother's feelings of ineptitude in this area and dissociating and denying her own wishes for more successful intimate relationships with men. The wish that the therapist meet the new man in her life involved a proxy evocation maneuver in which the therapist might be fantasized to be the proud possessor of intimacy feelings and actions that the patient unconsciously wished to avoid in herself.

*Case 3.* A young woman had subtly encouraged a previous therapist to act out sexually during her treatment. Early in a subsequent treatment, she began to exhibit seductive behavior which made the new therapist uncomfortable.

He was able, however, to resist these seductive efforts and the patient did not seem very unhappy about the seeming emotional distancing that accompanied his rather evident rejection of her overtures. She found the therapist to be somewhat stuffy compared to her previous therapists (she had worked with a number), but did not appear to feel rejected in any way.

Upon further reflection, the therapist remembered that this young woman had been repeatedly sexually abused at the hands of her father during childhood. She had often felt devalued and debased by her own passive resignation and acceptance of his sadistic assaults on her innocent young body. It now seemed clear that her seductive overtures with all of her therapists were sadistic reenactments of the sexual brutalizing at the hands of her father. The wish to dominate was far more important than the wish for sexual intimacy in her seductive behavior.

Interestingly, the therapist did not find the patient's seductive behavior to be very sexually enticing. His discomfort and subsequent distancing feelings reflected dissociated aspects of the patient's reactions to being seductively approached by her father. The patient, of course, did not feel able to distance herself from or reject the father's overtures during her childhood. The therapist, in the present, became a proxy container for these dissociated wishes to control and neutralize the sexually assaulting object.

*Encounters with the Object Representation*

We are often invited by the patient to experience aspects of significant environmental figures from their current or early life. In a certain sense, we are invited to temporarily put on the hats of these figures and become like them for the patient.

*Case 1.* A man came with his wife for a first couples session and behaved in a rather aggressive fashion. He repeatedly bombarded the therapist with questions regarding his training, experience with doing couple's therapy, and particularly wanted to know how and why the therapist had been chosen by his wife. By the end of the first meeting the therapist felt that he had been thoroughly grilled and did not know how well he had passed this man's tests.

During the next few couple's meetings, it became clear that, at least in part, the assaultive questioning attack on the therapist was a prelude to what was in store for the wife. The therapist was, momentarily, used as a proxy and displacement figure for the wife. The wife was, shortly thereafter, repeatedly peppered with questions as to the motivations for various actions and nonactions she had exhibited during the marriage.

The active and controlling "narrator" role taken by this man with both the therapist and his wife soon was revealed to be a defensive reversal of his sense of passivity and timid acquiescence to many of the latter's demands earlier in the marriage. This man attempted to camouflage his more passive and dependent wishes beneath a surface veneer of intimidating activity and bravado. His unconscious dread of once more being controlled and somehow emotionally under the thumb of both his wife and the new therapist was temporarily warded off by his assuming the role of active interrogator and narrator.

Both the wife and therapist were repeatedly invited to feel intimidated and controlled by this outwardly very active and "in charge" sort of man. By exerting counterphobic control over the therapist he unconsciously hoped that one day he might obtain a truer sense of equality, strength, and control with his wife.

*Case 2.* Two different women patients, both of whom experienced a severe sense of deprivation and abandonment by their fathers, expressed a similar pattern in relationship to their therapist. Each became extremely dependent upon the therapist, having transferred the idealized absent father figure onto him.

Their extreme dependency needs had to be repeatedly explored as well as the idealized object representations stemming from deficiencies in relation to the father. Each of these women expressed their dependency needs in a somewhat different manner. One expressed such needs by turning to the therapist for advice, even when she seemed able to think through and solve a particular problem quite well by herself. The other seemed always to be disappointed when the therapist asked for her own associations rather than offering a comprehensive interpretation of her dreams. At one point, she commented that it did not pay for her to bring in dreams, since the therapist did not seem able to do much with them.

In the transference for both women, the therapist represented both the longed for, idealized father and the symbiotically merged mother. Much of the therapeutic work involved interpretations of the disappointments with both mother and father. The anger toward these disappointing parental objects needed to be brought to the surface and expressed transferentially with the therapist who temporarily became a substitute for these objects.

*Case 3.* A therapist presented a case for supervision with which she had been having a great deal of difficulty. She was working with a young woman who had been severely sexually abused during her childhood. This patient was initially quite guarded and insisted that she could not remember the specific nature of the sexual abuse during initial phases of the treatment. The therapist was finally able to establish sufficient trust so that the woman began to become less guarded and began to express her feelings and thoughts much more openly. She still could not remember, however, the nature of the sexual abuse which had definitely occurred during her childhood.

She did reveal that her mother was a severely disturbed woman who somehow had been involved in the sexual abuse primarily perpetrated by her father. She could remember nothing more about the specifics of what took place.

Suddenly there was a breakthrough in the treatment and the patient began to remember, in some detail, the specific forms in which she had been physically and sexually abused. After recounting a few traumatic memories, she suddenly entered an extremely difficult period with her therapist. She became very cold and rejecting toward her therapist and stubbornly resisted any attempts by the therapist to establish an atmosphere of comfort, closeness, or trust. The therapist began to feel more and more exasperated with the patient and began to insulate herself against a sense of rejection by the patient.

The therapist sought out supervision because of her increasing dislike for the patient and negative feelings during the course of the therapeutic work. She felt continuously rejected by the patient who refused to open up any further, and if anything, was more closed and unrewarding to work with than she had been at the beginning stages of the treatment. The therapist did not like her negative feelings toward the patient and noted that she usually did not react this strongly and negatively with her other patients.

The supervisor asked for the specifics with regard to the sexual abuse that the patient had been able to recall from her childhood. The therapist warned that they were extreme and quite horrible and proceeded to relate that the patient had been severely physically and sexually abused by both parents. On numerous occasions, the mother would force the patient to submit to sexual intercourse with the father in her presence. On some of these occasions, anal penetration occurred with the mother's assistance by opening the patient up to the father's assaults.

Both the supervisor and therapist shuddered upon the recounting of these dreadful incidents of sexual trauma from the patient's early history. It also dawned on both, however, that a paradoxical dilemma confronted the therapist with this severely traumatized patient. By offering the patient an analytic treatment involving requests that she open up and share experiences, the therapist was transferentially replicating the most painful paradigms from the patient's past. The therapist had to contain projective identifications whose object relational characteristics she herself found to be extremely alien and abhorrent. The projectively identified object representations of the severely disturbed mother who repeatedly sexually degraded her daughter by opening her up to the father's assault was unacceptable to the therapist's ego and self system. In many ways, she preferred to keep a closed communication system with this particular patient rather than confront the awful significance of the object representational meaning of the patient's resistances.

The therapist had to accept role assignments in the transference that she (who preferred to see herself as a warm, helpful, and caring individual) found too uncomfortable and unpleasant. Her ultimate task, however, was to patiently contain these disturbing object representations while ultimately working toward a differentiation of her wishes to open the patient up to the treatment from those repeatedly exhibited in the past by the patient's severely disturbed and dysfunctional mother and father.

## CONCLUSIONS

Although encounters with the self representations during the course of treatment have been somewhat arbitrarily differentiated in this chapter from those with the object representations, it is not always very easy to make such distinctions. As Kernberg (1975b) has noted, the typical object relational unit involves a self representation, an object representation, and a linking affect. Every self representation is linked to an object representation in the context of a particular affective state. The same is true for every object representation.

The therapist's containing task with regard to the self and object representations produced through projective identificatory interactions with patients is not a very abstract one. Although the concept of projective identification has often seemed murky and unclear, it has become more and more useful from a contemporary object relational perspective.

Both Sandler's (1976) notions about role evocation and enactment and Bollas' (1987, 1989) updating of Winnicott's (1965) early conceptions about object usage, work well together in helping us to conceptualize the very real and emotionally powerful demand characteristics inherent in the transference and countertransference relationship between patient and therapist. The contemporary therapist must gain a greater awareness of and receptivity to the communicative importance of the self and object representations projectively identified and counteridentified back and forth during the course of psychoanalytic treatment. Individual therapists need to gain a greater appreciation of the systems implications of projective identificatory phenomena that seem quite familiar to therapists such as Scharff and Scharff (1987) and Scharff (1992) working from a couples and family treatment perspective.

There is no need to play back for the patient these representational processes in an active or manipulative fashion, as has been previously recommended by paradigmatic therapists (Nelson, 1962b,c; Spotnitz, 1969; Strean, 1970a). A flow of object usage and role evocation processes are naturally inherent in every treatment. Every transference and countertransference inter-active situation has certain enactment demands contextually embedded within it.

The therapist's task is to sensitively contain these projective identifica-tions and ultimately play them back in a sufficiently metabolized form so that they can be used by the patient to move toward the maturational goals of the treatment.

Projective identificatory interactions (and the self and object representa-tions contained therein) are inherent to both pathological and nonpathological interactive aspects of the psychotherapy process. The therapeutic importance and communicative value of these object relational processes should not be underestimated. The success or failure of the treatment may very well hinge upon the effectiveness with which they are handled.

# Chapter 8

# THE NEED TO PROTECT THE OBJECT

The *object usage* features of containing functions explored in the previous chapter raise the importance of the therapist's ability to demonstrate to the patient that she is not in need of protection from the toxic representations and associated affects unconsciously embedded within the patient's psyche. The therapist must also show an ability to tolerate action demands and role assignments during the course of treatment.

Historically, the importance of conceptions with regard to protectiveness have evolved and been underlined during the transition from a classical psychodynamic and ego structural model of psychotherapy to an object relational one. Conceptions with regard to the functions of objects and their linking affects have markedly changed during the course of this theoretical transition. The object can no longer be viewed as an arbitrary and least essential factor in a primarily drive determined equation, but must now be viewed as the primary focal point for the internalization processes underlying diverse forms of psychopathology and the treatment interventions required for them.

Every therapist is rather quickly confronted with the perceived deficiencies of the early objects via the patient's narrative. Many patients, however, deny or gloss over painful affects that might have been expected to be present in the context of such early object insufficiencies. When the therapist becomes curious and inquires about the possibility that the patient might be feeling a need to protect early objects from criticism, the response is often one of surprise and skepticism. The patient finds it difficult to imagine why she would need to protect her parents from exposure to the possibility of criticism. Such puzzlement clearly minimizes the impact of their dysfunctional or even toxic interactions with each other and with the patient over the years.

The mystification of many patients with regard to this issue often camouflages a dread of exposure of the parents to the critical judgments perceived as being inherent in the process of therapeutic inquiry. Much seems to be at stake for these patients were they to yield to an affectively powerful and critical confrontation with the parents' aberrant behavior and attitudes. The transference and countertransference interactions with the therapist, therefore, must frequently become a testing ground for the initially tentative and hesitant exposure of early object insufficiencies. The way in which the therapist allows herself to be used for self and object representational projection and for the role enactment expectations, will be carefully monitored by the patient and will set the stage for therapeutically empowering internalizations and initiatives toward maturational change.

The patient's deeply felt but largely unconscious loyalty to pathological introjects frequently forms a primary object relational core to her psychopathology. This fact has often been overlooked or taken for granted and has seldom received the systematic study that it requires. Treatment interventions, too, seldom incorporate systematic forms of explorative inquiry into the motivational patterns underlying these protective reactions.

## PROTECTIVENESS OF THE OBJECT IN BORDERLINE AND SCHIZOPHRENIC PATIENTS

It is interesting to note that the issue of protectiveness was first systematically studied in therapeutic work with the most difficult and severely disturbed patients. Colson (1982) directly addressed the protectiveness borderline patients manifest toward the family systems in which they have been pathologically enmeshed. The features of their early object relational environment that were most destructive are overlooked by such patients, as if to forestall the ultimate affect storms and rage reactions that might ensue. The ultimate dread, according to Colson, is of the grief and mourning reactions which are unconsciously sensed as being capable of facilitating the separation and individuation potentialities of these patients.

Unconsciously, borderline patients feel an intense need to protect the ego damaging early objects with which they have become symbiotically ensnared, even at the cost of their own freedom to separate and individuate. Indeed, any movement toward separation or individuation provokes unconscious feelings of disloyalty and intense anxiety. It is hardest for these patients to confront the various pathological ways in which the parents used them and the symbiotically enmeshed roles they took on as fixers and helpers of these severely damaged early objects.

Searles (1975) made a similar point with regard to schizophrenic patients. He reported the discovery during the course of intensive psychoanalytic work with these patients that they were transferentially reliving thwarted ambitions to repair damaged parental object representations. In his countertransference reactions to these severely disturbed patients which were carefully documented, Searles noted imperative hopes on their part that he would be enabled to repair certain defects in himself. Thus, his strongly obsessive–compulsive orientation which was contributing to an emotional shield between himself and many significant figures in his outer world, needed repair and change, according to one of his most profoundly disturbed patients. He felt that each of his severely disturbed patients was subtly attempting to get him to notice and change some aspect of his personality or behavior.

Searles began to decipher more instances of free associative derivatives indicating the need to open himself up to his patient's curative efforts. His genetic reconstructions led him to the insight that the parents had neglected these curative aspirations on the part of their severely disturbed child and, therefore, never opened themselves up to a mutually curative and freeing process of ego potentiation and maturational change. The therapist, according to Searles, must not make this mistake, and instead, should be continuously aware of her patient's deeply felt curative hopes and efforts. A receptivity to such efforts may become an important vehicle for mutual ameliorative change in therapeutic work with schizophrenic patients.

Searles in no way restricted this significant observation to work with the most profoundly damaged and disturbed patients. He found it to be central to an understanding of the deepest motivations of a diverse group, including much healthier patients. Every patient, at some point during treatment, will engage in an exploration of aspects of the therapist in need of repair. How the therapist responds to these frequently subtle and camouflaged overtures often is linked to her comfort and receptivity to effectively utilizing the countertransference for purposes of allowing the patient to expose her own flaws and ultimately, to help her to become a more whole and less dissociated, conflicted, or defensive person.

The object relational roots of these pervasive and frequently neglected protectiveness strivings need more systematic study. There is a need for clarification of what is at stake when the therapist is greeted with a protective reaction. To parallel the question frequently asked by Paula Heimann, according to Bollas (1987), "who is being protected and helped during these interactions and by whom," it would also be interesting to know why it is so important that someone be protected and from what dangers.

OBJECT RELATIONAL ASPECTS OF PROTECTIVENESS

Object relations theorists, by placing the self and object representation and linking affects at the center of therapeutic work, have suggested the importance of protective attitudes and motivational reactions. The issue of an excessive concern for the object was initially raised in Klein's (1940, 1946) description of the intense reparative efforts typically seen in both children and adults who have attained the *depressive* position. The angry and sadistic assaults, fantasized earlier during the paranoid position against significant part objects such as the breast, lead to a strong sense of guilt and active reparative strivings, once the depressive position has been maturationally reached.

Fairbairn (1952b) studied a similar phenomenon, at yet an earlier and more primitive level, in his notion of the different etiological roots of schizoid and depressive psychopathology. Whereas the schizoid patient feels an intense need to protect the object against her love feelings (felt to be highly destructive), the depressed patient feels an equally intense need to protect the object against her feeling of hate and more aggressive tendencies.

According to Fairbairn, both the schizoid and depressive patient share an intense need to protect the object, but from different motivational tendencies. In one type of patient (schizoid), love feelings and impulses are sensed to be extremely dangerous for the well-being of the object. In the other type (depressive), aggressive feelings and impulses have equally dire implications.

Winnicott (1963) has pursued this issue a bit further and has delineated a normal developmental phase in which caring for the object does not appear to exist and should not be required to exist. The mother, instead, is required to undergo the thankless task of tolerating the sadistic and ruthless assaults from her infant. She must not intrude upon the visions and fantasies of omnipotent powerfulness during this significant stage. She must merely exhibit her capability of withstanding and surviving the most vicious and uncaring assaults possible on her person. Winnicott (1947) qualifies this observation, however, by noting the tremendous feelings of anger and hate built up within the mother while undergoing the uncaring use of her by her infant. He parallels this with a similar sense of hate in the therapist who is required to undergo similar forms of object usage at the hands of her patient.

The fact that the mother experiences intense feelings of hate does not necessarily mean, however, that she is incapable of containing the uncaring object usage by her infant. Both her availability for such forms of use, and her unavailability, can be signaled in a variety of ways. She may communicate a sense of fragility or distaste for being used in a sadistic and uncaring fashion. Or, she may exhibit an intense need to be cared for or shielded from unpleasantly aggressive assaults on her person. In perhaps the worst scenario, she might even avoid or abandon her infant in response to uncaring assaults on her.

It is not hard to imagine that, paradoxically, an excessive sense of caring and protectiveness might evolve from such forms of maternal distaste for aggressive, uncaring usage by the infant. Winnicott (1963, 1968) has been interested in clarifying the object relational roots of the sense of concern and caring for the object. It might be important to clarify the psychological roots of excessive forms of caring and concern for the object. Whereas both Klein (1946) and Winnicott (1963) emphasize the aggressive implications of object usage that may have been difficult for the parents to contain, Fairbairn (1952b) stresses the fact that, at a still earlier and more primitive phase, the loving implications of object usage may be difficult for certain parents to contain.

It can be inferred from such object relational considerations that, under certain circumstances, a parent may convey the need for protection against naturally occurring feelings, impulses, and motivational states in their infant. This may occur at relatively early or later points in the infant's developmental history. Depending upon how strong the parent's need for protection tends to be, the infant or child may develop a greater or lesser sense of the danger-ousness to the parent of these inner psychic occurrences. Of course, the child's natural aggressiveness and sensitivities to parental affect and need states will be significant factors as well, in the degree to which they sense a need to protect parental figures and others in their external environment from inner psychic states, impulses, and action tendencies.

Fairbairn (1952b) argues that introversion is linked to the splitting and fragmentation of inner ego states resulting from the handling of libidinal strivings by parental objects. Winnicott (1965) has made a similar argument for most forms of psychopathology which he considers as resulting from environmental deficiencies. The implication in most object relations theories is that psychopathology stems from failure in environmental input and a lack of good enough parenting. The excesses in caring, concern, and protec-tiveness (frequently at the expense of self-strivings and needs) are seen in many patients. They may be viewed as complex results of an inner psychologi-cal readiness to respond in an excessively concerned and protective fashion toward the object world. There is also a sense (based upon past object rela-tional contact with significant parental figures) that such excessive protec-tiveness is required for the well-being and survival of these objects.

"THEY ARE ALL I HAVE"—A FAIRBAIRNIAN
EXPLANATION OF PROTECTIVENESS IN NEGLECTED OR
ABUSED PATIENTS

Fairbairn (1952b), while struggling to comprehend and conceptualize the evolution of the superego structure from his own unique object relations perspective, came up with an interesting observation about children who have been severely maltreated at the hands of their early parental objects. He noted that the abused child seldom remembers the specific instances of maltreatment by their parents. The parents, on the other hand, have no problem remembering such incidents. Fairbairn explored the dissociative (hystericlike) mechanics underlying the superego evolution in such children and questioned Freud's use of a very different model based upon the mourning and melancholy reactions of depressed patients for explicating the identificatory internalizations underlying the superego.

Fairbairn's preference for a return to the earlier dissociative mechanisms utilized by Freud (1905b) to explain hysterical phenomena, is consistent with his own emphasis upon a similar explanatory approach to understanding schizoid phenomena. Indeed, the conceptual centrality of dissociative mechanisms for understanding a diverse range of psychopathological states is basic to Fairbairn's object relational thinking. Thus, the maltreated or abused child must split off the bad objects and dissociate them from each other, more idealized expectations regarding them (i.e., the ideal object), and more ideal forms of ego and self structure (i.e., the central ego).

The abused child's failure to remember and report instances of abuse is linked for Fairbairn to the ultimate schizoid phenomenological dilemma that such children unconsciously dread and therefore defend against in a dissociative fashion. They dread the possibility of losing the one object that has at least bothered to reach out and contact them (admittedly, in a physically or sexually abusive manner), were they to remember and, even worse, expose publicly the damaging contacts with that object. Were they to lose that object, they dread the possibility of falling into a deep abyss of despair, loneliness, and even more primitive ego and self fragmentation.

Neglected or abused children feel a deeper need to cling to and protect the neglectful or abusive parents than do children who have received the "average expectable" and "good enough" parenting alluded to by Hartmann (1939) and Winnicott (1965). Dissociative mechanisms of splitting and repression often serve an important defensive function for such children. Such mechanisms allow the child to protectively cling to the only parental objects that they possess.

The recent literature on the psychopathology and treatment of abused children, particularly sexually abused children (Courtois, 1987; Herman, 1992; Davies and Frawley, 1994) tends to validate Fairbairn's conceptualizations regarding this issue from a clinical viewpoint. It can be paradoxically inferred from such literature that the best way to make a child protective toward a parent is for that parent to be severely abusive toward that child. Indeed, in many clinical instances the sexually abusive parent will be more clingingly protected than the more emotionally detached and outwardly less interested parent. The underlying feeling appears to be, "He (or she) offers me some feeling of contact."

The protectiveness of maltreated children will tend to continue outwardly, until they further mature and possess sufficient ego autonomy to go off more on their own. They often continue such intensely motivated attitudes of protectiveness toward internalized objects throughout their subsequent lives. The early dread of abandonment by the internalized bad objects continues to be manifested via an excessively caring and protective posture toward these objects. From Fairbairn's conceptual perspective, the central ego and self structures cling loyally and protectively to the split-off bad objects and ego and affective states associated with them. From a broader psychoanalytic conceptual perspective, *introjects* can be inferred as being internally established to maintain a continuous empathic and fantasied contact with the original ego damaging objects.

These introjects are stubbornly and loyally clung to, even in the face of threats to their continued maintenance in the form of potentially new and more benign object attachments and relationships. The therapeutic relationship is one such newer attachment which is perceived as threatening to the powerful and stubbornly maintained object ties implicit in pathological introjects.

PROTECTIVENESS AND THE CONCEPT OF INTROJECTS

Much of the conceptualizations regarding introjects stem from the ideas proposed by Freud (1917) regarding the prolonged nature of the mourning process in depressed patients who have repressed the ambivalent and hostile aspect of their original attachment to the departed object. The concept of depression as a turning against the self of the unconscious anger originally felt toward the object, flows rather naturally from Freud's thinking regarding the merciless self-laceration typical of pathological mourning states. The depressed and melancholic individual, thus, attacks herself, instead of the dead or departed object which is no longer available for attack. The object, on the other hand, is idealized and shielded from hostile feelings.

Freud's original thinking about depression viewed it as an affect (not very differentiable from melancholia or sadness), which is linked to an internalized object that repeatedly attacks the self in a direct reversal of the ways that the self originally wished to attack the object. The kernel of Freud's earliest ideas of the superego as an affectively painful and self-punitive introject are contained in his thinking here.

The largely self-punitive and prohibitive nature of Freud's view regarding the superego (1923) can be directly traced to this earlier (1917) depiction of it as an introject involving a great deal of self-criticism. Its melancholic and potentially depressive character involves a reflexive sparing of the object from critical or aggressive attack and instead a turning of these aggressive feelings against the self. Although Freud did not comprehensively explore the protective aspects of superego internalizations, he certainly alluded to them in his notions with regard to the ego ideal (1921) and in his early connection of pathological mourning and depressive phenomena to identificatory structures emanating from the loss of an object. Much of the theory of depressive and masochistic phenomena (more comprehensively delineated in chapters 2 and 11) can be traced to these early notions of Freud regarding introjects following upon the loss of objects. The fact that the object ends up being internalized in a highly self-punitive fashion, stems in great part from the need to protect the object from dissociated feelings and impulses of a hostile nature.

It is not surprising, therefore, that many depressed and masochistic patients utilize their severe superego introjects to protect the objects in their outer world against latent angry feelings and aggressive impulses. The fact that many such patients idealize their object representations while critically devaluing their self representations, is linked to an intense need to protect the object.

In many ways, feelings of caring and concern for the object are involved in the harshness of the superego introject. As Schafer (1960) has noted, idealizing tendencies and feelings regarding a *loving and beloved* object are involved here as well. The fantasy of the superego as a protective, loving internal object is very much involved in the tenacity with which painful symptoms, inhibitions, and character traits are clung to, despite available opportunities for therapeutic change.

Much of the ego syntonic and seemingly comfortable nature of character pathology can be viewed, in this light, as an unconsciously loving and loyal attachment to nonfunctional and even toxic introjects. Giovacchini (1984a) has made an important distinction between functional and nonfunctional introjects. Thus, many traits, attitudes, and motivational tendencies are internalized through intimate and continuous contact with parental figures. Some of these psychological characteristics are useful and quite adaptive whereas others are highly maladaptive. Therapeutic work with character disorders makes it clear that there is often a stubborn loyalty to dysfunctional character traits which essentially are introjects that need to be protected against the perceived dangers of change. The tenacity and resistance to change often seen in character disorders will be more fully explored in chapter 12. The point that needs to be made now, however, is that there is an intense attitude of protectiveness toward the introject which can be seen in many patients who stubbornly cling to painful, unpleasant, or dysfunctional modalities of interaction and behavior.

The issue of loyalty is an extremely important one, in assessing aspects of protectiveness implicit in various forms of psychopathology. Ultimately, many neurotic and characterological manifestations involve an unconscious and loyal attachment to introjects and the object representations symbolized by them. The original objects, as Freud (1917) and Fairbairn (1952b) have noted, were not necessarily good ones. Most typically they have been good and bad or predominantly bad ones. Nevertheless, they are sufficiently beloved to be stubbornly identified with, despite their painful and dysfunctional qualities. Indeed, according to Fairbairn (1952b) they are identified with precisely because of their badness. There is very little reason, in Fairbairn's conceptual model, to internalize a good object. Such a notion of introjects, although quite relevant to the intense loyalty often seen in pathological identificatory structures, flies in the face of the more mature and healthier identification processes alluded to by White (1963) that were discussed in chapter 4.

What we frequently discern in many patients is a stubborn loyalty to pathological introjects. This is most obvious with highly self-critical, depressive, or masochistic patients. It is also evident, however, in many nondepressed patients, particularly during phases of intense resistance or negative therapeutic reaction. Both the pathological introjects and the false selves alluded to by Winnicott (1960) are stubbornly and protectively clung to during the most resistant moments of treatment.

## PATHOLOGICAL FORMS OF LOYALTY TO THE OBJECT

Many patients put their lives on hold, unconsciously remaining intensely loyal to early unrewarding and highly deficient objects. Paradoxically, the more deficient and inadequate the object has been in the past, the more likely it is to be internalized in a highly protective fashion. The converse also appears to be clinically true. Thus, more adequate and competent parental objects inspire far less irrational forms of protectiveness and loyalty. Indeed, another paradox seems evident here. More competent parental objects encourage separation–individuation, and hence, more potential for appropriate forms of object usage and the possibility of being discarded in a relatively unconcerned manner.

As Winnicott (1960, 1963, 1968) has suggested, the possibility for the evolution of *true self* functioning may be considerably enhanced through relatively unconcerned forms of object usage. A diminished requirement that the object be protected, frees the budding true-self potentialities. An excessive need to protect the object, on the other hand, stifles latent self-potentials. The need to busily protect various objects from aspects of the self (particularly the truer ones), leaves little time or energy for self-actualization and expression. Indeed a too intense attitude of loyalty and protectiveness toward the object leads to a constriction and stifling of these inherent self-potentialities. Nonfunctional introjects and false self representations are rigidly clung to by individuals who have always felt the intense requirements of protecting dysfunctional, generally useless, and even destructive early objects. The false self, in many ways, emanates out of an unconsciously felt need to protect the vulnerable parental object against aspects of the true self. In certain individuals, the loyalty to early objects supersedes and interferes with the evolution and protection of significant aspects of the true self. Separation–individuation, assertive forms of self-expression, and emergent aspects of the true self are frequently seen as threatening to the safety and well-being of a vulnerable object. Significant aspects of the self must be dissociated or projectively identified into proxy objects, to protect the early objects.

Negative therapeutic reactions at various points during treatment, but particularly toward the latter phase, may occur as a result of intense loyalty reactions. The regression and loss of true self-potential and emergent ego functioning, so commonly seen during the termination phase of treatment, stems at least in part from a dread of abandoning the pathological introjects and early dysfunctional objects via separation–individuation and successful self-management. The hopefulness and potential for courage of the termination phase of treatment is seen as too sharp a separation and disloyal rejection of the connections to pathological early objects. The regressive pull, at such hopeful points, is toward the familiar ties to pathological introjects and associated false self functioning. By regressing, the guilt-ridden patient feels more loyal to the familiar dysfunctional objects of childhood. The true self implications of a successful termination of treatment are seen as acts of disloyalty and disconnection from pathological early objects.

The reconnection to these familiar pathological objects is, paradoxically, comforting and reassuring. A similar process is frequently seen to occur at moments of maturational growth and characterological change during the middle phases of treatment. For certain patients the extreme guilt feelings at moments of separation–individuation or major characterological shifts can lead to major treatment resistances. The nature of guilt and its ties to protectiveness need to be better understood.

## GUILT AND PROTECTIVENESS

Freud's conceptions of affect, reviewed more fully in chapter 1, have largely centered about negative feelings such as anxiety, anger, depression (melancholy), and guilt. He did not give much attention to the positive affects which have been more extensively focused upon in the present volume. Affects, according to Freud's later view (1926), have significant signal functions warning of an impending drive-determined danger situation. The sexual and aggressive drives were seen as motivating actions which were perceived as leading to potentially painful and punishing responses from the external environment (i.e., separation, castration, or loss of the love of a superego object). Guilt was viewed as an affective result of an internal structural conflict between the id and superego or ego ideal. Unconscious sexual and aggressive impulses might easily conflict with internalized moral standards, once the superego was established as a culminating structural resolution of the oedipal phase. Prior to the oedipal resolution and superego internalization, more externalized dangers and threats of abandonment (rather than guilt feelings), kept excessively hedonistic, narcissistic, or aggressive behavioral tendencies in check.

The superego for Freud (1923) was a significant maturational accomplishment which allowed for an *internalized* monitoring and affective signaling system (primarily relying upon the affect of guilt) to check and inhibit various forms of pleasurable or aggressive actions toward objects in the outer environment. Guilt is intrinsically linked to the superego, and according to Freud, probably does not exist prior to the oedipal resolution (at about 4 to 6 years of age). Later object relational theorists have tended to follow Klein's (1940) hypotheses that the superego (and hence guilt) can exist at a much earlier oedipal phase of development. Klein (1940, 1946) and Ogden (1986) have delineated a conceptualization of guilt as linked to the transition from the relatively guiltless sexually and aggressively fused *paranoid position* to the more reparative, caring, and concerned *depressive position*. The latter guilt-filled phase occurs as soon as object constancy and a sense of historical subjectivity has been established (prior to 2 years of age). The superego, too, already exists as a structure by this early developmental phase, as do oedipal psychodynamic issues.

Winnicott (1963, 1968) appeared to follow along with Klein's formulation with regard to the reparative motivations linked to both guilty and depressive affects. The strong wishes and needs to repair an object damaged via primitively fused sexual and aggressive actions during the earlier paranoid position are also emphasized by Winnicott. He notes that the capacity for concern (and, implicitly, reparative wishes and actions) is linked to a guilty response to the aggressive object usage that has occurred earlier upon the mother and her body. Once guilt and depressive affects are more predominant, the capacity exists for concern and reparative protectiveness toward the damaged maternal object. From these conceptualizations, however, it is difficult to envision caring concern or protectiveness without an unconscious memory or history of some form of sadistic or aggressive attack upon a significant early object.

Protectiveness for Freud may be seen as a reaction formation or guilty response to sexually motivated aggressive attacks upon the object. Thus, the oedipal child unconsciously feels guilty for death wishes toward the father and a wish to replace him sexually with the mother. The younger child (according to both Klein and Winnicott) also feels guilty and wishes to repair the objects (breast, mother) that have been damaged via the assaultive, unconcerned attacks of the paranoid position. The wish or need to protect the object is basic to Freud's, Klein's, and Winnicott's positions, but at different developmental phases. All three view the fantasized damage of the object as unconsciously linked to a need to reparatively restore it and protect it from further assaults. Protectiveness, thus, in all three theories is linked to a need to repair a damaged object and to avoid further attacks upon it. The oedipal child must protect the mother against further damage to her breast (from the Kleinian and Winnicottian perspectives), and must protect the father against death wishes and desires to replace him in a sexual relationship with his wife. For Freud, the latter occurs via the internalization of the father in the form of a protectively loving and critically punitive superego.

All three theoretical paradigms view protectiveness and excessive caring and concern for the object as a guilty response to unconscious fantasies of attack upon it. The negative affects of guilt must be present for caring and concern to occur from these perspectives. A surer, more ego autonomous, and less conflicted view of guilt and conscience is not articulated by either of these three positions. The idea of objective and rationally based guilt feelings is largely neglected by these theoretical models. Of course, such largely rational guilt feelings (in response to objectively assessed internal moral failings) do exist, just as do the ego autonomous and nonconflictual competency strivings elaborated in chapter 4.

Objective and rationally based protectiveness strivings (which certainly do exist as well) are intrinsically linked to these more rationally determined guilt feelings in relatively mature, competent, and high-functioning individuals. Such protective motivational tendencies are quite different from the more pathological forms of protectiveness under discussion in the present chapter. They do not usually interfere with adaptive ego functioning, true-self expression, and separation–individuation capabilities. They are instead natural manifestations of the self-critical, loving, and protective functions of a maturely articulated and internalized superego structure. The more pathological protectiveness patterns under discussion, on the other hand, are linked to more primitive superego internalizations and irrational feelings of guilt.

In the more pathological cases of protectiveness, a considerable degree of *survivor* guilt is evident, in response to potentially successful ego accomplishments. This occurs in the context of either intense abandonment anxiety or a dreaded loss of primitively introjected objects that continuously delimit and critically attack true self-activation and separation–individuation strivings. There is a tenacious need to protect pathological and dysfunctional introjects, at a huge cost to adaptive ego functioning and self-potentiation. The guilt feelings motivating such forms of loyalty to self-limiting introjects and false self functioning are highly primitive and essentially irrational in nature. Weiss, Sampson, and the Mount Zion Psychotherapy Research Group (1986) have offered a solid discussion of the dynamics of survivor guilt and its conceptual linkage to abandonment depression and separation–individuation impairments. They offer plentiful examples, in a relatively neurotic context, of individuals who severely inhibit ego and self-potentialities due to an unconsciously experienced dread of separating from a damaged but emotionally significant object.

Survival guilt reactions can severely inhibit ego functioning and need not solely occur in response to an object who has been lost via abandonment or death. Such reactions occur even in response to the fantasy of abandoning or letting go of an object via successful achievements, true self expressiveness, or enhanced separation–individuation capacities. Such forms of guilt are intrinsically linked to the need to protect early objects. The therapist's mode of handling the various tests, projective identifications, and object usage demands and role enactment expectations of the patient (as elaborated in chapter 7) will be important factors determining the success or failure of the treatment.

THERAPEUTIC GOALS AND STRATEGIES

The primary goal is to diminish the excessive concern and caring for pathological early objects that is manifested in the form of tendencies toward protectiveness. Another important goal is the alleviation of primitive and irrational guilt feelings associated with separation–individuation, true-self expression, and various competent and successful activities. These first two goals are linked to a third one, which is the diminishment of the tenacious sense of loyalty to dysfunctional introjects and the early objects linked with them.

All three goals can be attained through a perseverative focus throughout the treatment upon the varied manifestations of the need to protect the object. The excessive caring and concern for early objects need to be repeatedly ferreted out and explored with the patient. Thus, a man who complained continually about his wife's various failings and frustrating tendencies, while consistently protecting his parents and overlooking the existence of similar traits in them, was asked why he never complained about these traits in his parents. He was struck by this observation, but attempted to rationalize that these tendencies were somewhat different in his wife than in his parents. He quickly became aware, however, of the probable folly of such a track and seemed truly curious about this difference in the objects of his complaints. Indeed, his wife was probably the transferential foil for his protectiveness toward his parents. Although she certainly did many things to frustrate him, they were not nearly as significant as the frustrating ways that his parents had dealt with him.

As an experiment, the therapist suggested that the patient attempt to short-circuit the complaints regarding the wife by focusing instead on the parallel ways in which the parents had frustrated him. The patient was actively encouraged to diminish his excessive caring, concern, and protectiveness of the inner parents and to experience the considerable resentment and complaints he truly felt regarding their interactions with him.

Another patient continuously attacked himself for a failure to treat his sister well while she was alive and an even greater failure to properly mourn her death some years back. In many ways, his life was kept on hold, at least partially, due to intense unconscious feelings of survivor guilt. Why should he survive and thrive, he felt, when he had neglected his sister so badly? This patient, of course, needed to explore the ambivalent feelings toward the sister which underlay his difficulties in more successfully mourning his loss. His current attitude of protectiveness toward the sister (reflected in his repeated self-flagellation and inhibited capacity to successfully move on with his life) had to be, at least partially, punctured via an exploration of the many ways in which he had hated his sister and the various ways that she had encroached on his life during childhood.

Ultimately, the strategies for technically handling the attitudes of protectiveness as they manifest themselves during treatment is to constantly alert the patient to their existence and, ultimately, the deleterious impact they are having on the patient's capacities for effective love and work.

In many cases, the object usage interactions, which could never be fully expressed with the parents, who were perceived as being too vulnerable for such role enactments, may have to be expressed instead in the transference relationship with the therapist. Ideally, the therapist will be used more effectively and will survive these enactments in a relatively hardy and resilient fashion. If the therapist continually confronts the need to protect her and wonders about why this should be the case, the patient will eventually stop being protective and begin using the therapist in a more outwardly critical and aggressive manner. The therapist's ability to survive such assaults and ultimately connect them to the unconsciously hated but protected early objects will free the patient to more fully separate from these objects.

The disloyalty and diminished concern for the early objects acted out in the transference will eventually free the patient to express their true-self potentialities and give up their loyalties to the *frozen introjects* alluded to by Giovacchini (1984a). Subsequently, they will initiate a more authentic and effective mourning process which will culminate in a successful termination of the psychotherapy relationship via a solid internalization of the therapist's positive ego attributes and affect tolerance capabilities.

A great deal of negative enactments and struggle, however, will need to take place in the relationship with the therapist, before a patient can be coaxed to give up her intense loyalties and protectiveness of early dysfunctional objects. The therapist's capacity to maintain attitudes of empathy, analytic curiosity, and hopefulness, in the context of aggressive object usage and assaults on her professional identity will assure an ultimately successful outcome. The diminishment of the patient's latent attitudes of protectiveness via a conveying of the therapist's capacity to take and survive her *best shots* will naturally occur via the object usage enactments in the transference and countertransference relationship. The therapist, by accepting and even inviting a relatively uncaring attitude from the patient, paradoxically, increases her capacity to care more authentically, rationally, and spontaneously.

CASE ILLUSTRATIONS

*Case 1*

A young professional woman had been struggling for years with a wish not to be like her mother in her relationships with men. Three relationships that she had during college, however, brought her a bit too close to her mother for comfort. All three relationships were apparently with extremely narcissistic men who treated her cruelly, ultimately rejecting her for other women. Since then, she had been very insulated against intimate relationships with men and had been living a rather independent existence focused largely about her professional work.

Her mother frequently conveyed a great deal of concern regarding the patient's life-style and the possibility that she might never marry and produce grandchildren for her. The patient saw her mother's concerns as largely narcissistic and felt constantly angry at her mother for expressing them. She intensely disliked a certain quality of desperation that she repeatedly sensed in the mother's frequent suggestions for things that she might do to enhance her possibilities for finding a mate. The patient felt that her mother exhibited similar desperation in her own life, in repeatedly running after the father (an alcoholic who alternated between being abusive toward the mother and herself and abandoning them) and imploring him to stay with her and her young daughter.

The patient, an only child, had always dreaded the symbiotic attachment that evolved in her mother's relationship to her. She also felt considerable disdain for her own vulnerable attitudes in the three significant sexual relationships that she had allowed herself to risk. She had spent the last few years hardening herself to the fact that she might be able to survive quite well (without becoming desperate like her mother), if a man were never to be in her life. Two obstacles to this insular and self-protective goal, however, were explored during treatment.

Her therapist (a male) had kept annoying her by wondering about the impact of her narcissistic and indifferent father upon her extreme reluctance to risk further relationships with men. Any mention of her father annoyed the patient who had not been in communication with him for many years. He never remembered her birthdays, unless reminded to do so by her mother (who still maintained a relationship with him). When asked to discuss him in her treatment, the patient expressed resentment at "wasting" her time in this way. She wondered why the therapist was so interested in him, since he had played such an insignificant part in her life for many years. She recently wrote a long angry letter to a male cousin detailing many complaints about the way he was treating her. She became quite annoyed when the therapist suggested that she might consider writing a similar one to her father.

The patient angrily insisted that the father would never be able to comprehend such a letter and that it would be a waste of time and effort. She seemed surprised when the therapist suggested that she might want to *protect* the father from the angry feelings that would be expressed in such a fashion. The patient clearly was oblivious to her lifelong need to protect this man (much as her mother had always done). The revulsion of being anything like her mother made it difficult for her to imagine such a motivation for her avoidant behavior vis-à-vis her father.

Interestingly, but not surprisingly, she had been similarly avoidant with her therapist who had always felt an almost *antiseductive* attitude in the transference and countertransference interaction. Dreams suggesting an eroticized component to the transference had always seemed to have nothing to do with her feelings or wishes toward the therapist. The patient had, however, been able to channel much of her angry feelings toward her father, admittedly in an avoidant and oppositional manner, into the transference relationship with the therapist. The therapist felt the need to contain a certain degree of rejection and seemingly emotional indifference during the course of treatment interactions with the patient. There had been a sort of collusive agreement not to look at the strong feelings (both positive and negative) that must exist in relationship to the therapist.

In many ways, the therapist felt the need to protect the patient against any premature exposure of the more intimate and affectful aspects of the treatment relationship, much as the patient had felt an unconscious need to protect the father against her own deeply felt feelings. By becoming less protective of the patient, in this regard, the therapist was better able to help the patient both to free herself of the counteridentificatory bind she had created with her mother, and to become aware of the protective motivations underlying her avoidance of potentially hostile and confrontational communication with her father.

## Case 2

A second patient exhibited intense protectiveness during her childhood, but behaved very differently in her interactions with her therapist. The patient was severely sexually abused by her father during childhood. The mother, as is typically the case, remained mute and provided no protective shield whatsoever for her young daughter against the father. Indeed, the mother always seemed like a passive and unrelated figure throughout the patient's life. The father, on the other hand, came across as a powerful person who at least contacted the patient, admittedly in a sadistically manipulative and abusive fashion. Considering the degree of abuse experienced at the hands of her father, the patient had established, for many years, a surprisingly accepting and understanding attitude toward him. It was as if he was her only hope for emotional contact of some sort, since the mother seemed pathetically hopeless and unreachable.

In a previous therapeutic encounter a sexual relationship had evolved during the course of treatment. During the early phase of her current therapy, she was somewhat seductive, but seemed comfortable with the therapist's unresponsiveness. She proceeded, however, to regress quite severely and in an almost psychotic fashion during early phases of the treatment. She had the annoying habit of repeatedly calling the therapist with lengthy messages between sessions. These messages were extremely vengeful and bizarre and felt like a sadistic assault.

The therapist felt as if his answering machine (clearly a substitute for himself) were being bombarded by these frequently sexualized and sadistic messages. The last straw (at least for the therapist's tolerance) was a bizarre message that was so lengthy that it took up the entire quite liberally provided tape, leaving a sound that gave the impression that the machine was broken. The therapist angrily confronted the patient during the next session, emphasizing that he refused to be a further victim of the patient's assaultive behavior. The patient laughed at the therapist's seemingly impotent rage and merely noted that he was obviously not aware that answering machines immediately cut off (but are not broken) when a message proceeds to the end of the tape.

From a somewhat cooler position, it gradually dawned upon the therapist that he was being sadistically manipulated by the patient, in much the same way that the father had abusively manipulated her during childhood. The patient agreed to a voluntary psychiatric hospitalization, following which she came back into treatment to work much more productively on the object relational roots of her difficulties. Projective identifications could be more fully explored as a need for an object usage experience with the therapist that, not surprisingly, greatly resembled the way she had been used by her father. Her need to protect her father (and, equally so, her sad, passive mother) from her rage had led to continuous acting out of an extremely impulsive and self-destructive nature during her adolescence and young adulthood. Given her intense need to protect both parents from her rage over their dysfunctional interactions with each other and with her, she felt that she had no choice but to act these feelings out destructively against herself.

A continued exploration of her protectiveness and unconscious attitude of loyalty to both parents, ultimately, led to a greater comfort with separation–individuation and a more satisfactory mourning of the losses she experienced during childhood in being confronted with such extremely dysfunctional parenting. She began to pull away emotionally from her parents and to establish an independent existence. Her underlying competencies increasingly came to the fore as her therapy progressed.

CONCLUSIONS

Both cases reflect, from quite different psychopathological perspectives, the importance of exploring protectiveness as a central motivational attitude in the early object relational experiences of patients who have experienced varied forms of dysfunctional parenting. Although both cases involve severely traumatic object relational experiences of an extremely disappointing nature, protectiveness can be found to exist in much healthier and far less disappointing relational contexts.

The paradoxical attitude of protectiveness and loyalty toward relatively disappointing early objects can be clinically observed in patients across the spectrum of ego strength and psychopathology. As Fairbairn (1952a,b) has noted, all sorts of neurotic adaptational maneuvers, ultimately, can be traced to a core schizoid dilemma involving dissociated ego, self, and object representations. Many patients tend to split off and dissociate the protective aspects of their feelings toward disappointing early objects. They prefer to blame themselves, self-destructively act out, or externalize blame onto significant figures in their current environment such as a mate, child, or therapist, rather than truly feel the rage and disappointment, and ultimately mourn the loss of their unsatisfying and far from ideal early objects.

As Fairbairn (1952b) has suggested, the need for an ideal object is quite great during childhood, and its satisfying existence is the sole assurance of a solid, coherent, and unfragmented central ego and self structure. Anything short of such good enough parenting (Winnicott, 1965) or "average expectable environment" (Hartmann, 1939) will inevitably lead to some form of dissociative behavior and heightened protectiveness and tendencies toward loyalty. Paradoxically, the greater the degree of disappointment with these early objects, the greater the need to protect them, either via tenacious maintenance of nonfunctional introjects (Giovacchini, 1984a) or via an equally stubborn clinging to false self tendencies and refusal to experience and openly express truer aspects of the self (Winnicott, 1960).

The basic therapeutic task, hence, has two significant components. The therapist must first provide a reparative experience of object usage which was never fully available during childhood. Second, the therapist needs to assist the patient in a difficult mourning process that has been largely frozen and avoided prior to the treatment. The therapist, both by being curious about latent protective tendencies and by vividly and repeatedly demonstrating the fact that she does not need such forms of unconscious loyalty and protection, ultimately frees the patient to give up these intensely ego depleting and energy sapping defensive efforts and to separate from early objects, more adequately mourning them in the process.

# Chapter 9

# THE WISH TO STOP THERAPY: OBJECT RELATIONAL IMPLICATIONS

The need to protect the object, which was explored in the previous chapter, is very powerful and has important ramifications for psychoanalytic treatment. It is particularly linked to an extreme loyalty to pathological introjects which somehow must be protected against the seemingly intrusive assault of goals and expectations built into the psychotherapy process.

The therapist's ideals and expectations for maturational growth involve an implicit or even explicit valuing of separation–individuation and a broader range of affects and affective attitudes, including more positive ones such as joy, exhilaration, hopefulness, and courageous risk taking. Most of these positive affects and affective attitudes can only be experienced following a separation from and mourning of early pathological objects. The gradual awareness of this need to let go of early object attachments can be quite threatening for the patient who may prefer to end the treatment rather than internalize newer, healthier, and more potentially joyful object relationships.

The need to hold onto and protect pathological objects from the onslaught of therapeutic expectations for separation and change is evident in subtle and yet definitive ways throughout the treatment process. A male patient had been resisting for many months interpretations regarding his refusal to have sexual relations with his wife. The rigidity with which he clung to this reluctance to change his sexual behavior was connected to the similar rigidity of his parents, every time that he had come up with a suggestion for change, during childhood. On one occasion, after noting that he had been able to make love with his wife the previous night, he proceeded to speak critically of various qualitative aspects of the sexual experience. He went on to seriously consider the fact that he might have to more actively proceed toward separation and divorce.

He seemed puzzled when the therapist noted the paradoxical juxtaposition of his breakthrough regarding sexual relations with his wife and the almost simultaneous consideration of the need for a divorce. It seemed as if the breakthrough and possibilities for change in the sexual sphere was so threatening that it had to be countered via a resurgence of stubborn clinging to older attitudes and feelings of hopelessness regarding any possibilities for change. The stubborn loyalty to these old affective attitudes masked the dread of change, letting go, and mourning the pathological objects associated with them.

A young woman who was being treated for a severe hair-pulling condition, said repeatedly, "I can't stop it." The therapist, attempting to maintain a more continuously optimistic affective attitude, repeatedly responded, "Yes, you can stop, yes you can." During one particular session, the patient changed her statement to, "Maybe, I can stop doing it." The therapist responded with some elation and hope which she attempted to conceal from the patient, fearing that this might make her feel too pressured and self-conscious.

Not so surprisingly, the patient abruptly terminated the treatment shortly after that momentously hopeful session. Paradoxically, it appeared that both the patient's and therapist's feelings of elation and hopefulness had to be dashed and destroyed, inferentially, out of an even greater need for loyalty to internalized pathological objects and the need to protect them.

The unconscious sense of protectiveness toward early objects, often occurs at the expense of the establishment of new and maturationally beneficial object attachments. It may also lead to the disruption of such attachments, once they do occur. A male patient remained a bachelor until he was well into his forties. Interestingly, he became engaged to a woman and ultimately married her, shortly after his mother's death. His strong and deeply felt need to protect the mother (whom he felt had been dealt numerous raw deals in her life) was continually explored throughout treatment. The fact that he had repeatedly been unsuccessful in maintaining a long-term committed relationship in the past was explored. This was seen as partially related to strong attitudes of devotion toward the mother and a need to protect her from sensing his separateness and individuation.

The fact that the mother's death might have freed him at last to actively pursue a woman and successfully commit himself to her seemed self-evident to both the patient and analyst. The patient had a great deal of difficulty, however, in exploring feelings of anger that clearly lay beneath his strong sense of protectiveness toward the mother and others in his outer world. He could never be openly assertive with others, needing instead to shield them from those aspects of himself. He needed particularly to shield his wife (as he did his mother before her) from any sense of his angry or assertive feelings.

After a few years of treatment, the patient began to hesitantly express his more assertive side with his wife and others in his environment. He began gradually to relinquish the habit of protecting others from his anger and more aggressive feelings. This newer attitude began to manifest itself at work, where he had been satisfied with the most passive efforts and meager competitive success. This had been a great bone of contention with his wife who repeatedly attacked his therapy as not being at all helpful in making him more competitive and successful in his professional endeavors.

At one point, the patient came in and stated that he was tired of hearing his wife's complaints about the therapy and so he had decided to quit treatment. The therapist felt angry toward the wife and even more exasperated and angry with the patient for not standing up more assertively to her assaults upon the treatment. Focusing the anger more directly toward the patient was helpful, in that it could be used to more effectively explore the patient's own dissociated feelings of anger toward his wife.

By working on the projective identificatory component, the therapist was able to help the patient, at least partially, to own his anger at the wife. He began to own some of the anger over her intrusiveness, in a way that he seldom could with his mother. He decided eventually to continue with the treatment, despite his wife's protestations about it not being helpful.

Interestingly, the patient now began to assert himself in a much more competitive fashion at work. His work focus was so much greater that he obtained a monthly award for productivity for a continuous period of six months in a row. He was ecstatic about these accomplishments but was somewhat surprised when the therapist noted the fact that this newfound success had occurred almost immediately after a decision to terminate treatment.

He saw very little connection between these two events and wondered why the therapist insisted upon connecting them. The therapist responded that the patient's strong need to protect both himself and the wife against his assertive and competitive potential might have been unconsciously involved in his wish to prematurely terminate, particularly at that point in treatment.

The capacity to integrate aggression more effectively into love and work activities was very threatening to the precious early object attachments of this patient, particularly to his mother whom he had always shielded against such feelings and impulses. The mother had made it clear that she was uncomfortable with his self-assertive side. She had, however, wished that he was more assertive with others and particularly in the academic and work spheres. Since he had experienced the need to dissociate his assertive potential with her, he could not very easily express it in these other areas.

The intense feelings of loyalty and need to protect an object against certain aspects of the self tends to generalize and become a pervasive aspect of characterological functioning. Other objects are reflexively protected against these self representations. This patient developed an intense and reflexive protective reaction with his mother and subsequently began to shield others around him (i.e., employer, colleagues, wife, the therapist) from confrontations with his more aggressive and assertive self representations. There was a stubborn and oppositional quality to his refusal to show his competitive and assertive potential to his mother via motivated attainments both at school and at work. It was as if he said to himself, "Yes, I will shield mother from my aggressive tendencies, but I will also withhold from her any expression of my competitiveness via academic and work motivations and success."

The secret and well-camouflaged need to displease mother was an important dynamic for this patient. His capacity to own such feelings more directly with mother, wife, therapist, and authority figures at work became an important working through insight during the subsequent course of his treatment. Thus, his wish to prematurely terminate the treatment had important object relational significance. It involved a complex condensation of two distinctly different object relational attitudes, the wish to protect the mother from his assertiveness and the opposite wish to attack her via cutting off his budding competitive aspirations. The attitudinal piece involving the wish to protect the mother was transferentially displaced to the wife via his passive willingness to go along with her demands that he terminate the treatment. The deeply camouflaged anger at the mother, on the other hand, was transferentially expressed via the same submissive action, but with the implication that the therapist would be deprived of an opportunity to experience his impending spurt of competitive success.

Thus, in many situations involving a request to prematurely terminate treatment, it is helpful for the therapist to review the object relational implications of such a decision. The dynamics of intense loyalties to pathological objects need to be explored. Attitudes of protectiveness which may camouflage deeply dissociated angry feelings toward early objects need to be unraveled and explored as well. Projective identificatory aspects of the therapeutic interaction need to be noted, as well as subjective and objective countertransference reactions in the therapist.

### THE DYNAMIC SIGNIFICANCE OF THE WISH TO STOP TREATMENT

The wish to stop treatment is a very complex one and has manifold dynamic significance. The mutual decision to stop treatment typically leads to intense feelings of both a positive and negative nature. There is a sense of exhilaration over the impending liberation from the drudgery of the treatment. There is also a feeling of joy with regard to the opportunity to competently and autonomously perform self-analytic functions that have been internalized from the therapist's interpretive interventions. The internalization of an *analytic introject* emphasized by Giovacchini (1984a) and of *self-soothing* functions alluded to by Stolorow and Lachmann (1980), can often lead to a smooth and relatively joyful transition away from the psychoanalytic treatment relationship.

When the decision to stop treatment has been a mutual one, the therapist is relatively free to offer the *celebratory* response alluded to by Bollas (1989) to the successful implications of the patient's impending separation from the treatment process. Many therapists, however, have difficulty in expressing such feelings, as do their patients. Difficulties with the expression of positive affects (such as celebratory feelings of joy and exhilaration) may, therefore, permeate the termination phase of treatment leading to regressive patterns and negative affects such as helplessness, exaggerated melancholy, mournful, depressive despair, and intense feelings of separation guilt and anxiety.

The termination literature (Ticho, 1972; Schafer, 1973; Novick, 1982; Viorst, 1982; Schachter, 1992) contains many discussions of the various difficulties experienced both by patient and analyst, once a mutual decision to terminate the treatment has occurred. Schafer (1973), in particular, emphasizes the need to confront the relative imperfections of both patient and analyst at such a point in the treatment. The normal mourning process, at this time, consists of the further resolving of latent idealized self and object representations, omnipotent strivings, and perfectionistic tendencies in both patient and analyst.

## THE PATIENT'S RELUCTANCE TO RADICALLY REDECORATE AN "INNER APARTMENT"

Therapists such as Giovacchini (1984a), who have worked with relatively severe character disorders, seldom overlook the patient's intense loyalty to pathological introjects. Giovacchini has repeatedly noted the difficulties such patients experience in yielding up their nonfunctional introjects and replacing them with more functional *analytic introjects*. The therapist's strong wishes to facilitate such a process of substitution, however, may lead to a conflict with the patient's unconscious need to loyally persevere in maintaining intact the more pathological self and object representations associated with early life experiences.

A young woman, whose case will be more fully explored in chapter 11, exemplifies many of the issues of loyalty that are best not overlooked in the context of therapeutic zeal for inner object relational change. The patient, who presented with severe bulimic symptomatology, had lost her mother to cancer at quite at an early age. She was sent away to live with her grandmother for a few years. Upon her return to her home, she discovered that the father, much too quickly for the patient's comfort, chose to remarry and brought the new wife into the family home. The stepmother proceeded, quite naturally, to make changes and redecorate the home.

The patient, being quite young, initially expressed no reactions to the stepmother's redecorating. She did, however, become embroiled in various conflicts with the stepmother, particularly in the area of eating and food. She stubbornly refused to submit to the stepmother's efforts toward diminishing her overeating behavior and reducing her weight. Her subsequent bulimic symptoms became the central focus for her treatment.

One aspect of the patient's identification with her terminally ill and dying mother was metaphorically captured in a repetitive series of dreams consisting of apartments in varying states of ugliness and decrepitude. The therapeutic exploration of the significance of these repetitive dreams led back rather consistently to an experiential sense of what the dying mother's inner and outer environment must have been like. The patient, by keeping both her own outer apartment and her inner psychic states messy and extremely unpleasant, was revealing her deep feelings of loyalty and protectiveness toward the mother's role in her early life experience.

She refused to follow the stepmother's and father's lead in redecorating the family abode. She also stubbornly resisted the stepmother's efforts to curb her appetite, reduce her weight, and thereby enhance her inner psychic apartment, body and self image. The intensity that the stepmother brought to her redecorating efforts became a great problem for the patient. She stubbornly refused to be redesigned by the stepmother and brought a similarly stubborn attitude of resistiveness to the therapist's efforts to redecorate her inner psyche and bodily self-images.

The ultimate resolution of her intense resistances required a continued awareness on the part of the therapist of the patient's stubborn loyalty to pathological self and object representations. Unlike the patient's stepmother and father, he had to be very sensitive to the disruptive and painful implications of his wish to redecorate her inner psychic apartment. The patient's attitudes of loyalty and protectiveness had always to be noted and respectfully interpreted. Feelings of frustration, helplessness, and impatience had to be contained for long periods of time during the treatment, while an attitude of optimism regarding the possibility for inner object relational shifts was maintained. Many treatment impasses with difficult patients can be traced, at least in part, to an unconsciously loyal clinging to pathological self and object representations. The insensitivity of wishing to redecorate too quickly the patient's inner apartment is an apt metaphorical expression of the object relational dilemma. This is particularly apparent at moments of impasse or intense resistance to the treatment.

At such points, it might be most important for the therapist to contain and ultimately metabolize via interpretation the intensely loyal and protective aspirations underlying the temporary therapeutic stalemate. While acknowledging the strong need to protect and hold onto the pathological objects, the therapist patiently holds out some optimism and hope for their ultimate relinquishment and the substitution of more therapeutic ideals and internalized object relations.

The therapist's gradual awareness of the deleterious impact of her zestful and enthusiastic wish to cure the patient can, paradoxically, allow the patient sufficient resistance space to get past her dread of disloyalty and abandonment of pathological objects. The therapist's capacity to recognize and more effectively utilize intense countertransference feelings, rescue wishes, and therapeutic strivings with patients who have strong needs to cling loyally and protectively to early pathological objects ultimately can allow for a productive and positive treatment outcome.

## COUNTERTRANSFERENCE AND PROJECTIVE IDENTIFICATORY ISSUES WITH PATIENTS WHO WISH TO STOP TREATMENT PREMATURELY

The therapist is repeatedly tested by the patient's resistances during the course of the treatment. Patients who come late or repeatedly miss sessions establish particular forms of object usage and role enactment interactions with the therapist. Often, these resistive actions are projective identificatory in nature, putting feelings of rejection and abandonment into the therapist that have been difficult for the patients in their own lives. As Ogden (1979) has emphasized, they watch the therapist's metabolic functions like a hawk, wondering how the therapist will handle these feelings that they themselves have found so difficult. The therapist's capacity to contain and metabolize such feelings more effectively than the patient experienced in childhood interactions with their parents may allow for a beneficial reinternalization process by the patient.

Patients who come late or miss sessions threaten the therapist with feelings of helplessness and abandonment. The ultimate threat and potentially most treatment destructive resistance, however, occurs via a stated wish to terminate treatment at a point that the therapist considers premature. The therapist experiences feelings of helplessness, at such points, possibly mixed with a sense of disappointment and resentment. The deeply engrained therapeutic strivings and ideals come to the fore. Images of the patient's perfectability (at least in accordance with the therapist's ideals for the patient), which are about to be frustrated, lead to a great deal of conscious or unconscious resentment of the damage perpetrated by early objects upon the patient. Termination of a lengthy therapeutic relationship, similarly, leaves a certain degree of grieving to be done by both therapist and patient for the object relational shifts that never fully took place. Premature termination, however, is a much more upsetting experience for the therapist who must grieve alone for the ego damage perpetrated via early pathological objects on the patient. The patient has typically dissociated angry or sad feelings in response to early object deficiencies and has deposited them with the therapist who has become the patient's full fledged proxy.

The patient fully prepared to terminate the treatment before more comprehensive therapeutic work can be done on these damaging early object relationships, unconsciously wishes to protect these objects from the potentially disruptive scrutiny of a continuing psychoanalytic interaction. The therapist ends up feeling the dissociated feelings of helplessness, abandonment, and resentment that the patient was never able to effectively express with their early objects. This is a very important *test* for the therapist, much as Weiss, Sampson, and the Mount Zion Psychotherapy Research Group (1986) have emphasized in their approach to transference and resistance analysis. Should the therapist, somehow, pass the test and the patient reconsider the decision to terminate, a significant and benign reinternalization process may ensue.

Certain strategies and approaches may be helpful in effectively utilizing the induced countertransference feelings and projective identificatory interactions at such points of therapeutic impasse.

### Therapeutic Goals and Strategies

It is, perhaps, most essential that the therapist, through self-analysis, get in touch with the latent affects and affective attitudes (both positive and negative) that the patient threatening to quit treatment prematurely may be actively dissociating. Thus, negative affects such as separation anxiety, guilt, disappointment, helplessness and impotent rage are nowhere to be found in the patient but are abundantly experienced by the therapist. More positive affects and affective attitudes of courage, hope, joy, and optimism are seemingly nowhere to be found in either patient or therapist at such moments of impasse, although they may be another essential aspect of what is being dissociated via the difficulties in the projective identificatory interaction.

It may be helpful for the therapist to wonder aloud about these dissociated affects. She might ask the patient why she is now feeling so helplessly angry or guilty regarding the thwarted goals of the treatment. If she is feeling frustrated and angry at a significant figure in the patient's life (parent, wife, husband, etc.), she might ask why this might be the case, hinting at the proxy nature of the interaction. She can allude to more positive dissociated affects as being also thwarted via such a premature decision to terminate. Thus, the potential for hope or to risk joyful therapeutic change is being avoided by the wish to terminate.

It may be somewhat easier for the patient to reown negative feelings of abandonment and disappointment than more positive affects which have been much more dissociated and may seem largely unrelated to the present treatment impasse.

In certain circumstances in which the therapist must initiate an impending termination of the treatment due to illness or geographical relocation, it is important to explore the counterphobic and counterdepressive defenses utilized by the patient. Thus, the patient may even more prematurely wish to terminate the treatment, protecting the therapist from feelings of disappointment and rage and depriving both of the opportunity to work through together and mourn the relationship, in the time remaining.

Also of considerable strategic importance is the focus upon object relational issues of protectiveness and loyalty to pathological introjects that may underly the patient's wish to terminate the treatment prematurely. As was evident in the case material provided earlier in this chapter, many patients unconsciously are enacting the roles of captains, loyally going down with their family ships, by threatening to foreclose their treatment too early. Sensing the potential threat of treatment for their symbiotic enmeshments with pathological early objects, they prefer to cut the treatment rather than allow it to perform its ultimate separation–individuation functions. It is, therefore, most important that the therapist be alert to the issues of loyalty and protectiveness and actively share them with the patient, particularly at a point in the treatment in which the patient has threatened to prematurely terminate.

Finally, the therapist needs to be aware of her intense wishes to cure the patient and *redecorate* her inner object relations and psychic world. The dangers of such zealous aspirations for the patient's unconsciously protected and loyally internalized objects needs to be sensitively acknowledged. The patient's need to loyally and protectively stay close to these pathological early objects should be explored as a significant factor underlying the willingness to disrupt and potentially terminate the evolving therapeutic bonding.

The open exploration with the patient of the countertransference wishes to redecorate the patient's inner object world can, occasionally, be helpful in informing the patient of how threatening such aspirations might be for the loyally maintained and protected object attachments. It can be even more helpful if the therapist finds a way to understand and modulate such motivations by self-analysis, slowing the treatment down to a pace that is less threatening for the patient and his or her protectively shielded internalized objects. The trick, of course, is to maintain some affective attitudes of hope and optimism with regard to the possibilities for therapeutic change, under such demanding and containing circumstances.

# Chapter 10

# OBJECT RELATIONS IN THE NEGATIVE

# OEDIPAL CONFLICT

The dynamic significance of the Oedipus conflict was explored in chapter 5 in terms of the positive affects that are so frequently overlooked in expositions regarding its various clinical and theoretical aspects. The focus, in that chapter, was largely upon the positive Oedipus complex in which the child competes with the same sex parent for the sexual and loving attention of the opposite sex parent. The complete oedipal conflict also consists of a dyadic preoedipal phase and a triangular negative oedipal phase. The latter phase will be the central focus of the present chapter which will offer an explication of it from an object relations perspective.

There has not been much interest in exploring the various psychoanalytic ramifications of the negative oedipal configuration alluded to by Freud in the "Ego and the Id" (1923). The wish by a girl to compete with her father for her mother and by a boy to compete with his mother for his father has been duly noted by a few psychoanalytic theorists (Karme, 1979; Jaffe, 1983; Blanck, 1984; Blos, 1984; Frankiel, 1991), but has not been very deeply or comprehensively assessed.

The bulk of the theoretical and clinical formulations regarding this conflictual issue have been well within the context of Freud's original drive theoretical paradigms. Thus, the sexual and aggressive drive implications of the attraction and wish to compete for the same sex parent have been high-lighted in most studies. The projection of aggressive and sexual drive tenden-cies onto the opposite sex parent has led to the assumption of a dreaded retaliatory response to the child's competitive sexual aspirations toward the same sex parent. The fantasized dangers of abandonment, castration, or loss of superego support, as alluded to by Freud (1926) in his more ego psychologi-cal formulations of the *signal* aspects of the anxiety affect, apply as much to conceptions of the negative oedipal conflict as to the classical conceptions of the positive oedipal configuration.

It is frequently assumed that the negative oedipal conflict has a distinctly homoerotic cast. Thus, the longings by a little boy to replace his mother in a sexual or loving relationship with his father, or by a little girl to do the same regarding the love of her mother, is automatically assumed to have homosexual significance. Why else, it is often argued, would a child so intensely and competitively seek out the love of their same sex parent? So long as such aspirations remain tentative and temporary, they mesh well with Freud's (1924a) assumptions regarding the normal constitutional bisexuality of all human beings. Should they become more fixed conflictual determinants in a given individual, than it can be assumed that a greater than average degree of femininity in a male or masculinity in a female must exist.

The classical model has a variety of ways for conceptualizing the strongly driven attraction by the child for the same sex parent, above and beyond the notion of constitutional bisexuality. The ideas that a female child or woman might unconsciously protest her femininity, perhaps due to envy of the seem-ing phallic advantages of the male, or that a male child might unconsciously devalue his masculinity out of envy of the ability of his mother to give birth to a child, have been proposed as aspects of the bisexual manifestations frequently observed. Strong identifications with the opposite sex parent have been noted in many children for fleeting or longer periods, during the course of their sexual development.

The male child, in particular, is faced with the maturational need articu-lated by Greenson (1968) to disidentify from his mother who is his initial primary identification figure. The powerful identificatory connection to the mother in little boys has been delineated from a classical Freudian perspective by various theorists (Jacobson, 1950; Kestenberg, 1956; Jaffe, 1968) who have noted the strong maternal feelings and procreative wishes in male chil-dren. The difficulty of integrating such feminine identifications and aspirations with more masculine strivings in boys and men is, perhaps, one of the reasons for Freud's assertion (1937) that, for men, negative oedipal issues are the most formidable and difficult aspects of psychoanalysis. An analysis, should it broach passive feminine wishes in a male (and the negative oedipal psycho-dynamics that underlie them) can become quite stormy and resistant, given the threat to masculine identity structures. Most men find it difficult to integrate their feminine identifications and wishes for loving closeness to their fathers with their masculine identifications.

Although women, too, do not very easily integrate negative oedipal aspirations, this is not because of a gender-specific need to disidentify with their mothers, as is true for men. As in the case of men, the partially homosexual implications of such aspirations make them extremely threatening and difficult to approach during the course of psychoanalytic treatment.

Culturally sanctioned gender roles, although currently being questioned from a feminist perspective (Chodorow, 1978a,b; Benjamin, 1992) have historically prescribed an active and dominant stance for males and a more passive, nurturant, and interpersonally receptive stance for females. The negative oedipal constellation has often seemed threatening, therefore, due to the departure from these prescribed gender roles in the form of passive fantasies of a receptive nature in the male and more active and dominant fantasies in the female.

The paranoid and sadomasochistic dimensions have also been seen as highly relevant for understanding negative oedipal psychodynamics. Paranoid types of projective defenses are seen as typically occurring in response to the ego alien homosexual connotations of negative oedipal fantasies. Such defenses may also be a response to unconscious sadistic fantasies and impulses. Freud's (1919) original work regarding the oedipal connotations of beating fantasies has been updated by Novick and Novick (1972). The Novicks see beating fantasies as having differential significance for girls (where they may provide a brief transitional step toward the consolidation of a more solid feminine identification) and for boys (where they appear to have a more pathological significance). According to the Novicks, in boys these fantasies are linked to sadomasochistic fixations and attitudes toward their mothers. Negative oedipal fixations would also appear to be linked to this group of fantasies in young boys.

Negative oedipal psychodynamics, thus, tend to be viewed from a classical perspective as pathological forms of fixations and regressive tendencies which interfere with a maturationally appropriate resolution of the issues of the oedipal phase. Reich (1933) depicted the negative oedipal configuration as a *passive feminine* reaction formation in males against their unconscious phallic oedipal aspirations. The negative oedipal constellation, thus, has typically been depicted (Karme, 1979; Jaffe, 1983) as being associated with intense feelings of castration anxiety and aggressive counterreactions. In both boys and girls, there is a pathological and regressive shift away from the castrating father and mother and a defensive identification with the parent of the opposite sex. The little boy seems thereby to say to his father that he need not beat him up or castrate him, since he is actually a little girl or woman.

The little girl wishes to placate her angry mother by positing a wish to identify with her father rather than competitively possess him sexually as a love object. Classical psychoanalytic conceptions of the negative oedipal conflict and its various transference and countertransference configurations have been severely delimited as a result of Freud's drive theoretical biases. His emphasis upon notions of constitutional bisexuality, sadomasochistic forms of aggressive fantasy, paranoia, and homosexuality have not been sufficient in explicating the complexities of negative oedipal phenomena. A more contemporary emphasis upon object relational aspects and cultural normative shifts away from a stereotypical and rigid patriarchal definition of gender roles have opened up some newer pathways for understanding negative oedipal aspirations and conflicts.

## NEGLECTED OBJECT RELATIONAL DIMENSIONS OF THE NEGATIVE OEDIPAL CONFIGURATION

Freud's drive theoretical assumptions often led to an understatement of the central significance of actual object relational encounters in the evolution of pathological states of inner psychic conflict. Greenberg and Mitchell (1983) have stressed this point repeatedly in their systematic review of classical Freudian and later object relations theoretical paradigms. More classically trained analysts, too, have somewhat hesitantly moved toward an integration of object relational and interpersonal perspectives in their theorizing. This has been particularly evident in their theoretical study of the Oedipus conflict.

Object relational aspects of oedipal conflicts have been emphasized more and more by theorists (Greenspan, 1977; Chodorow, 1978b; Kaufman, 1983; Blanck, 1984) who have begun to explore the importance of preoedipal determinants such as separation–individuation, object constancy, and narcissistic self and object representational fusion tendencies that underlie oedipal constellations. The idea that the specific and unique characteristics of the object milieu must be fully understood in order to comprehend a given individual's oedipal dynamics has come more and more to the fore. The environmental feed cycle stressed by object relational theorists such as Winnicott (1965) and Giovacchini (1984a) must be systematically assessed as a component of the oedipal configuration. Thus, an understanding of over- and underprotective aspects of the environmental milieu can be helpful in understanding particular oedipal configurations.

Simon (1991) has stressed the significance of counteroedipal features of the object milieu in response to particular oedipal aspirations. Thus, overly seductive, or attached or unattached, intrusive or disinterested parental reactions can have significant effects upon the process and outcome aspects of oedipal conflict resolution. Freud's largely drive theoretical focus led to a neglect of the specific stimulus characteristics of the object milieu in determining particular forms of oedipal psychopathology. The negative oedipal conflict is clearly heavily determined by specific object relational configurations.

Thus, an object milieu consisting of a very powerful but largely distant and unavailable father and an indulgent, overprotective mother may have similar and yet different negative oedipal impact upon a male child and a female child, all else being equal. The loving, attentive, and identificatory gaps will be differently felt by both the male and female child. The male child may end up on a perpetual quest for a strong and loving father figure to substitute for the gaps felt in relationship to his own father. There may be a temporary homoerotic quality to the clingy relationships that he forms with male authority figures. The ultimate need to disidentify with the more actively available and nurturing mother may lead to a temporary or more permanent pulling away from and distrust of intimate relationships with women. The female child, on the other hand, may also feel the father's distance as a rejection and may seek out a strong father substitute in her relationships with men. After finding a fatherly man she can trust, she may eventually settle into a dependent and clingy relationship with him. Given the solid (albeit overprotective) character of her identificatory relationship with her mother, she may not need to establish homoerotic or clingy relationships with women.

Of course, this hypothetical example is an oversimplified presentation of certain negative oedipal configurations that may ensue in a male or female child, in response to a particular parental object milieu. The important thing to note is the significance of the specific object relational environment in determining which one of the many possible negative oedipal conflict resolutions is chosen by a particular child.

Negative oedipal conflicts are typically a response to specific deficits in the object milieu. Thus, an absent father in the home environment of a male child or an absent mother in the environment of a female child may set off an intense feeling of object hunger and an incessant quest for same sex substitute love objects. This may be a transient or more permanent interpersonal response, depending upon a complex range of temperamental, characterological, object relational, gender identity, and constitutional bisexual factors in that particular child.

Feminist analysts such as Benjamin (1992) have recently begun to outline the *agentic* rather than dominance factors that are so essential to the object usage characteristics of many oedipal and negative oedipal relationships. The experience of the mother or father as an object rather than an agentic self, thus, have a very powerful impact upon the intersubjective and identificatory behavior of children. Agentic lacks in the father will have a particularly devastating impact upon the male child. Such lacks in the mother will have a particularly devastating impact upon a female child. The object hunger and subsequent substitutive negative oedipal quests of such children is strongly colored by the deficiencies felt, particularly in relation to their same sex parents.

From a contemporary object relations perspective, it is now possible to redefine the negative oedipal conflict as a form of object hunger and love strivings for substitute same sex objects to replace various deficient aspects of the original attachments to primary parental objects of the same sex. Specific family dynamic aspects, such as dominance or submissiveness, activity or passsivity, powerfulness or impotence in the same sex parental milieu are quite important in determining the character of a particular negative oedipal constellation. Qualities such as intersubjective agency perceived as present or lacking in the same sex parents, however, may be even more important. Certainly, interpersonal and object relational qualities of the same sex parent such as presence or absence, interest or disinterest, affective engagement or disengagement are equally important in determining the object hunger and negative oedipal substitutive quests of particular individuals.

Negative oedipal conflicts, psychopathology, and regressive tendencies are thus being redefined, from an object relational and intersubjective perspective, as forms of object hunger for reparative same sex relationships as a substitute for deficient aspects of counteroedipal and negative oedipal responses on the part of same sex parental figures. The importance of the opposite sex parent must be stressed as well in determining the severity of a given negative oedipal conflict. Above and beyond their own emotional availability to their opposite sex child they must not be threatened by the object relatedness of that child to their marriage partner. If anything, they must be willing to joyfully celebrate the object attachment between their child and the same sex parent. While the preoedipal importance of a comfort on the part of the opposite sex parent to the bonding of children to their same sex parent (particularly the mother) has been fairly commonly noted, there has not been similar importance placed upon this form of bonding in the negative oedipal sphere.

A father, thus, needs to be comfortable with the bonding of his daughter to a mother perceived as being powerful, active, and agentic. A mother, similarly, needs to be comfortable with the negative oedipal bonding of her son with his father. Various aspects of the couple relationship between the parents will certainly be quite relevant to the degree to which such identificatory bonding interactions can be successfully maintained between same sex parent and child. All things being equal, a happily married couple will be able to provide negative oedipal bondings more satisfactorily than will an unhappy couple. A certain degree of emotional maturity and freedom from narcissistic tendencies and feelings of deprivation are required both in the same sex parent and in the opposite sex parent, in the provision of adequate negative oedipal and oedipal bonding opportunities for their children.

The negative oedipal constellation can be viewed, as in the classical analytic position, as a transitional oedipal dyadic configuration between the preoedipal phase and the triadic positive oedipal phase. It has a triangular character and requires, for successful passage through it, two relatively mature and narcissistically undamaged parents who can relate lovingly and with mutual respect both to each other's agentic needs and to the bonding needs of their opposite sex child with the same sex parent. Just as was emphasized in chapter 5, a celebratory reaction to the negative oedipal bonding between parent and child (by both parents) assures an ultimately successful resolution of the conflicts of this particular developmental phase.

Certain object relational characteristics in both parents allow for successful negative oedipal bonding experiences between their marriage partner and children of the same sex.

## PARENTAL PROVISION OF TRANSITIONAL NEGATIVE OEDIPAL OBJECT EXPERIENCE FOR THEIR CHILDREN

As was previously elaborated in chapter 5, parents need to provide their children with a platform for launching courageous overtures of a sexual, aggressive, and lovingly intimate nature toward the parent of the opposite sex. A certain degree of risk taking and courageous affective attitudes are required in the child to allow for an expression of deeply felt object hungers and object usage needs toward the parent of the opposite sex. A similar degree of courage is required to risk the expression of such object needs for the parent of the same sex.

Ogden (1989) has introduced a number of interesting ideas regarding the transitional oedipal configurations of a dyadic nature by which a same sex parent prepares their child for a positive oedipal experience with the opposite sex parent. The parent is capable of being used by his or her child in this way as a culmination of satisfactory object relational encounters of an oedipal nature with their own opposite sex parent.

A similar form of transitional object relatedness can be provided by the parent for their child who must navigate the conflicts of the negative oedipal phase. A mother may joyously prepare her daughter for courageous entry into an oedipal attachment with a beloved father through her oedipal experiences with her own father. Similarly, she may prepare her daughter for a equally courageous negative oedipal encounter with herself via her internalized negative oedipal experiences with her own mother.

A father, too, may utilize internalized object experiences to provide transitional oedipal and negative oedipal experiences for his son. His past oedipal relationship with his own mother, if joyously received and accepted by his parents, allows for a similarly joyous containing identificatory interaction with his own son. The father, thus, provides his own internal oedipal experiences in a dyadic projective identificatory interaction with his son, thereby subtly encouraging the son's budding courageousness and willingness to risk an oedipal triangular encounter with him and his wife.

At a negative oedipal level, the father subtly utilizes memories of his father's receptivity to his own childhood bonding overtures to provide an encouraging milieu for his male child's budding wishes to express his paternal bonding needs.

Since the heart of the negative oedipal experience culminates in some sense of object hunger, the parent who can most effectively utilize his or her own negative oedipal experiences in a transitional object fashion will provide the best hope for a successful resolution and minimization of the residual object hunger in their same sex child. Father and son bondings of a negative oedipal nature have a somewhat different structural character than mother and daughter bondings of this sort. This stems, at least partly, from the fact that the mother and daughter bonding has typically been solidly cemented via earlier preoedipal attachments and connections of a fairly symbiotic nature. The daughter's subsequent movement toward disidentification or counteridentification with her mother, therefore, may conflict with her negative oedipal bonding aspirations.

The son, on the other hand, has not had as much preoedipal experience of a symbiotic nature with his father (although this pattern has been somewhat reversed in contemporary fathering patterns), and hence has a less ambivalent and conflictual attitude with regard to his negative oedipal bonding wishes. His bonding needs may be stronger and he may feel more frustrated by the father's seeming unavailability, unreceptivity, or disinterest in gratifying these relational needs. The ultimate sense of object hunger and unsatisfactory resolutions of the conflicts and needs of the negative oedipal period would, therefore, more likely be greater for the male than for the female child. The father's role in the negative oedipal phase, thus, can be assumed to be of a very central nature.

The negative oedipal phase, from the perspectives being offered in the present chapter, need not be viewed as a vague and poorly understood transitional period between the dyadic preoedipal phase and the fully triangular positive oedipal phase. Rather it can be viewed as fully triangular and parallel to the positive oedipal phase. Transitional object relational provisions and counteroedipal responses of a positive affective character on the part of the same sex parent can facilitate a successful passage through this phase.

Although both mothers and fathers have central counteroedipal role functions and responsiveness requirements during this phase, the role of the father is perhaps most central due to his being typically less available during the earlier preoedipal phases of his son's development. Thankfully, there have been noticeable cultural shifts away from the stereotypically rigid view of the father as a distant superego figure who provides an oedipal identification experience of separation and individuation from the mother and little else of a more relational nature. The expectations for fathers to provide nurturing and growth promoting experiences of a preoedipal, negative oedipal, and oedipal nature for their sons and daughters have increased markedly during recent years.

## NEWER VIEWS OF THE FATHER'S ROLE IN FACILITATING A BENIGN RESOLUTION OF THE COMPLETE OEDIPAL EXPERIENCE

One hopes that the considerations in the previous section regarding the father's role in the negative oedipal phase have not created the impression that his role with his son is more significant than that of the mother with her daughter. Both the mother and father have extremely significant object relational and intersubjective functions requiring role modeling for their same sex children of their inner sense of agency, potency, activity, sexuality, and openness to a broad range of affects (especially of a positive hedonic character) for purposes of social learning and internalization. The mother, however, as has been previously noted, has typically been at the center of social and intersubjective engagement from the earliest periods of infancy and during the course of the more dyadic and symbiotic involvements of the preoedipal period. Both male and female children form highly intimate identificatory attachments with the mother whose attunement capacities and positive affective expressiveness facilitates their resolution of the central issues of the preoedipal period.

The need to separate from and partially disidentify with mother and to establish a more intimate bonding connection with father occurs both in female and male children. The need to disidentify from mother and establish an intimate connection with father for purposes of masculine identification would appear to be more intense in little boys than is the negative oedipal bonding needs of little girls with their mothers. A father's negative oedipal role with his sons, thus, has at least a dual function of intersubjective intimacy and masculinity enhancement. The mother's negative oedipal role with her daughters, since a great deal of the feminine identificatory needs have been met earlier, tends to be more solely centered about motivations for interpersonal and intersubjective intimacy.

The delineation of the various aspects of the father's role with children has been undergoing tremendous change. Broad cultural shifts have been occurring which have softened the traditional patriarchal image of an active, potent, hypermasculine father figure who promotes a sense of separation–individuation and disidentification from mother in both his male and female children. Recent writings with regard to the role of fathers both with sons and daughters (Cath, Gurwitt, and Ross, 1982; Tessman, 1983) have stressed a more relational father who is more capable of empathic attunement and intersubjective intimacy with his wife and children. Feminist authors (Chodorow, 1978a,b; Benjamin, 1992) have been critical of the stereotypical male image of an active, dominant, and highly agentic figure who can be idealized but cannot comfortably relate on an affective or intimate interpersonal level.

The capacities of fathers for object usage in Winnicott's (1968) sense of that term on a preoedipal, negative oedipal, and oedipal level has expanded greatly. They are now expected to allow themselves and their children a broader range of affects and affective attitudes, at all three phases of oedipal development. They need not wait out the preoedipal phase, allowing their wives the sole responsibility for nurturant functions with the children, but instead, may participate fully and with far greater mutuality in the empathic attunements and identificatory tasks of that dyadic phase. A man's capacity to share his positively internalized mother and father with his wife can facilitate her nurturant functions and sense of agency. His availability to his children, in a similar fashion, facilitates their successful progression through the three phases of oedipal development.

The father's ability to intimately share inner transitional objects (both mother-in-father and father-in-father) with his wife and children can vastly facilitate the resolution of the various conflicts of the oedipal period. His ability to joyously celebrate the gratifications of preoedipal, negative oedipal, and oedipal strivings in his children has a very self-enhancing function as well.

From a contemporary and postfeminist perspective, cultural expectations regarding fathering emphasize a flexible mix of agentic, nurturing, relational, and intersubjective functions. A similarly broad range of functions is expected with regard to the mother, as well. The loving mutuality, interpersonal and sexual intimacy of the parental couple can enhance a positive internalization by the child of that couple imago during the negative oedipal and oedipal phases of development. Excessively dissociated couple relationships and identificatory functions in which the mother must be the solely nurturant object and the father the agentic selfobject, on the other hand, may impede the child's progression through the various phases of oedipal development.

Case material will next be provided to illustrate various aspects of the resolution of object hunger clinically encountered during the negative oedipal phase. In each case example, the patient copes, in his or her own unique fashion, with deficient experiences with a same sex negative oedipal object who has been unable to provide a joyous celebratory encounter with their own internalized parental objects.

## CLINICAL ILLUSTRATIONS

*Case 1*

A male patient had never felt satisfied with his father's seeming disinterest and extensive professional activities which often kept him away from home. He had frequent fantasies of an intimate relationship to a strong male figure with whom he was able to establish a warm, loving, and mutually supportive relationship.

From childhood through adolescence, he frequently established relationships with older males, both in his family and within the neighborhood. These men would take him under their wing and share their interests and skills with him.

After a brief period of homosexual experimentation in adolescence, he shifted quite comfortably into a solidly heterosexual orientation.

In his later career, he established significant relationships with older men who briefly became his professional mentors. He always felt warmly toward these men and frequently maintained outside social relationships with them as well.

He was able to marry successfully and was an excellent parent to his two children, a son and daughter. His relationship to his son was especially warm, supportive, and caring. He felt a strong need to provide both children with the empathic and involved fathering that were so frequently absent in his own childhood.

During the course of treatment, he had been able to successfully mourn the deficiencies he felt in relationship to his father and to internalize a warmer and more empathically attuned sense of masculinity and fatherhood from the intimate relationship with his male analyst. Subsequent to the insights and relational learnings of his intensive therapeutic experience, he was able to effectively diminish his unconscious envy of the intimate fathering experiences that he felt essential for his two children. He was able, instead, to joyfully empathize with the intense gratifications provided by the fathering interactions with his children, particularly his son. He also felt gratified and pleased to provide both intimate nurturing and fathering experiences for his wife. Benign internalizations obtained from early childhood with his nurturant and involved mother and from relationships with male authority figures (including his analyst) allowed him to be an effective father and husband.

*Case 2*

The patient was unable to establish a warmly intimate and caring relationship with either her mother or father. Her father was severely neglectful and indifferent to her emotional needs for relatedness during childhood. He eventually moved away from the family and maintained almost no further contact with her mother or herself.

She found it difficult to trust men in her subsequent sexual relationships and was especially hurt by a series of relationships to men with whom she fell in love but who eventually rejected her for other women. She began increasingly to distrust herself in relationships with men and to seek out the greater comfort of close relationships with female friends, some of whom were married and some of whom were not.

She maintained an ambivalent relationship with her mother who constantly prodded her to establish more relationships with men. She stubbornly resisted the mother's prodding which she felt was not empathically based and sought out, instead, empathic connections with her female friends.

Her early object relationship with her mother provided her with a negative view of a woman's relationships to men, both through the mother's frustrating and unhappy relationships to the patient's father and to her own father and paternal grandfather. Her mother was in no way able to enjoy the patient's positive attributes and achievements. The relationship to her mother, although somewhat more trustworthy and dependable than the relationship to her father, was nevertheless, joyless and unempathic.

She sought more positive affects and empathic attunements via supportive connections to a group of female friends. Her willingness to move away from the safety and empathic supportiveness of such same sex object attachments was marred, however, by the seeming riskiness of relationships to men. Her friendships with women were far more comfortable and created somewhat of a barrier to a warm, feelingful, trusting relationship with her male analyst for some time in her treatment.

She found the courage eventually to risk such a transferential experience with her analyst and in relationship to a man with whom she successfully established a loving relationship.

The male analyst facilitated this transition in part by maintaining an empathic internalized connection to loving feelings experienced with his own parents and grandparents, and sharing them via the empathic projective identificatory interactions with the patient.

*Case 3*

This patient moved geographically quite far away from his immediate family to a distant city where he began to work for an uncle who had established a very successful business venture. His family of origin consisted of an actively nurturant and somewhat controlling mother and a passive, ineffectual, and emotionally detached and distant father.

The uncle always seemed to awe the patient with his self-confidence and assertive tendencies. He established a rather deferential and subservient relationship to the uncle who seemed so pleasantly different from his passive and emotionally unavailable father. He seemed comfortable in establishing a mentor object attachment to the uncle as a substitute for his unavailable and essentially unpalatable identifications with his father.

This uncle eventually provided the patient with the thrust toward disidentification with his mother which the father had been unable to provide. He began to feel more and more self-confident and assertive, and eventually was able to even express these new-found feelings of assertiveness with his uncle.

The uncle's provision of a transitional object usage experience (via an empathic sharing of his masculine identificatory experiences with his own father) were very helpful in resolving the patient's negative oedipal conflicts. Certainly, his male analyst's sharing of similar transitional object experiences paralleled those shared with the uncle and augmented the patient's needs for an internalization of more benign and functional same sex identifications and object representations to augment those so painfully lacking in his relationship with his father.

*Case 4*

The patient's mother was absent for significant periods during her early childhood. She was left in the care of the maternal grandmother who had few emotional resources, but who nevertheless nurtured her the best that she could.

The patient had never known her father who had abandoned the family before she was born.

Although extremely intelligent and forever hovering on the verge of success in her professional career, she was never quite able to maintain a continuous period of professional success. Her relationships with men were typically sadomasochistic and extremely frustrating and unsatisfying. Her relationships with women friends, on the other hand, were much more comfortable, trustworthy, and satisfying. They were often felt to be the sole source of gratification and solace in her life.

As in the second case described above, she utilized female friends to internalize the warmly nurturant, bonding, and identificatory experiences that were so sorely lacking in her earliest relationships with her mother and maternal grandmother. Neither her mother nor her grandmother was able to provide her with the transitional negative oedipal object experiences (mother-in-mother) that she so desperately needed.

She was particularly in desperate need of a strong father experience which she in no way seemed able to arrange for herself. She chose men who were always emotionally unavailable. She was able to allow herself this experience, however, in a transitional fashion via a relationship to a very emotionally strong and reliable older female mentor who had been a former employer and had become a close friend. She always felt able to fall back upon this woman for emotional support during periods of instability and crisis. This woman could provide her the strong father-in-mother experiences that were always felt to be lacking throughout her early life. She was also able to provide her with the strong mother-in-mother experiences that were deeply needed.

The therapeutic goal for this patient, as was true for the second patient, was to eventually internalize enough transitional and positive affectively toned identificatory experiences of a preoedipal, negative oedipal, and oedipal nature (mother-in-mother, father-in-mother) to allow her to risk an oedipal attachment of a more object constant and, one hopes, emotionally rewarding nature. Her relationship with her male analyst provided some experiences of that sort and might eventually provide her with a launching pad for loving attachment to a man with whom she might risk a long-term and successful relationship.

CONCLUSIONS

All four cases reflect varying coping strategies with the object hungers stemming from deficiencies in early preoedipal, negative oedipal, and oedipal object relationships. The negative oedipal aspects of these cases reflect either intense object hunger for relationships with a same sex parent or same sex substitute objects. They also reflect the use of such object experiences as defenses against very threatening and seemingly dangerous object attachments of a positive oedipal nature.

Interestingly, the female cases reflect both the hunger for negative oedipal attachments and the use of such attachments as transitional objects which defend against much more threatening oedipal object relationships. The male cases reflect more clear examples of negative oedipal object hunger and usage experiences of a compensatory but largely nondefensive nature.

Thus, there is some preliminary evidence for the possible hypothesis of divergent transitional object usage patterns for males and females, as they struggle to cope with negative oedipal conflictual and deficiency experiences. It is not assumed, however, that the patterns revealed in so few cases reflect a more general gender pattern. Such a more universal pattern could only be discerned in an empirical study of a large sample of treatment cases.

Nevertheless, the transitional object hunger and usage aspects of a patient's life experiences offer a useful means for assessing and psychoanalytically ameliorating their negative oedipal object deficiencies and conflicts. In the future, it might be interesting to more comprehensively explore the negative oedipal conflict from a gender perspective. The extremely deleterious impact of the father's parental deficiencies and absence as both a nurturing and agentic identificatory figure has extremely significant but probably differential impact upon negative oedipal configurations for males and females. Such deficiencies, certainly, have as much object relational significance as the more commonly noted maternal insufficiencies.

All three phases of the complete oedipal conflict need to be more comprehensively assessed from both an object relations and gender perspective.

# Part III

# Character Structure

# Chapter 11

# THE RELUCTANCE TO EXPERIENCE POSITIVE AFFECTS: A CHARACTEROLOGICAL FORM OF RESISTANCE

Patients are often seen in clinical practice who have a great deal of difficulty in tolerating positive affective experiences. These patients cut across the spectrum of psychopathology stemming from the largely neurotic forms of personality difficulty, at the one end, to the more clearly narcissistic and borderline types of problems, at the other end.

SOME SUBTLE SHIFTS IN THE METAPSYCHOLOGICAL
MODEL FOR CONCEPTUALIZING AFFECT AND RESISTANCE
RESULTING FROM THERAPEUTIC EXPERIENCE WITH
CHARACTER DISORDERS

The concept of resistance has always been linked with affect and has been a very fertile one in the psychoanalytic literature. Freud's gradually dawning awareness that patients do not always voluntarily cooperate with the process of therapeutic amelioration offered by the psychoanalytic process is documented in his various classical contributions to both the metapsychological and clinical aspects of this phenomenon (1915a,b,c). His earliest conceptions were based upon the libido theory and implied an ego that essentially dreads instinctual feelings and impulses, even those of a rather positive and pleasurable nature. Quite early in his work, he espoused a sort of toxic discharge model in which he envisioned unpleasant tension states as being a direct result of the ego's tendency to dam up quantities of libidinal energy. According to Freud's earliest (1895, 1986) metapsychological model, too much pleasurable affect was conceived as being a threat to the ego and as precipitating defensive maneuvers of a primarily repressive nature. These repressive defenses eventually led to the building up of excessive quantities of libidinal energy and the clinical experience of neurotic frustration and anxiety.

Gradually, as he became increasingly interested in more structural aspects of the ego (1923, 1926), Freud began to shift away from his toxic discharge model in which anxiety was depicted as the end product of the ego's repressive maneuvers against libidinal impulses, to the currently accepted metapsychological model. In this model, anxiety is viewed as having cognitive signal properties which initiate the broad variety of ego defense maneuvers described by Anna Freud in her classical contribution to ego psychological theory (1936).

The signal theory of anxiety, in which anxiety is viewed as a precipitant rather than a resultant end product of the ego's defensive maneuvering, has been an essential aspect of our current metapsychological conceptions of both the ego defenses and the phenomenon of resistance to the psychotherapy process. Thus, unpleasant anxiety states are seen as signals to the ego that a dangerous situation is impending and that an inhibition of various behavioral and expressive strivings is required.

Freud's metapsychological contributions, as they were further elaborated by Anna Freud and the ego psychologists (Schafer, 1954; Rapaport, 1960; Hartmann, 1964), rather consistently emphasized the precipitation of defensive maneuvers and inhibitions of various ego expressive functions as the primary clinical data base underlying the phenomenon of resistance. Once the ego dimly recognizes, even at a preconscious or unconscious topographic level, some impending danger situation, it quickly calls a halt to expressive strivings. This tendency is clinically manifested in various neurotic symptoms and is a major form of resistance during psychotherapy. The concept of inhibition has been central to our understanding of repetitious aspects of neurotic resistive behavior. When asked by an analyst to lie on the couch and free associate, the neurotic patient experiences a tendency to freeze up and inhibit the potentially spontaneous flow of her thoughts and feelings. This resistance to the analytic process tends to delay it and prolongs neurotic suffering. It also allows for a continuation of the various inhibitions that underlie that suffering.

The structural theory of inhibition and resistance has been derived from clinical experiences with neurotic patients. The signal anxiety conception has been neatly translated into the notion that most neurotic symptoms are basically *ego dystonic,* and thus, can be ultimately unravelled and resolved with the help of a positive therapeutic alliance. The ego of neurotic patients is assumed to be defending against potentially painful experiences and as operating under a continuously unpleasant and inhibiting state of anxiety. The implicit promise of the psychoanalytic treatment model that it can substantially reduce that anxiety, eventually allows for an ameliorative working through and consequent diminishment of repetitiously resistive neurotic behavior.

Patients with character disorders, on the other hand, as emphasized in the incisive contributions of Wilhelm Reich (1933), do not manifest such ego dystonic reactions. They are quite comfortable with their neurotic tendencies and protect them via an almost impermeable characterological armor and virtually intractable resistance behavior. The ego syntonic aspects of characterological disturbances have been clinically documented in numerous ways and have led to a rather subtle shift in our metapsychological theory of resistance and its various ego inhibitive properties. Whereas neurotic patients quite clearly manifest a dread of potentially painful anxiety experiences via their conflictual and defensive behavior, those with character disorders are much freer of anxiety and indeed seem to be virtually unaware of the painful affect of anxiety. These are severely constricted individuals whose characterological organization and defensive structures are too fragilely maintained and shaky to tolerate a broad and differentiated array of emotional experiences of either a positive or negative emotional nature. Whereas the neurotic patient anxiously inhibits expressive behavior and impulses out of a dimly felt dread that some unpleasant or noxious experience might ensue, the character disordered patient is relatively free of anxiety, and if anything, seems to be motivated toward a reduction of potentially positive experiences and affects. Modern clinical work with character disorders and ego damaged patients has emphasized their unconscious dread of potentially pleasant affective experiences. The theory of anxiety and resistance has been fertilely applied to clinical work with neurotic patients. There has, however, been a subtle shift in the treatment of more primitive character disorders toward a different sort of metapsychological model, as a result of clinical experiences.

Object relations conceptions have been melded into both the metapsychological and clinical model for understanding the characterological forms of resistance manifested by ego damaged patients. Current contributions to a therapeutic understanding of more primitive patients emphasize the pervasively *narcissistic* roots of their resistive behavior. Due to various ego defects, these patients cannot tolerate a state of empathic relatedness over an extended period of time. The potentially positive and ego-enriching aspects of object relationships, therefore, cannot very easily be made available to such patients. They suffer, as Balint (1968) has noted, from a *basic fault* in their ego structure, and capacity for object relational experience which makes it virtually impossible to sustain a benign or rewarding interpersonal relationship.

Their potential for further ego maturation and personality differentiation is severely restricted as a result of this incapacity to sustain and contain positive object relational experiences.

In a series of clinical and metapsychological contributions Giovaccini (Giovaccini, 1975a, 1979; Giovaccini and Boyer, 1967) has brilliantly described the introjective and identificatory limitations implicit in the ego functioning of character disordered patients. He has further developed a treatment model for psychoanalytic work with such patients. His basic premise is that more primitively fixated patients maintain concrete and narcissistic modes of object relatedness as an expression of their defective ego structural equipment. They rigidly persevere in repetitively unrewarding object relational patterns and project potentially positive introjects and interpersonal experiences into others in their outer environment. They cannot contain positive object relational experiences very easily and are prone to projectively identify positive affects into others who are required to play out the role of proxy container for such benign affects.

Giovacchini further specifies that the rigid maintenance of continuously unpleasant and unrewarding object relational encounters is a primary diagnostic feature of the more primitively organized patient. Due to their defective and rather nonfunctional introjects, these patients cannot effectively internalize potentially benign affects and object relational experiences. If anything, they are threatened by such potentially positive experiences. It is as if the maturational potential of certain benign interpersonal relationships creates a very threatening environment for the character disordered patient. Signal anxiety occurs, paradoxically, in response to topographically preconscious and potentially positive affective experiences. These patients are more comfortable when they can continuously reexperience their early and decidedly unpleasant object relational experiences.

Mahler (1952), Winnicott (1965), and a number of other object relations theorists have contributed greatly to our understanding of the dread such patients have for positive, benign, or maturationally enriching interpersonal experiences. The very defective early object relational encounters with parental figures, particularly the lack of a good enough maternal experience at the critical stage of rapprochment, has led to a developmental fixation at a preseparation level in patients who manifest narcissistic character pathology. The ultimate dread, clinically discernible in the resistive behavior of such patients, is of any benign environmental circumstance that might potentially lead to ego development or any object relational experience associated with enhanced ego autonomy, or expressive spontaneity. At the root of the resistances manifested by such patients, we repeatedly discover an intolerance, bordering upon a disdain, for positive affective experiences and object relationships.

The therapeutic task, in working with such patients, is repeatedly confounded by this resistive tendency. Somewhat in contrast to the neurotic patient who forms a therapeutic alliance with the preconscious or unconscious goal of eventually reducing anxiety affects of an ego dystonic nature, these patients unconsciously dread the maturational and object relational enhancement potential of the therapeutic process. They cannot as easily form a therapeutic alliance, and their resistances have a primitive object relational character. They resist positive affective experiences in a very pervasive and tenacious fashion. A primary focal point of the treatment must be the repeated analysis of this very rigidly engrained and characterological resistance pattern.

### CLINICAL EXAMPLES OF THE RELUCTANCE TO EXPERIENCE POSITIVE AFFECTS

Certainly, the discomfort with positive emotional states is a common enough form of psychopathological expression. Many neurotic patients express this difficulty in the form of relatively inhibited reactions to opportunities for self-actualization. A good example is the patient who develops a case of stage fright over an upcoming theatrical performance, following an extended period of rigorous preparation and disciplined practice of a particular musical skill or talent. The psychodynamic implications of such a relatively temporary inhibition of talents and exhibitionistic strivings has frequently been conceptualized as a response to unconscious oedipal fantasies and wishes which conflict with conscious and preconscious values, ego ideals, and rules for proper social conduct. At a more behavioral level, an attitude of shyness seems to be observable which does not allow for a smooth and comfortable expression of various exhibitionistic strivings in such patients.

A similar form of reluctance can be seen in patients manifesting more severe forms of character pathology. Many depressed patients become extremely uncomfortable when confronted with some complimentary or potentially positive ego experience. One patient in particular expressed this discomfort in her mode of dress which involved the most frumpy and unappealing clothing possible. It seemed as though her choice of clothing was designed to deemphasize her various feminine attributes and potential sexual appeal. She clearly needed to protect herself against a positive regard or seductive approach by a man. This reluctance to experience positive sexual affects was, of course, manifested as a transference resistance in her interaction with her therapist and formed a central metaphorical theme which needed to be worked through during her treatment. Another patient recoiled at the possibility that she might be considered an interesting or worthwhile patient by her analyst. She frequently criticized the paltry nature of her free associations and was very critical toward her dreams which did not seem worthy of her analyst's interpretive interest or attention. Her reluctance to experience herself as an interesting, valuable sort of person was an important manifestation of her depression and needed to be explored as a resistance during the course of her psychotherapy.

Patients manifesting severe weight disturbances most commonly express this form of resistance during their treatment. An anorexic patient could not enjoy a meal without punishing himself by vomiting afterwards. But this self-punitive gesture was not deemed sufficient. He subsequently had to swim consecutive laps at a local olympic pool for three hours straight, until he was reassured that he had not gained a single pound as a result of ingesting the food. He feebly attempted to rationalize his compulsively ritualistic behavior by mentioning the intense athlete's high and spiritual feeling of uplift that he experienced at the end of his exercise. His intolerance for the pleasures of food was evidently camouflaged by a severely compulsive and self-punitive anhedonic regime of physical exercise.

Bulimic patients, too, frequently manifest an incapacity to tolerate potentially pleasurable activities, particularly those centering about experiences with food. Thus, a young woman tended to go through an elaborate ritual of preparing her food in a special way, putting on the television, and getting under her bed covers for a relaxing eating experience. She subsequently, however, had to pay for the pleasurable nature of the experience by expelling the contents of her stomach via violent vomiting episodes. She would frequently do this until her face became chalky white and ghostlike in appearance. The pleasures of food were, paradoxically, quite intolerable to this patient. A number of themes were evident in the story of her life which contributed to at least some clarification of the psychodynamic significance of her bulimic intolerance for the pleasures of food.

Her mother had died after a chronic period of illness when she was 5 years of age and she had never had the opportunity to adequately mourn her loss. Indeed, she recalled coming home from a pleasurable play activity with a friend on the day her mother had died. A crowd of sad mourners had gathered at the home. She could not understand why they seemed so sad, but she specifically recalled their frowning reactions to her seeming gaiety and unawareness of the tragic event that had just occurred. She was clearly made to feel guilty for her emotional spontaneity and playfulness. She was subsequently sent away from the home to stay with a grandmother while her father attempted to deal with his deep sense of depression and loss. She returned to her home two years later, and her father soon remarried. Her relationship with her stepmother was a very stormy one that largely centered on this woman's explosive rage reactions to the patient's food binges and tendency to forage through the refrigerator in a seemingly excessive fashion. The stepmother's efforts to curtail her evidently compulsive food pleasures were experienced in a very harsh fashion by the patient. She always felt in conflict with her stepmother, at least in part, as a result of those food interactions, and resentfully experienced her father as being too weak to intercede actively and effectively on her behalf.

The patient gradually became more and more resentful of the stepmother's presence within the home. This was the same home that her father had previously lived in with her deceased natural mother. Any effort on the part of the stepmother to change some decorative aspect of the home was met with deep feelings of resentment by the patient. She felt, probably correctly, that the stepmother was attempting to erase her natural mother's presence from the home. The stepmother's very great enjoyment in homemaking and decorative activities only enflamed her resentment and rage. The patient began to hoard souvenirs and memorabilia of her natural mother, in a desperate effort both to preserve her presence and to ward off her stepmother's intrusiveness.

Her need to protectively maintain introjects and identifications with her natural mother became a central psychodynamic theme in her life. This identificatory process became increasingly pathological, in that she felt impelled to identify with the depressed, chronically pain-ridden, and dying mother of her early childhood, as a means of warding off any potential identifications with her seemingly unacceptable stepmother. Of course, as a result of this resistive pattern, even the more positive and competent aspects of her stepmother could not be effectively internalized.

Although she rather feebly attempted to idealize her natural mother and to depreciate her stepmother, this idealizing effort further curtailed any possibility for more benign object relational experiences and identificatory interactions with her stepmother who, in many ways, was a very competent and emotionally healthy sort of person. The need to guiltily protect the idealized mother's memory increasingly led to the maintenance of pathological, depressive, and extraordinarily anhedonic behavioral attitudes. Her guilty reluctance and incapacity to sustain any enjoyment in experiencing food became the most prevalent expression of this pathological identificatory process. Her expressive behavior was thus permeated by a guilty, depressive anhedonia which was the psychodynamic bulwark of her bulimic symptomatology. Her tendency to expel food that she had voraciously gorged herself with was unconsciously linked to a need to undo any of the pleasures that food symbolically represented to her.

This pathological introjective process, thus, was the dynamic core underlying her psychopathology and was manifested in the form of a very pervasive resistance during the course of her treatment. The resistance had characterological features which made it relatively intractable and certainly very difficult to permeate therapeutically. She could not tolerate the pleasures of food or pleasures of any other nature over a sustained period due to an unconscious association of such pleasures with the loss of her depressive, chronically pain-ridden mother. She, too, had to keep herself in a chronically deprived, depressed, and pain-ridden state as an unconscious act of loyalty to this natural mother whose loss she had never had the opportunity to effectively mourn. She was pathologically identified with a dying mother whose ego and affective functioning had been severely impaired as a result of a chronically debilitating physical illness. This severely constricting identificatory process had object relational characteristics which pervasively interfered with her capacity to be competent and enhance her self-esteem through appropriate forms of competitiveness and self-assertion.

She could not internalize and identify with some of the very healthy, competitive, and self-assertive aspects of her stepmother due to a frozen sort of introjective process which was associated with the genetically grounded failure to mourn and psychologically separate from her natural mother. The bulk of the transference work during the course of her psychotherapy, therefore, involved a repeated analysis of her characterologically engrained resistance to the pleasurable affects associated to food experiences. She was given many interpretations, frequently in the form of dynamic reconstructions of the painful object relational experiences she must have had as a young child faced with the loss of a pain-ridden but much beloved mother. The identification with her natural mother was repeatedly stressed as the dynamic core underlying her anhedonic difficulties. Her reluctance to form a maturationally higher level of identificatory attachment with her stepmother was also repeatedly clarified.

Her ultimate resistance, of course, was to the powerful and maturationally facilitative aspects of the therapy process itself. Her therapist, by continuously empathizing with her incapacity to tolerate the pleasurable affects associated with the ingestion of food, and by repeatedly interpreting the dynamic roots of this resistance pattern, was eventually able to offer her a more benign containing experience than was possible during her childhood. She attempted to resist the therapist's more permissive attitude toward the pleasures of food in many ways, and, thereby, was able to rigidly hold on to her bulimic psychopathology.

The therapy could only become effective via an extensive analysis of her resistance to pleasurable experiences (symbolically contained in her bulimic symptom) which eventually crystallized itself in the form of a transference resistance. She needed to be made aware of how frightened she was of yielding to the maturational pulls of the therapist and his therapeutic environment. His optimistic expectation that she might one day give up her pathological identification with a depressed, pain-ridden, and dying mother was felt by her as very threatening. Indeed the interpretive exploration of her early

experience of maternal loss which she had for so long kept out of her awareness, was initially very difficult for her to internalize. She repeatedly returned
to an acting out of her depressive tendencies via her rigidly engrained bulimic
behavior patterns.

The therapist's seeming resiliency and comfort with such symptomatic
regressions, however, had a benign and ego supportive effect. Despite the
patient's pessimism with regard to the possibility of ever curbing her symptoms, the therapist remained undaunted and convinced that the interpretive
model being utilized would eventually have a benign effect. Continuous reminders with regard to her incapacity to tolerate pleasurable experiences
(particularly those involved in eating), also had a clearly ego supportive
and maturationally facilitative impact. Following each bulimic symptomatic
recurrence, the therapist repeatedly reminded the patient of her dread of the
pleasurable experience involved in incorporating food into her body.

The patient's various protests with regard to the unpleasant distorting
effects that the food might have on her body image were duly noted but were
not accepted by the therapist as sufficient cause for the patient's compulsive
need to immediately rid herself of the ingested food by vomiting. Her dread
that she might gain weight and look ugly, one of her rationalizations for the
vomiting which always followed the ingestion of large quantities of food, was
gradually seen as a superficial defensive cover for her more basic resistance to
pleasurable experiences.

The patient rigidly held on to a dread that her symptom might be incurable. The therapist, on the other hand, continually made her focus on the
possibility that she might have a much greater fear of pleasurable experiences.
Should she allow herself to retain and thereby enjoy her food, she might then
begin to allow herself to contain other enjoyable and maturationally beneficial
experiences. The therapist repeatedly emphasized the patient's seeming incapacity to tolerate and internalize a more benign environmental milieu. Her
home environment had to be as unpleasant as the hospital-like environment
that her mother probably had to face throughout the course of the patient's
childhood. The patient felt guilty whenever she began to experience a more
benign and less chronically ill and ego incapacitating sort of milieu. Her
paradoxical incapacity to allow herself benign object relational experiences
was the primary resistance that needed to be explored in treatment. Indeed,
the central transference resistance was manifested in the form of a reluctance
to experience optimism in the therapeutic environment. She needed to hold
on to the dread that she might never be able to give up her bulimic symptom.
Her recurrent bulimic regressions ultimately involved a need to inject the
pessimism she experienced during the course of the symbiotic attachment
with her natural mother into her relationship with the therapist.

The containing task for the therapist was to tolerate the pessimism engendered by the patient's repeated symptomatic regressions without himself becoming unduly pessimistic. Ego resiliency needed to somehow be incorporated into the therapeutic environment in the form of a continuing optimism with regard to the patient's eventual potential for sustained positive and more alive sorts of experiences. Each protest by the patient that she was essentially incurable had to be met with a therapeutic clarification and reminder with regard to her dread of positive object relational experiences. The patient's insistence that her symptom was intolerable and anxiety producing (an implicit statement with regard to its ego dystonic character) had to be repeatedly translated into a formulation of her much more basic fear of the possibility for sustained ego resiliency and more benign and maturationally facilitative object relational experience. The therapist's repeated reminders with regard to this very central resistance pattern eventually had a beneficial effect. An internalization process began to be evident both in her relationship to the therapist and to her stepmother.

Whereas she had always previously become embroiled in essentially masochistic sorts of sexual relationships, she met a young man who was able to treat her more positively. Her capacity to tolerate and sustain a nonmasochistic relationship occurred simultaneously with a decision to go back to school. She chose a very difficult scientific field involving the need for great intellectual discipline and scientific rigor. She also chose a field requiring that she compete with men rather than idealize them in a submissive and masochistic fashion. Her increasing self-confidence at school (where she had previously felt a sense of failure due to intense experiences of test anxiety) spilled over into an intense desire to redecorate her apartment. She began to compulsively reorganize and reshape the depressing and morbid environment in which she had been living.

Her intense decorating efforts, of course, paralleled the home reshaping activities manifested by her stepmother that had begun earlier in the patient's life and continued up to the present. Her capacity to tolerate the identificatory aspects of this behavior allowed for a furthering of her ego development and a new experience of both attachment to and competition with her stepmother. She began to shift from a preoedipal attachment to her depressed mother to an oedipal level, conflictual–identificatory relationship with her stepmother. She was able to markedly increase her self-esteem due to this new receptivity to identifications with the adaptive behavior of her stepmother.

In conceptualizing the marked ego enhancement and maturational growth that occurred in this case, it is important to emphasize the primary ego restorative effects of the continued analysis of the patient's seemingly intractable resistance to positive affects. At an object relational level, this patient repeatedly manifested a reluctance to internalize beneficial and maturationally facilitative sorts of interpersonal experiences. She dreaded benign and maturationally high level experiences in a similar fashion to the way that the neurotic patient dreads and becomes inhibited by unconscious signal anxiety. In contrast to the more neurotic sort of patient who may become inhibited due to an unconscious castration fantasy, this patient and others like her tend to unconsciously dread the giving up of primitive, essentially toxic introjects and object attachments. A primary ego ameliorative benefit can be attained from a continuing analysis of that dread and its expression in the reluctance to tolerate positive affective experiences.

Various patients manifest in subtle and not so subtle ways their dread of positive affective experience. Some patients cannot tolerate a compliment with regard to some personality or ego attribute. These patients tend to blush and communicate an intense discomfort with such benign affective experiences. Most depressed patients are involved in primitive object relational attachments which can be conceptualized as toxic introjects. These introjects radically distort their ego functioning and capacity to internalize more benign affective experiences. The anhedonic features of the symptoms manifested by such patients can be seen as characterologically engrained and essentially structural forms of resistance.

Quite often, the reluctance to internalize positive affects can be noted in a sequence analysis of the themes introduced during a psychotherapy session. Many patients manifest their intolerance for positive object relational experience via a subtle shift in the mood and affective tone of the session. One patient, a chronically depressed woman, exhibited this tendency in a session that she began by describing a very exciting and pleasurable day she had recently experienced. She noted that on that particular day, she felt alive in a way she had not felt for a long time. She ended the day by going to a movie that she had been looking forward to seeing for some time. She thoroughly enjoyed the movie and was so excited when it was over that she absent-mindedly stumbled on the balcony steps, severely twisting her ankle in the process. She then went on to her more typical sort of laments and complaints about the thoroughly intolerable and unpleasurable nature of her current life situation. Her mood shifted in a sadder direction at that point. The therapist noted that she might be feeling discomfort over having experienced such an exciting and mood uplifting sort of day. She needed, therefore, to punish herself and to get in touch with the far more familiar feelings of sadness and pessimism with regard to her life. She was very uncomfortable about the buoyant start of her session, and therefore had to shift to a much more familiar complaining and lamenting tone.

Another patient manifested resistance to positive experience via a similar sort of a session. He began his session by noting that he had really been feeling ''on a roll'' lately. He had been making a number of successful sales at work and everyone at his place of employment had been responding to his seemingly boundless energy and enthusiasm. He felt very handsome and was receiving continual seductive offers from his secretaries. He went on to note that he had been vigorous and sexually potent with his wife for the first time in a long time. His very buoyant, excited mood continued for some time during the session but began gradually to diminish and to shift into a subtly sadder and more worried sort of affective tone. He brought up, once again, his concern about going crazy and having to be hospitalized. The dynamics of this concern had been analyzed many times during previous sessions. He became visibly sadder and less excited as the session progressed. The sequential affective shifts in the patient's session, as in the case of the previous patient, reflected his incapacity to tolerate and effectively internalize benign and maturationally ego enhancing experiences. He actually feared and hence had to avoid the maintenance of a buoyant and self-confident frame of mind over an extended period of time.

Many paranoid transferential reactions to the therapist also convey this form of resistance pattern. One young woman who had finally been able to rid herself of her undesired virginity via a very enjoyable sexual experience, opened up a therapy session with the conviction that the therapist quite clearly frowned upon her recent promiscuous behavior. The therapist seemed like a moralistic stuffed shirt who almost certainly judged her behavior in a negative fashion. The similarity of this judgmental behavior to the frowning face of her father throughout her childhood, however, when noted by the therapist, could not be completely overlooked by this patient.

The unconscious wish to avoid positive affective experiences pervades the therapeutic process with patients across the diagnostic spectrum of character pathology. It can be seen in neurotic patients, and in higher and lower level character disorders. It is a quite familiar pattern to most therapists that is discernible in the painful communications of a great variety of patients. The object relational and resistance implications of these communications, however, have not been focused upon sufficiently. The therapeutic technique for dealing with these resistances has not yet been clarified and fully elaborated.

## SOME TECHNICAL SUGGESTIONS FOR DEALING WITH THE RESISTANCE TO POSITIVE AFFECTS

Reich's therapeutic model for exploring and resolving characterological resistances has been clearly articulated in his classic book, *Character Analysis* (1933). His basic model for resistance analysis is well incorporated in the treatment model practiced by most dynamically oriented psychotherapists.

His essential recommendations stress the importance of focusing upon characterological resistance prior to more dynamic interpretive exploration and genetic reconstructions. He specifically suggests that genetic interpretations be held back from the patient until partial exploration and resolution of the main resistances of the patient has been initiated.

Reich stresses the centrality of characterological resistances and notes that they are hierarchically organized within a given patient's personality structure. Resistances are seen as structural features of personality and ego organization. The essential technical recommendation of Reich, therefore, is that ego structural features such as resistances, need to be focused upon prior to a deeper, more dynamic interpretive exploration of the genetic antecedents underlying these characterological resistances. He stresses the essentially hierarchical organizational structure of these resistances and notes that the more basic, cardinal resistances need to be explored and resolved prior to working with the more peripheral and less primary resistances.

Once a very basic or cardinal resistance has been discerned by the therapist, it needs to be focused upon in a repeated fashion with the patient. Reich notes that the typical sequence of characterological resistance analysis is a three-step process. The patient is told that she has a particular resistance. Second, the patient is informed *how* she is resisting; that is, the particular defensive maneuvers that she is utilizing in order to resist the therapeutic process. Finally, the patient is involved in an exploration of the dynamic issues underlying her resistances. Interpretations are offered of a genetic and more reconstructive nature.

This was the basic therapeutic model utilized with the bulimic patient alluded to above. Her resistances were explored in accordance with the three-step approach recommended by Reich. One difference, however, was the fact that a continuous interweaving of genetic–dynamic interpretation and more structural and characterological confrontations occurred during the course of her treatment.

The genetic and object relational features underlying her symptomatic behavior were interpreted on a continuing basis from the very beginning phase of her treatment. The more characterological and structural sorts of observations with regard to her reluctance to experience and internalize positive affects, were made from the beginning of her treatment as well.

Indeed, in this particular patient's treatment, the object relational and reconstructive interpretations were repeatedly offered at the earliest phases of her treatment and gradually were diminished and replaced by an almost sole focus upon her cardinal characterological resistance to experiencing positive affects. At an intermediate phase in her treatment the genetic and object relational dynamics underlying her symptom were repeatedly linked to her primary characterological resistance. Her reluctance to engage in the pleasurable experiences of eating were linked repeatedly through genetic interpretations to the early toxic environmental milieu she had experienced with her natural mother. As the treatment progressed, these object relational interpretive connections, particularly their impact on her identifications, did not have to be made quite as often. She began to internalize an understanding of the impact on her of her natural mother's death. She gained an emotional grasp of the toxic frozen nature of her maternal introject and its impedance of her capacity to make healthier, more functional identifications with her stepmother. Subsequently, the therapeutic focus shifted to a repeated exploration of the various symptomatic and behavioral manifestations of her incapacity to tolerate pleasurable effects. In the latter phases of the treatment, the therapist was forced continually to contain the optimistic affects that the patient could obviously not tolerate very well. This containing effect occurred by means of constant reminders regarding her reluctance to experience the positive affects which underlay her pessimism and dread that she might never fully recovery from her bulimic symptom.

It is suggested here that Reich's model for analyzing characterological resistances can be directly applied to the exploration and resolution of the reluctance to experience positive affects. His emphasis upon the need to always precede genetic and dynamic interpretations by a more structural focus upon characterological resistances, however, need not be followed too rigidly. Ultimately, an interweaving of the object relational features underlying the patient's psychopathology with the more structural and characterological resistance aspects, will need to be presented to the patient by means of interpretations. The pathological identifications underlying the resistance to positive affective experiences need to be interpretively explored in a solidly object relational fashion. Once the patient has a solid emotional and cognitive grasp of the deleterious impact of their reluctance to experience positive affects, they have begun to effectively work through the characterological aspects of the resistance.

Just as in other forms of character and resistance analysis, a great deal of patience is required on the part of the therapist. There are certain repetitious features to the technical handling of this very well-entrenched and characterologically engrained form of resistance. The therapist's task is to constantly remind the patient who is experiencing and reporting feelings of painful self-awareness and disappointment, of the defensive and resistive nature of these feelings. The patient makes it quite clear that she has never even considered the possibility that her depressive affects might be a resistive, anhedonic avoidance of more positive and pleasurable affects. The therapist's repeated reminders with regard to the reluctance to internalize benign emotional experiences are most often met with reactions of surprise and disbelief. The process of continued resistance analysis, however, eventually allows for a suspension of disbelief and a gradual internalization of the therapist's more optimistic attitudes and beliefs with regard to the patient's ego and maturational potentialities.

During the course of this process of resistance exploration and resolution, the therapist can and should maintain the position of technical neutrality recommended by Kernberg (1976b). Although empathically aware of the patient's depressive suffering and sense of despair, the therapist is most effective when she maintains a degree of objectivity with regard to the dynamic and structural factors underlying the patient's sense of pain. The repeated reminders to the patient that this sense of pain actually involves a preferred and unconsciously chosen defensive maneuver eventually allow the patient to work through the resistance to positive experience.

Nydes (1963), in his brilliant clinical contribution to the treatment issues involved in work with a group of patients that he labeled paranoid–masochistic characters, makes a number of technical suggestions similar to those being made in this paper. After articulating some of the dynamics underlying both paranoid and masochistic forms of psychopathology, Nydes notes, however, that the paranoid patient also has a deep dread of the successful actualizing of unconscious oedipal wishes. The various paranoid doubts and worries continuously expressed by such patients convey their fear of potentiating phallic ambitions.

The ultimate dilemma for both sorts of patients is that any inner sense of effectiveness is linked to an aggressive attack on an oedipal figure. Thus, a male patient who successfully marries unconsciously feels that he has aggressively attacked and defeated his father. He may, therefore, conceal his sense of victory by developing paranoid preoccupations that interfere with his sexual gratifications. He may become worried over his potency or masculinity as a means of punishing himself for an unconscious oedipal victory. Masochistic patients, on the other hand, may continuously sabotage themselves through a depressive depletion of energy and, thereby, avoid any competitive or assertive behavior that might lead to unconsciously dreaded phallic achievements.

Nydes recommends that both types of patients need to be constantly made aware of the unconscious guilt feelings that underlie their expressive behavior. The therapist's objectivity with regard to characterological features of these patients' psychopathology is his most effective tool. Nydes sums up his treatment recommendations with the following statement:

> From the above example, it is clear that one of the major therapeutic problems in dealing with the paranoid-masochistic character is to avoid the temptation to yield to the patient's diversionary tactics. The analyst's

inner emotional reaction serves as a clue to the patient's intention. To express such reactions often serves only to fortify the mechanism rather than to undermine it. In the predominantly masochistic phase an attempt is made to excite in the analyst a sense of great compassion for the hardship which the patient is enduring but to extend pity serves only to add to the patient's investment in suffering as a means of demonstrating his innocence. What may appear to be a ruthless denial of pity to the suffering masochist, is in effect a genuine respect of his strength. To extend pity where none is needed is to join the patient in his demonstration of inadequacy. To withhold pity tends to frustrate his need to be the victim and to confront him with his real effectiveness. Often, it is necessary to be sensitive to the patient's tone of voice, rather than to the context of what he is attempting to convey. He may speak of happy events with a subdued mournful affect as if to say, "Even though good things have happened, don't blame me: I'm really not happy." On the other hand, he may sound quite forceful and even exuberant when discussing the injustices and hardships to which he has been subjected. It is essential that the analyst understand the dynamics underlying the patient's mood rather than yield to the temptation to adopt the same mood while relating to the patient [1963, pp. 246–247].

Nydes recommends certain paradigmatic sorts of interventions that can be effectively utilized with such patients. Paradigmatic techniques mesh well with the contemporary object relations model of psychotherapy. Chapter 7 notes some of the features which overlap in the paradigmatic and object relations models of psychotherapy. The common feature underlying both Nydes' approach to treating paranoid–masochistic characters and the approach being espoused in this chapter is that resistance analysis is central to the therapeutic task. The sort of patients being described in this chapter are quite similar to the help rejecting complainers described by Nydes. The need to speak of happy events in a subdued, mournful tone, or to apologize for happy occurrences by undoing them in various self-defeating ways, is a primary resistance pattern which can be focused upon during the course of the psychotherapy process. Paradigmatic interventions of a humorous, playful, or ironic nature can also be effectively utilized to resolve these resistances.

The paradigmatic approach fits quite well with object relations conceptualizations and is a direct outgrowth of Reich's early recommendations of an irritative, therapeutic approach to exploring and resolving character resistances. Paradigmatic modes of resistance analysis have been clearly articulated in the contributions of Nelson (Nelson and Nelson, 1957; Nelson, 1962a),

Strean (1970a), and Spotnitz (1976). They offer a useful adjunct to the therapist struggling with the need to find a constructive means of utilizing countertransference feelings induced via the projective identifications of characterologically impaired patients. The intolerance for positive affects often expressed by such patients induces many unpleasant feelings in the therapist which can be partially contained via paradigmatic interventions. Ultimately, the therapist's optimism about the patient's capacity to internalize positive affective experience and to attain a higher maturational level of character functioning will provide the most effective form of containing experience for these patients.

CONCLUSIONS

Clinical experience with patients manifesting a reluctance to experience positive affects suggests the need for a reconsideration of Freud's original proposals with regard to the theory of anxiety and resistance. Both his original toxic theory of discharge (1895, 1896) and his later updating of resistance theory in the form of proposals with regard to the signal functions of anxiety (1926), imply a struggle by the ego to cope with either consciously felt negative affects or some preconscious awareness of the potential for such negative affects. Anxiety is theoretically depicted as a negative affect which operates as a signal to the ego that it must inhibit some course of action. Spontaneous and potentially pleasurable forms of expressive behavior are inhibited as a result of the dangers they unconsciously portend to the ego which, according to Freud's structural theory, must continuously monitor the external environment for such dangers.

Affective states of anxiety and the inhibitory processes that they initiate are both felt to be extremely noxious and unpleasant experiential conditions. They have adaptive potential, in that they allow the ego to defend itself against the variety of inner and outer stressors alluded to by Anna Freud in her classic work on the ego and mechanisms of defense (1936). They also, however, have a debilitating effect on the ego in its search for realistic and effective means of pleasure gratification. Inhibitions, by their very nature, restrict the possibility for pleasurable, self-actualizing forms of affective experience. It is the very unpleasant nature of the affects arising out of these inhibitory processes that ultimately leads to the possibility of a psychoanalytic approach to the neuroses.

The viability of a psychoanalytic model for treating neurotic symptoms, at least in part, stems from Freud's theories of signal anxiety and inhibition. The basic notion is that neurotic inhibitions are felt to be unpleasant ego restrictive states. It is the affectively unpleasant, essentially ego dystonic nature of these inhibitions and neurotic symptoms which eventually allows the patient to establish a therapeutic alliance with his analyst. The subsequently successful analysis and resolution of resistances to the therapeutic process can be performed thanks to the establishment of such a therapeutic alliance. Freud's metapsychological concepts of anxiety and inhibition are nicely applicable to the theory of psychoanalytic treatment of the neuroses. They are not, however, sufficiently explanatory of the various complications seen in therapeutic work with more disturbed and ego damaged patients.

Treatment experiences with patients manifesting character, narcissistic, or borderline disorders have led to observations that do not quite jibe with Freud's structural theory of anxiety. Giovacchini (1975a, 1984a) reports the interesting case of a woman who suffered from pervasive experiences of anxiety. Although her anxiety symptoms consisted of extremely unpleasant affective states, they were not truly ego dystonic. She needed these anxiety states to firm up her shaky sense of ego identity and feel a greater sense of inner aliveness. Anxiety for this woman did not have the signal function alluded to by Freud. Her anxiety did not initiate processes of ego defense. It was a primitive form of defense maneuver in its own right. Giovacchini concludes his case discussion with the following statement, "From the above one can see that the adaptive significance of anxiety is considered not merely in terms of its potential to lead to defense formation and thereby bring about ego integration, but it is considered also as a positive factor in its own right, one that can lead directly to a better equilibrium by enhancing ego feeling or narcissism" (1975a, p. 17). Of course, this is a very paradoxical statement when viewed in light of Freud's signal anxiety theory. Anxiety is not seen by Giovacchini as being either a noxious state of affect discharge or as an unpleasant affect signaling the need for ego defenses or other forms of inhibitory behavior. It is rather depicted as a positive factor allowing for a greater sense of self-articulation and narcissistic gain in a primitively fixated patient.

Anxiety evidently has a different structural and functional character within the psychic economy of more primitively organized and ego damaged patients than it has in neurotic and higher level patients. The paradoxical need to seek out anxiety and other forms of unpleasant affective experience can frequently be discerned in these patients. This paradoxical tendency to seek out unpleasant affects and to avoid more pleasant affects is particularly evident in the approach many such patients have to feelings of depressive anxiety. The relative incapacity to tolerate feelings of depressive anxiety, which Zetzel (1949) describes as a typical feature of certain neurotic patients, is not as evident in many primitively fixated patients. These patients, rather, tend to defend against potentially positive affective experiences. Their inhibitory tendencies and resistances seem ironically to get set off by the dangers posed by positive affects to their primitively organized egos.

There is often an anhedonic quality to the defensive and resistive tendencies of patients manifesting serious character pathology. The reliance by such patients on more primitive defensive maneuvers such as denial, idealization, splitting, and projective identification tends to be associated, on an experiential and object relations level, with a reluctance to experience more benign and potentially maturational self and object representations. This discomfort with more benign object relational encounters and seeming comfort with less pleasant forms of affective experience does not mesh very well with Freud's original or subsequent metapsychological formulations with regard to neurotic inhibitory processes. The reluctance to experience positive affects, thus, tends to be an ego syntonic and characterological form of resistance in more primitively fixated patients. A different metapsychological conception of anxiety is required to explain this form of resistance. The capacity of anxiety states, particularly depressive anxiety, to have a functional and structural utility for certain ego impaired patients, needs to be incorporated in a revised theory of anxiety and the inhibitory process.

There can be no doubt that the resistance to positive affects is linked to a form of superego pathology. In accordance with Freud's structural theory and its metapsychological elaboration in the work of the later ego psychologists (Hartmann and Loewenstein, 1962), the superego is envisioned as a precipitate consisting of ego ideals, values, and moral prohibitions. These evaluative tendencies are largely derived from authority figures who serve as identificatory role models. The severity and inhibitory restrictiveness of a given individual's superego is directly related to the severity of the superego of his or her role models.

The superego, in accordance with Freud's early formulations, is one end product of an effective resolution of the oedipal developmental crisis. The more severe the original oedipal conflict, the more severe is the superego structure resulting from the eventual resolution of that conflict. Schafer (1960) has alerted us to the potentially more loving features of the superego in healthier and better integrated individuals. One attainment from an effective psychoanalysis, according to Sandler (1960), is the ultimate dissolution of the infantile superego and its primitive injunctions against pleasure. This dissolution of primitive superego structures allows for the substitution of a more benign, permissive, and self-loving sort of superego structure.

Given their quite primitive and rigid superego structures, many severely disturbed patients are initially threatened by the therapist's efforts at exploring their reluctance to experience positive affects. They perceive the therapist's interventions as an endorsement of a hedonistic and excessively permissive life-style. The therapist, of course, has no such interest in imposing a hedonistic orientation upon his basically anhedonic patients. His interest, quite to the contrary, is in supporting viable superego structures and in replacing only those that inhibit the patient's potential for a maturationally higher level of experience and affective flexibility. The therapist's interest in resisted pleasurable affects is related to the maturational and object relational goals of the psychotherapy process. Ultimately, effective psychotherapy should broaden the range of affective experiences available to a given patient. It should also increase the object relational maturity of these affects.

The splitting mechanisms that Kernberg (1975b) has so convincingly delineated as basic to the defensive organization of narcissistic and borderline patients are, in part, a reflection of the primitive organization of their superego structures. Many borderline patients idealize and envy the self-actualizing and pleasure attainment capacities of others around them while, at the same time, depreciating their own capabilities for such ego attainments. These patients are basically fixated at the rapprochement developmental stage. They seldom attain object relational experiences of an individuated nature, nor can they allow themselves the pleasures often associated with such benign affective experiences. The difficulty in attaining a solid sense of separation and individuation is one major object relational feature of severe character disorders. This difficulty has been repeatedly noted in the theory of psychotherapy articulated by Winnicott (1965), Giovacchini (1975a, 1979; Giovacchini and Boyer, 1967); and Kernberg (1975b, 1976b). The developmental theory underlying the contemporary object relations approach to psychotherapy owes a great deal to the contributions of Mahler (1952). Horner (1979) has recently contributed a systematic elaboration of the developmental stages underlying various forms of severe character pathology.

We now commonly accept the fact that a major difficulty in primitively fixated patients is their incapacity to attain a true state of separateness and ego identity. Many characterological manifestations of psychopathology can be linked to such separation–individuation difficulties. The incapacity to tolerate pleasurable experiences is a manifestation of both a structural ego defect and an object relational impairment. Searles (1975) has poignantly described the inherent loyalty with which schizophrenic patients maintain their pathological object relationships and disorganized thought processes. He argues that a failure in the unconscious quest for curing a damaged parental introject is one major object relational feature in schizophrenic and other forms of severe character pathology. The schizophrenic patient, according to Searles, cannot allow herself a higher level of object relational attainment due to an unconsciously felt failure at curing a significantly ego damaged parent. There is so much unconscious quilt associated with the psychic act of separation–individuation that it becomes virtually impossible. There is a paradoxical sense of disloyalty associated with states of psychic health for such primitively organized patients.

A similar sense of loyalty to damaged parental introjects can be noted in the characterological manifestations of nonschizophrenic patients. Colson (1982) has recently described the need to protect the structurally damaged parental environment as basic to the transference resistances and countertransferences difficulties often experienced in therapeutic work with borderline patients. He makes the following points about the negative therapeutic reactions typically manifested by such patients:

1. In the initial phase, the opportunity that psychotherapy offers for growth threatens much that the patient holds most dear; in particular, it poses the prospect of eventual independence, fantasied by the patient to be destructive to both himself and his family.
2. As the patient begins to recognize all that he has sacrificed to ensure the family homeostasis and his ''special'' role in the family, he feels increasingly resentful, angry, and depressed.
3. As he takes steps toward individuation, he is confronted with a series of identity crises. That is, as he considers the promise of more mature functioning, he is also confronted with a loss of old, familiar, and predictable patterns of self-experience and of relating to others. The patient may panic in response to the uncertainty about where these changes will lead.
4. The patient experiences depressive emotion and a profound narcissistic injury after discovering the possibility that he can discontinue playing his protective, caretaking role. He comes to feel far less ''important,'' which is accompanied by a loss in the sense of purpose in his life and questions of a despairing nature about whether life is worth living. This phase may be accompanied by concerns about suicide or other forms of nihilism and self-destruction.
5. At times, the treatment process becomes a major obstacle to change. In an effort to save the pathological family from destruction, the patient employs treatment in a self-defeating way or talks interminably of the risks of making constructive changes in his life [1982, pp. 318–319].

Whereas healthier, more neurotic patients manifest such negative therapeutic reactions at a definitive point toward the end of psychotherapy, more primitive patients manifest such reactions fairly continuously throughout treatment. They basically resist treatment due to an unconscious appreciation of its capacity to enhance their object relational experience. The reluctance to experience positive affective experiences is a pervasive resistance feature noticeable during the course of the psychotherapy process with all patients. Oedipal dynamics are almost certainly involved in the paranoid–masochistic sort of transference reactions manifested by many patients to the therapist's efforts to explore and ultimately resolve this resistance. Nydes (1963) has emphasized these oedipal dynamics in explicating his theory of psychotherapy with neurotic characters. More primitive character disorders, however, tend to be fixated at a largely preoedipal level of object relational development. The fear of separation from a damaged and largely anhedonic infantile milieu is evident in the resistances of preoedipal patients. The psychotherapy process itself, from the very start, poses a dreaded danger to such patients, due to the maturational potential unconsciously perceived as inherent in that process.

More primitive patients dread, at an unconscious level, the benign and maturationally higher identificatory potential of the psychotherapy process. They sense that they will be asked during the therapeutic experience to give up anhedonic and pathological yet, nevertheless, loyally maintained introjects. The fact that they can substitute more benign, pleasurable, and maturationally ego enhancing identifications for these damaged introjects is not very reassuring to such patients. The therapist's task, therefore, is to constantly monitor and interactively explore this characterological form of resistance, particularly as it manifests itself in the reluctance to experience positive affects.

# Chapter 12

# BELOVED SYMPTOMS AND STASIS IN CHARACTER DISORDER

Patients manifesting character disorders have always been considered difficult to treat for a variety of reasons. From a classical perspective, the ego dystonic symptom neuroses have typically been juxtaposed against the ego syntonic character disorders. Whereas neuroses were seen as consisting of ego alien symptoms that unconsciously symbolize and express repressed drive impulses and wishes, character disorders were viewed as being comprised of structured, repetitious patterns of behavior that are quite comfortable for the ego.

From a classical psychoanalytic perspective, the neurotic individual is willing to tolerate the pain of a psychoanalytic explorative process in order to reduce the inner psychic pain and anxiety associated with neurotic symptoms. The patient with a character disorder, however, has no similar motive for inner psychological exploration and restructuring, at least in part due to a supposed freedom from painful symptoms, anxiety, and conflict. This rather simplistic mode of psychodynamic thinking, stemming from Freudian drive theory, led to assumptions that character disorders were essentially untreatable via psychoanalytic approaches.

A great deal of change has occurred in this area of psychoanalytic thinking. Reich's classical work (1933; Frank, 1992) has opened up a variety of approaches to making ego syntonic character structures and defensive maneuvers ego dystonic, and ultimately treatable from a psychodynamic perspective. Giovacchini's important contributions (1972, 1975b, 1984a, 1986) have virtually eliminated the simplistic discriminations between the treatable *transference neuroses* and the supposedly untreatable *narcissistic neuroses* (character

191

disorders). A great deal of optimism now exists with regard to the psychoanalytic treatment of a diverse variety of character difficulties. Kernberg's (1975b, 1976a,b, 1980a) and Kohut's (1971, 1977) important contributions have extended this optimism to the psychoanalytic treatment of borderline and narcissistic personality disorders. The augmenting of the ego psychological and structural models of Hartmann (1939, 1950) and Rapaport (1953a, 1960) with the object relational models of British analysts such as Fairbairn (1952a, 1963), Guntrip (1968), and Winnicott (1965, 1971) have further contributed to an optimistic extension of the psychoanalytic model to the treatment of severely regressed schizoid and schizophrenic characters and personality disorders. Josephs (1992) has expanded upon psychoanalytic treatment models for work with character disorders from a self psychological perspective.

Despite the increased optimism promulgated by the application of object relations conceptions in work with a variety of "difficult" characterologically impaired patients, tediously repetitive and severe resistances to change have nevertheless permeated the therapeutic work with these patients. A model for comprehending the intractable redundancy and seemingly static nature of character pathology can now be offered in a timely fashion, utilizing the interrelated affect theoretical and object relational principles being developed in the present volume. Such a synthesis of current affect theoretical and object relational conceptions can expand our understanding and technical leverage in therapeutically approaching the severe resistances to change manifested by these more difficult patients.

The more classical notions of repetition compulsion and traumatic reenactment alluded to by Freud (1912, 1914, 1920) can be updated from the contemporary perspectives provided in the present volume. The deeper affective and object relational meanings of entrenched character structures and resistances to the change implicit in the psychoanalytic treatment process will thus be explicated further. The conceptualization of *protectiveness* discussed in the object relations section of this volume defines a primary attitude toward internalized objects derived from early projective identificatory interactions with the parents which tends to be repetitively externalized and pervades the therapeutic milieu, making subsequent treatment interventions often seem difficult and even hopeless in work with character disorders.

The unconscious sense of loyalty to dysfunctional objects is subtly but prevasively embedded in the idiomatic nature of character structure and expressed via repetitious and often nonverbal mannerisms and idiomatic forms of self-definition. The lovingly idealized nature of relatedness to early objects has until now been noted but insufficiently emphasized in terms of the rigidly entrenched aspects of character structure and psychopathology.

Freud's earlier notion (1914) of repetitious acting out as a substitute for memory can be updated from a contemporary object relational perspective and applied to a deeper understanding of the significance of rigidly entrenched characterological styles, pathology, and resistances to the treatment process. The frequently *nostalgic* nature of the cognitive and affective memory and thinking process needs to be emphasized and further delineated as a relevant aspect of seemingly intractable character pathology.

## NOSTALGIC ASPECTS OF MEMORY IN CHARACTER DISORDERS

Throughout the present volume, there has been an emphasis upon the frequently overlooked difficulty with positive affects in many patients. This tendency is particularly enacted in patients manifesting characterological impairment. Such patients rigidly cling to idealized memories of early object relationships and their associated self representational states and linking affects. A number of theorists have explored this issue from a variety of object relational perspectives. Each of these perspectives offers a roughly parallel and potentially optimistic vantage point for understanding the nostalgic qualities of rigidly maintained character pathology.

### CHRISTOPHER BOLLAS

Bollas (1974, 1987, 1989, 1992) has argued rather convincingly that character structure involves a special form of memory of early object relational experience and associated affects. He creatively updates Freud's notions of acting out as a substitutive form of memory for repressed traumatic experiences with a conception of character as an expressive mode of translating early experiences with objects. Thus, for Bollas, certain early experiences with objects are captured in a structural fashion in an individual's characterological patterns. The memorial nature of character structure captures both the early experiences that are embedded in particular character patterns and the frequently intractable and repetitious quality of the behavioral patterns manifested as a result of those structures.

Bollas (1974, 1992) argues against a pessimistically static viewpoint with regard to character. He views stylistic modes of characterological expressiveness as idiosyncratic forms of linguistic communication of a generally interpersonal nature. An individual's personal idiom, true self, and sense of destiny (rather than fate) is conveyed through his character orientations. Characterological patterns of behavior (often nonverbal in nature) convey memories of the ego's earliest adaptational responses to aspects of the object relational environment. Much of the characterological domain of self-expressiveness consists of the communication of primitive forms of remembered experience that Bollas (1987) has labeled the *unthought known*. It is an expression in the here-and-now of the ego's earliest states of being in relation with primitive objects from the past.

The affective nature of characterologically grounded forms of primitive object relational memory is captured by Bollas' (1987) notion of the *conservative object*. He refers by this term to early forms of object relational experience that are conveyed through particular moods and feelingful states. A repeatedly experienced mood state, thus, may capture an early object relational encounter that can be interpersonally conveyed to another person but may remain virtually dissociated from conscious self-experience. Such mood states, when communicated in a therapeutic context, may be translatable into particular memories of object relational experiences.

Thus, according to Bollas' conceptions, characterological forms of self-expression and their associated affects consist of memories of early object relational experiences and encounters which may be largely of a preconscious and unconscious nature. Nevertheless, these object relational memories can be reconstructed both through intensive self-analysis or a psychoanalytic interaction.

Despite the seemingly compulsive, perseverative, and redundant nature of many characterological forms of self-expression, Bollas views such patterns as potentially open communicative systems. He decries the nosological categorizing of character styles and typologies (Shapiro, 1965) as implying closed systems with very limited communicative potential: "To regard character, then, as in the past, according to libidinal stages (i.e., oral, anal, phallic) or nosological type (hysterical, obsessional) is crudely to overlook the individual *parole* and to crush it back into a collective *langue*. Character is not an end product in stasis: its ''traits'' are *compelled to find expression* in the here and now'' (1974, p. 411).

The more static and redundant features observable in certain forms of characterological dysfunction are linked to the rigidified object usage and projective identificatory tendencies and frozen forms of dissociated memory storage typical of these disorders.

The therapist's task involves an enhancement of the patient's ego via a freeing of the primitive memories and associated affects repeatedly being communicated in a dissociated, unaware, and essentially nostalgic fashion through characterological communications of a projective identificatory nature.

## Thomas Ogden

Ogden has been one of the more important contributors to the clarification of the concept of projective identification and its implications for therapeutic work with severe character disorders and more primitively regressed patients. His formulations with regard to projective identification (1979, 1982) emphasize the interactive and communicative aspects of such processes, and like Bollas, stress their potential for open as well as closed system types of interpersonal interaction. Projective identificatory interactions, in accordance with Ogden's quite articulate and clarifying operational definition, involve an unconscious effort at placing an inner psychic content (thought, feeling, fantasy, motivational need, etc.) into another person for metabolic purposes. The way that person processes the projected psychic content is carefully monitored, and can be an unconsciously helpful or damaging experience for the original projector.

Projective identificatory forms of communications occur across the boundaries of a variety of social systems such as groups (Kissen, 1976, 1980a); families (Scharff and Scharff, 1987; Scharff, 1992); and couples (Scharff and Scharff, 1991), each of which may have open or closed systemic properties, depending upon the rigidity or flexible permeability of the boundaries of that system. Projective identificatory interactions in systems consisting of dysfunctional or characterologically impaired individuals, typically, have more rigid, perserverative, or closed system characteristics. Such communicative patterns are more likely to seem static and repetitive and to be unreceptive to possibilities for freer, more flexible, playful, and metaphorical forms of feedback.

Ogden's conceptual elaborations of the ideas of Melanie Klein regarding the *paranoid-schizoid* and *depressive* positions (1986), updated by his articulation (1989) of an even more primitive *autistic contiguous* position, are linked to his notions with regard to the systems properties of projective identificatory forms of communicative interaction. Every form of interaction, according to Ogden, is comprised of the dialectical polarities established by all three positions. Any given communicative interaction, however, may have a greater loading on a particular position, depending upon the degree of metaphoric possibility contained therein. Thus, projective identificatory communications, primarily at the level of the autistic–contiguous position, have a quite tangible, tactile, and essentially nonverbal character. Those at the level of the paranoid position have a rather concrete and ahistorical character. Those at the level of the depressive position have a fully historical and metaphorical quality.

Many severely dysfunctional and characterologically impaired systems are prone toward quite primitive forms of projective identificatory communication. The therapist must be receptive to more primitive forms of object usage and must be prepared to contain and metabolize primitive projective identifications in his work with character disorders. The outward redundancies of projective identificatory and object usage interactions with such patients frequently have an ahistorical and nonmemorial quality. Nevertheless, the essential therapeutic task is to translate those repetitive and seemingly static forms of characterological communications into the primitive object relational experiences and memories underlying them.

Ogden, like Bollas, views characterological enactments as projective identificatory forms of communication that camouflage the hidden memories and object relational encounters underlying them.

The nostalgic tendency to cling to early memories and experiences of an object relational nature and to provoke them in another (whether child, sibling, parent, or therapist) involves a form of object usage and enactment that is typical of character disorders. Once again, the therapeutic task involves the translation of the concrete, seemingly ahistorical action language implicit in the projective identificatory interaction into a more metaphorical, historical, and memorial form of symbolic communication. A great deal of the empathic, emotion-articulating, and creative aspects of psychoanalytic treatment technique are tested out during this process of translation and interpretive reconstruction.

## PETER GIOVACCHINI

Giovacchini (1975b, 1984a, 1986) has been one of the most prolific and creative contributors to the literature on psychoanalytic approaches to the treatment of character disorders. His study of the nonfunctional introjects internalized in a highly protective and self-esteem diminishing fashion via projective identificatory contact with dysfunctional parent role models, has clarified a great deal of the structural and psychodynamic aspects of severe character pathology.

His specific notion of the *frozen introject* (1984a) has helped articulate the blocked mourning typical in many forms of characterological impairment. This conception updates Freud's (1917) earlier notions of the mourning process and applies them to the internalization of frozen and protectively idealized objects which can, thereby, never be more effectively mourned and internalized. The normal mourning process can allow for an effective and ego enhancing process of identificatory introjection. Dysfunctional objects that have been protectively idealized in order to deny and dissociate the angry and aggressive feelings and impulses provoked by them, however, cannot be separated from and usefully internalized. Instead, they are internalized in a fashion that reduces competence and self-esteem. This is required in order to protect the original dysfunctional and incompetent objects from the assaults and devaluation merited by their personal inadequacies and identificatory insufficiencies. An endless struggle ensues, with the character disordered patient's ego sustaining the punishment and criticisms that ordinarily should have been directed at the inadequate parental role models.

The ego and self structures of character disordered patients, according to Giovacchini, are severely damaged via an internalization of essentially frozen, submerged, and nonfunctional introjects which contribute to the marked erosion of self-esteem and perceived competency typical of these psychopathological configurations.

The pathological form of introjective process is, at least in part, a substitute for the authentic process of remembering that appears too threatening and dangerous to the characterologically impaired patient. Rather than experience the painful, frustrated, and angry affects associated with a true memorial reconstruction of the damaging parental interactions, these patients substitute a highly idealized, dissociated, and outwardly nostalgic form of memory.

Giovacchini's notion of *externalization* (1984a) is perhaps one of his most important and creative contributions to the understanding and treatment of various forms of severe character pathology. This notion is somewhat similar to the conception of projective identification but involves a tendency to projectively recreate an entire environmental ambience that was traumatically experienced earlier in a given patient's life. As in Freud's (1914) conception of the active repeating rather than remembering of a passively experienced traumatic event, the externalization evokes the experience of an assaultive infantile environment (and the associated feelings of helplessness, vulnerability, and primitive defensive tendencies) in the other (friend, mate, or therapist), who must somehow struggle to make sense of the experience and metabolize it as effectively as possible.

Giovacchini argues that the countertransference readiness to be used by the patient as a container for the metabolizing and metaphorical reprocessing of these externalized forms of early environmental experience can ultimately be ego supportive and structuring for the patient. This is in accordance with the conceptions of object usage (Winnicott, 1971), projective identification (Malin and Grotstein, 1966; Ogden, 1979, 1982), and Bollas' (1987) notions with regard to the effective use of the therapist's self in the countertransference with primitively organized patients.

The patient's memories of early ego assaults resulting from traumatically deficient and emotionally painful environmental experiences, are repetitively recreated and reexperienced in the form of these externalizations in the therapist's self and environmental experience. There is a dissociated and nostalgic character to these externalized experiences which ultimately will need to be translated into more therapeutically useful and historically veridical forms of remembering.

## CASE ILLUSTRATIONS

### Case 1

The patient, previously described in chapter 3, was a young man who repeatedly reenacted the severe physical and psychological assaults experienced during childhood at the hands of both parents. He did this in one of two ways: He either repetitiously berated and devalued himself, insisting that he was incapable of independently functioning in the outer world, or controlled, manipulated, and devalued his wife by symbiotically enmeshing her in his severe agoraphobic world. By crippling himself, much as his brutally unempathic parents ended up crippling him and his siblings, he established a loving monument to their cruelty. This nostalgic monument to their cruelty was endlessly replayed through his severe characterologically based impairments.

Rather than remember and mourn the damage perpetrated by the dysfunctional parents, and the angry, critical affects associated with their impact upon his self-esteem, the patient preferred to emulate their sadistic assaults upon himself. His therapist ended up feeling angry at the parents and at the helplessness he was forced to feel, due to the recalcitrant and resistant nature of the patient's symptoms. Although the therapist felt perpetually angry at the ego damaging parents of the patient's childhood, the patient never fully owned up to such feelings so that an effective process of mourning could be initiated.

The therapist began to feel more and more frustrated, helpless, and eventually angry at the patient who seemed to be stubbornly rejecting the change potential inherent in the therapeutic relationship. Sadistic feelings had been transferred in some fashion from parent to child (patient) to therapist. The recreation of a cruel, sadistically unbudgable environment had been effectively created in the therapist's office which felt more like the prison yard atmosphere permeating the patient's infantile environment than like a milieu full of hopefulness and therapeutic potential.

The nostalgic form of remembering the painful and frustrating features of early infantile life experiences had effectively created a stasis in the treatment environment from which there appeared to be no freedom or salvation. The more useful and constructive forms of remembering (which can lead to a successful mourning and letting go of past toxic experiences), had been severely foreclosed and blocked via an ego and therapy crippling form of nostalgia and recreation of the most toxic features of the infantile environmental milieu.

*Case 2*

A man with a severe addictive problem endlessly reminisced about the *exciting* visits with his father. The father was an extremely irresponsible and unpredictable man who, following the separation from the mother, would honor the patient and his siblings with a visit every two or three weeks. On some occasions, he would take the patient along to his favorite watering holes and introduce him to the many women who seemed also to find him very exciting. The patient felt quite aware of the superficial, shallow, and self-serving quality of the father's visits, but nevertheless found them to be the most exciting and exhilarating aspects of his childhood.

These visits punctuated a rather dull and unexciting childhood existence in which the patient felt cooperatively and protectively ensnared in a relationship to a seemingly pleasureless and martyred mother who forbade hedonic excess of any sort either for herself or her children. The father, on the other hand, came across as a defiant hero, a sort of "Diamond Jim Brady," who uninhibitedly flaunted his willingness to live a life full of abandon and excess, even if it might be detrimental to his health and well-being.

The patient's nostalgic and idealized memories of his father were the only buffer that he felt he had against his anhedonic and excessively controlling mother who repeatedly sought to forbid him a pleasureably vital sense of life.

Unfortunately, the nostalgic memories of an idealized father became associated with a severe addictive problem with a great deal of self-destructive potential. The incapacity to mourn the father and view his painfully frustrating absence and self-centered indifference more objectively, was paralleled by a similar incapacity to view the dangerous nature of the addictive disorder more objectively. Both involved highly idealized self and object representations and linking affects of a hedonically exciting nature. The essential superficiality and self-destructive potential of the identificatory interactions with both father and drugs were logically but not necessarily emotionally evident. The stasis and intractable characterological resistances in this case were, thus, associated with a highly nostalgic and exciting attachment to extremely dangerous objects (father, drugs).

To give up either felt like facing a tremendous loss with nothing palatable or equally exciting to substitute in its place. The nostalgic memorial process was locked into place. To give up the affects provided by the exciting father (drugs) threatened a reunion with the affectively apathetic, controlling, and pleasureless mother of childhood.

*Case 3*

A young woman, aspects of whose treatment have been described in chapters 8 and 11, had developed a severe eating disturbance which made her life extremely unpleasant. The addictive features of this disturbance were linked to an extremely loyal attachment to her natural mother and a refusal to identify with her stepmother who (too quickly for her own mourning capacities) wished to eliminate certain aspects of her natural mother's presence from her home and life.

The intractable and stubbornly resistive nature of the patient's eating disorder partially involved an intense nostalgic linkage to unconsciously retained memories of the various unpleasant aspects of her natural mother's illness. She repeatedly was able to relive through her bulimic symptoms some of the dimly remembered unpleasantries of her natural mother's extended illness, prior to her death.

During the course of psychotherapy, she was able to reconstruct the painful linkages between her mother's suffering and her own self-perpetuated suffering as a result of her highly unpleasant bulimic rituals. Her symbiotic attachment to her idealized natural mother was pervasively enshrined and symbolically captured through the bulimic discomfort that she repeatedly forced herself to endure.

This patient was unable effectively to mourn her natural mother's death and internalize her in a more benign fashion. Instead, she felt it necessary to relive nostalgically the painful ending of her mother's life via uncomfortable and abhorrent bulimic behavior patterns.

As she began to relive in her treatment the dissociated traumatic memories surrounding her mother's death, she was able to both mourn the loss of her mother more effectively and gradually give up her painful eating disorder. The fact that she was now able to mourn the loss of her natural mother allowed her to establish a much better relationship with her stepmother and to internalize some of her positive attributes. The nostalgic attachment to the natural mother through a seemingly intractable and painful symptom was replaced via the mourning process by a less toxic but nevertheless sad series of memories.

*Case 4*

A male patient helped his therapist appreciate some of the truly stubborn, unyielding, and unempathic aspects of both of his parents via certain subtle aspects of his characterological demeanor expressed repeatedly and resistively during the psychotherapy interaction. While he had found his parents' behavior extremely unpleasant and offensive and had vowed to never be like them, he subtly tended to recreate them through certain stubborn forms of resistance. In many ways, the parents had squelched the patient's spontaneity and assertiveness through the unempathic and unyielding united front that they had established repeatedly during the course of his childhood. The therapist began gradually to understand the patient's nostalgic connection to the parents' stifling behavior, as his own therapeutic endeavors were repeatedly shot down, and ultimately stifled as a result of the patient's responses to them.

The patient, of course, could see no connection whatsoever between his own tendency to repeatedly discourage and find fault with the therapist's formulations and reconstructions, and the similarly fault-finding and rejecting manner in which he was treated by his parents during childhood. To agree with any of the therapist's formulations and reconstructive efforts would be tantamount to validating his spontaneity and creativity. Since he had never had his own spontaneous ideas and suggestions validated by his parents during childhood, he could not perform such a validating function for his therapist.

In many ways, it was more important to vividly convey and reenact with the therapist the toxic and unreceptive handling by the parents than to more insightfully explore the transferential patterns stemming from them that were occurring during the course of the treatment relationship.

As the nostalgic qualities of this form of enactment were repeatedly noted by the therapist, an increasingly playful and spontaneous ambience began to pervade the treatment relationship. The therapist was gradually allowed to share formulations that could be at least tentatively validated by the patient. The patient was thereby enabled to begin to perform a function that he had never experienced with his parents.

The nostalgic connection to the consciously disavowed and abhorrent aspects of the parents' behavior and responsiveness was gradually dissipated. Characterological changes of a positive nature ensued from the gradual severing of this memorial and identificatory connection to the parents. As the therapist was allowed to feel validated for his creative efforts, the patient was enabled more and more to risk a less constricted mode of relatedness in his external world.

### CONCLUSIONS

Most characterological patterns of a seemingly static and resistive nature involve subtle forms of memory. The repetitive reenactments implicitly contained in a given characterological pattern, although often having a concrete and ahistorical quality, can eventually be explored from a more metaphoric

and historical perspective following an extended period of playfully interactive object usage and projective identificatory containing and metabolizing
on the therapist's part.

As Bollas (1974, 1987) has emphasized, a seemingly static and closed
system sort of nosological encounter with a rigidly structured and prescribed
characterological pattern can be gradually converted to a more open system
in which therapeutic maturation and change is possible via a patient process
of containing and countertransference exploration. The frustrating aspects of
therapeutic work with various forms of character pathology can be tremendous
due to the seemingly static and intractable nature of these structural patterns
of behavior. The frustration can be considerably diminished, however, via
continued awareness and active probing into the affective and object relational
significance of these characterological patterns.

The highly constricting and nonfunctional introjects that patients with
character disorders repeatedly enact out of an unconsciously devoted, idealized, and protective attachment to dysfunctional infantile and childhood objects, need to be continuously flushed out and interactively explored during
treatment. The more playful, creative, and spontaneous the treatment interaction the better. Of course, these patients who have experienced tremendously
constricting and unspontaneous childhoods will repeatedly need to frustrate
the therapist whose goals are clearly the opposite of those repeatedly experienced during childhood.

The need to externalize and recreate a frustrating, oppressive, and highly
constricting environment similar to that experienced in childhood is perhaps
one of the more definitive ways in which patients with character problems
approach the treatment situation. The freedom to change and eventually eliminate painfully unrewarding characterological patterns, which is clearly inherent in the treatment situation, is often seen unconsciously as a threat to loyally
maintained attitudes of protectiveness and nostalgia toward early objects.

The paradoxical devotion toward early objects, many of whom have been
severely frustrating, dysfunctional, and intensely disappointing, is evident
in most patients exhibiting characterological difficulties. This devotion is a
pervasive feature underlying the repetitious and rigidly entrenched forms of
characterological stasis manifested by those patients. These patients create
memorials to their dysfunctional, unavailable, and damaging infantile objects
by, paradoxically, not remembering them.

To truly remember their pathologically idealized objects, these patients
would have to confront the painful realities of the harm that they have done
in various ways during childhood. The dissociated anger would need to be
owned, and then an incipient process of more effective mourning could be
begun. A great sense of disloyalty would have to be tolerated, and eventually,
also a truer feeling of sadness and inner emptiness.

The gradual erosion of the nostalgic memorial connection to damaging infantile and childhood objects, although providing tremendous maturational and therapeutic benefits, is a very painful process which requires an expansion of the affect array typically experienced by the patient. In some cases negative affects such as anger and resentful hostility must be reowned. In other cases, positive affects and affective attitudes such as joy, exhilaration, pride, optimism, and courage must be reowned. Such affect reownership almost always involves an unconscious sense of disloyalty and failure of the attitudes of protectiveness that have always previously pervaded the inner object relational world of the patient.

The dread of disloyalty is one of the motivational energizers which has continuously fueled the nostalgically maintained characterological symptoms and resistive stasis. The psychoanalytic process which continuously values and provokes more veridical forms of remembering, always prods the patient in a direction antithetical to the nostalgic attitude of loyalty and protectiveness. The therapeutic alliance can eventually be tested enough and is solid enough to allow the patient to hesitantly risk the attitude of disloyalty that she has always unconsciously dreaded. The pathological objects of childhood can eventually be given up (as can the characterological symptoms and static resistances), as a result of the empowering and freedom enhancing qualities of the therapeutic relationship.

The object usage and successful containing features of the therapeutic relationship also ensure a benign maturational outcome in work with patients manifesting character pathology.

A continued focus upon the nostalgic qualities of the memory process can facilitate an eventual thawing of the frozen introjects and free a more authentic process of mourning.

Ultimately, the benign, ego enhancing, affect expanding, and enriching features of the therapeutic process can be internalized as a replacement for the gaps left as a result of the now more adequately mourned objects and remembered experiences from the patient's past.

# Chapter 13

# CHARACTEROLOGICAL DEPRESSION IN PRIMITIVELY ORGANIZED PATIENTS

## ENERGIC AND NARCISSISTIC FEATURES OF DEPRESSION IN PRIMITIVELY ORGANIZED PATIENTS

Depression as a characterological process is pervasively reflected in the depletion of psychological and physical energy so commonly noted in more regressed patients. Many such patients tend to be martyred, ever-suffering individuals who are forever lamenting the frustrating and painful nature of their life experiences. The capacity for creativity, competitive mastery, and selfhood is extremely impoverished in these patients. This is nowhere more evident than in their chronic complaints with regard to the futility of their existence and their inability to gain pleasurable satisfactions and a sense of mastery over seemingly insurmountable situations. They pervade the therapeutic environment with a sense of hopelessness, helplessness, and despair. The therapist must continually confront and overcome his own sense of pessimism and despair in working with such patients. Pessimism is projected into the therapist, and his primary containing task consists of a struggle to regain a sense of purpose, optimism, and positive therapeutic focus.

The primitive ego identities and weakened adaptive capacities of these patients contribute to an extreme impoverishment of their internal energy systems. It is this energy impoverishment which most directly has an impact on their self-esteem and capacity to regulate the oscillation between positive and negative affects and mood states. They are developmentally arrested individuals with a diffuse sense of ego identity and impaired self-esteem. Jacobson (1971) has documented the impact of depression on the self-esteem

205

of more primitively organized patients. She repeatedly notes the ego–superego conflicts and traumatic early histories that are central structural and psychodynamic determinants underlying depressive experience and behavior. She also offers considerable clinical data regarding the impaired capacity for self-esteem and mood regulation in severely disturbed patients with depressive tendencies.

Kohut (1977) has emphasized the narcissistic impairment in primitively organized patients which is manifested in their tendency to oscillate between grandiose, omnipotent, and hypomanically, energized self-evaluations and much more pathetic, energyless, and self-deprecatory tendencies. He argues that the lack of parental empathic response and mirroring, due to the parents' own narcissistic difficulties and self-absorption, contributes to the patient's deficiencies, creative blocks, and energy depletion tendencies. Kohut alludes to a causal connection between narcissistic insufficiencies and impaired self-esteem regulation and energy depletion—particularly in the sphere of creative functioning. He offers clinical material to document this relationship. Thus, many narcissistic patients suffer from marked inhibitions and energy impoverishment in their creative strivings and work efforts. Kohut notes repeatedly their incapacity to channel their energies productively into creative work.

The creative work blocks of narcissistically damaged individuals are symptoms associated with energy depletion and a lack of effective capacity for thermostatic regulation of self-esteem and positive affects. There is a primary ego defect and developmental arrest in such patients which eliminates their capacity to be creative and productive, to experience and exhibit the self in a positive fashion. They cannot regulate their positive and negative affects and mood states and most of their inner experience is pervaded by pessimism, loss of energy, and negative affective states. These narcissistic deficiencies and associated creative and adaptive energy impairments give a masochistic cast to their interpersonal relationships and intrapsychic experiences. These patients have an incapacity to sustain energy and positive affective experiences. They increasingly become chronic complainers who derive secondary gains from negative attention-seeking behavior. These patients are experts at self-sabotage. They pathetically attempt to restore some sense of psychic equilibrium, self-esteem, and mastery via continuous behavioral outpourings of self-laceration and lamentation.

Stolorow and Lachmann (1980) have recently studied some of the associations between narcissistic impairment, energy insufficiency, and impairments in the capacity for self-regulation of moods and affects in primitively organized patients. These authors repeatedly point out the deficiencies in affective self-regulation and energy supply which underlie masochistic and depressive behavior. They state: "In an individual with a diffuse or dissolving self-representation, the masochistic search for acute experiences of pain can be understood as a means of acquiring a feeling of being real and alive and thereby re-establishing a sense of existing as a bounded entity, a cohesive self'' (1980, p. 32). Stolorow and Lachmann do not overlook the more commonly noted dynamic implications of masochistic behavior as a manifestation of oedipal conflicts, but instead focus upon the narcissistic characteristics of such behavior in developmentally arrested individuals. As a result, masochistic and depressive tendencies are seen as primitive efforts to shore up the shaky self-esteem and energic imbalances of more primitively organized patients.

Depression and masochistic behavioral tendencies can be seen as characterological forms of psychopathology. Such behavioral manifestations involve a striving toward an increased sense of self-articulation and more energetic and positive affectively colored psychic experience. Depressive and masochistic symptoms are essentially characterological defensive maneuvers. Repeated complaints and self-lacerations in primitively organized patients are paradoxical efforts at restoring psychological energy and self-esteem. The incapacity to sustain positive affective experience in many such patients leads to efforts at self-restoration and reenergizing via masochistic characterological defenses.

## Case Illustrations

### Case 1

A fairly attractive but slightly overweight young woman entered treatment because of depressive difficulties. Her depression was manifested in an inability to marshall sufficient energy to clean up and organize her home and in considerable unhappiness and dissatisfaction in the relationship with her husband. She also noted a difficulty in sustaining sufficient energy for creative work endeavors. She had considerable writing talent but did not feel able to produce a finished piece of literary work. Her pervasive writing block was merely one example of her primitive ego identity, impaired self-esteem, and depressive lack of energy for creative and work activities.

Her narcissistic needs were organized around an extremely idealized romantic attachment to a man who seemed almost totally indifferent to and disinterested in her. She felt madly in love with this man, but never seemed able to engage his interest or affectionate feelings. He always seemed cold and distant and gave her repeated messages of his disinterest by withholding any form of emotional commitment or viable sexual relationship. Nevertheless, she continued to obsess about the possibility of a sexual relationship. She repeatedly compared her husband, whom she experienced as too passive, inept, and emotionally hungry himself to provide for her romantic needs, to this very phallic and idealized man who seemed much more able to gratify her romantically and sexually.

Due to the pervasiveness of her romantic preoccupations, she was unable to sustain any energy whatsoever for either household work or creative activities. She was also too depressed and symbiotically enmeshed in the relationship to her 2-year-old son to clean up her home and to begin some form of work outside the home to enhance her self-esteem. She was extremely dependent upon her parents, particularly her mother, who paid for the therapy but constantly complained about the fact that it would probably turn the patient against her. Her symbiotic attachment to her mother was replicated with her son. Both relationships, in part, submerged her potential for ego autonomy and creative energy. She dreaded her son's separation–individuation and transition to nursery school, just as she dreaded her own forced separation–individuation from her mother. In a certain sense, she was pleased by the child's regression and the recurrence of his intense clinging to her, following a childhood illness.

Her own separation–individuation was imposed upon her against her will, due to early life experiences. She had a twin sister who suffered a calamitous genetic defect which kept her a virtual physical vegetable from birth. This sister required extensive attention from her parents, both of whom were educators. The parents were energetic individuals who devoted most of their considerable energies to the handicapped twin sister. The patient experienced being sent to sleepaway camp at an early age as rejection and abandonment by her parents. She felt intense rage toward her twin sister who had robbed her of love and affection from her parents. At still another level, she felt identified with the paralysis and physical incapacity of her twin. She internalized the sister's paralysis in the form of a depressive energy depletion and incapacity to perform either simple household chores or more complex creative work. She unconsciously felt that functioning too energetically and capably might lead to rejection and abandonment by her mother.

She also tended unconsciously to rebel against the ego ideals of her parents via her depressive and lethargic behavior. She constantly displayed her lack of energy and inability to cope with household chores to her parents, who took pride in being energetic people capable of mastering difficult and demanding situations without becoming depressed. In a sense, she was a container for their dissociated depressive affects. They were too energetic, efficient, and goal-oriented to allow themselves the luxury of even brief depressive states.

Initially she was almost totally unaware of her unconscious dread of the potential identifications with her energetic and seemingly competent parents. Her mother needed to be constantly buoyant, active, and zestful in performing her daily functions. She took pride in her capacity to manage a household including a handicapped daughter while maintaining a full-time teaching position and managing a summer camp which she ran with the father. The patient, on the other hand, was always melancholic and self-absorbed. She was forever lamenting the deprivations in her marriage and fantasizing about an extramarital affair. She brooded in a morose way about her deprivations and the lack of pleasurable satisfactions in her life. She could not even begin to grasp the significance of her negative identity structure (i.e., identification with a physically handicapped twin sister who somehow maintained a symbiosis with the mother through her handicap), and unconscious dread of identifications with her more potent and effective parental figures. She feared that functioning on a higher and more energized affective level might rob her of the symbiotic level of relatedness that was never sufficiently gratified during her childhood.

Her continuous suffering, loss of energy, and adaptive insufficiencies had evolved into an elaborate masochistic character defense. She cloaked her latent talents, positive affects, and energies beneath this form of narcissistic character armor. Her masochism and depressive lack of energy was an effort at establishing the ego boundaries and sense of self-definition that she was deprived of in early childhood due to her parents' tendency to focus most of their attention on the damaged twin sister. Separation–individuation, ego autonomy, and adaptive and creative functioning were associated with an intense feeling of neglect and emotional abandonment during the course of early phases of the patient's object relations. Pathological identifications with the damaged twin and an unconscious dread of the more competent parental identifications provided her with some compensatory emotional gratifications.

During the course of treatment, she was encouraged to explore the characterological significance of her depressive symptoms. An empathic and mirroring therapeutic model similar to that described by Kohut (1977), Kohut and Wolf (1978), and Stolorow and Lachmann (1980) was utilized. It was juxtaposed with the character analytic and interpretive model contained in the writings of Reich (1933) and Nydes (1963). In chapter 11, a therapeutic model was described for working with the dread of positive affects manifested by primitively fixated patients. It will be further delineated in the present chapter.

## STRUCTURAL FEATURES OF THE DEPRESSIVE TENDENCY IN DEVELOPMENTALLY ARRESTED PATIENTS

The primary structural deficits underlying severe depressive character disorders can be traced to the nature of their preoedipal ego and superego development. The ego and superego can both be viewed as systemic matrices of psychosexual and psychosocial stages which have broad implications for affective, cognitive, and behavioral subsystems. During the course of maturation, a given individual must successfully traverse the oral, anal, and phallic–oedipal modalities. Her early object relational encounters must provide the empathic mirroring or *containing* experiences to allow for the development of high level ego functions (i.e., reality testing, ego strength, identity and constancy of self and object representations) and superego functions (i.e., internalized moral code, self-loving, and prohibiting functions). Object relational inadequacies during the course of the preoedipal period are manifested in the basic faults described by Balint (1968). These faults are structural deficits and inadequacies which can be manifested through affective (depressive mood states), cognitive (exclusively concrete thinking), or behavioral (acting out, explosive, and implosive impulsive reactions) disorders. Brickman (1983) has focused upon these structural deficits as forms of pathological superego development.

Normal superego maturation during the preoedipal period involves a gradual renunciation of narcissistic impulses and object relational expectations. The desperate need for a symbiotic or merger selfobject who can be idealized or depreciated is replaced by the internalization of the realistic ideals for excellence and moral code of beloved parental objects. Schafer (1960) has focused upon the structural aspects of superego and ego ideal formation and has noted the fact that every superego identification with parental ideals involves a complex condensation of id, superego, and ego factors. Thus, the superego and ego ideal of the child tends to be a compromise formation containing the ideals modeled by both parents. Superego maturation occurs during the course of a complex social learning process, with both parents supplying the ideals and role models. The child consciously and unconsciously sifts through parental ideals and establishes self representations and identity structures that are relatively functional and coherently organized.

More primitively organized patients, however, have remained pathologically fixated at preoedipal phases of ego and superego development. These fixations are manifested in various forms of cognitive, affective, and behavioral impairment. They are also manifested via a heavy reliance upon pathological defensive maneuvers. The object relational features and pathological defensive functioning in borderline disorder has been comprehensively delineated by Kernberg in a series of writings (1975b, 1976b). He emphasizes the pervasive utilization of primitive defenses of splitting, projective identification, idealization, and self-depreciation by borderline patients, due to their structural ego and superego deficits and their consequent need to deny painful aspects of reality.

The borderline patient often has an externalized superego. Her internalized ideals and values are not very coherently organized and her sense of identity is very diffuse. Due to a heavy reliance on splitting mechanisms, contradictory self-evaluations, mood swings, and impulses predominate. Feelings are experienced across the affective extremes between hypomanic excitement and depressive apathy. At the apathetic end of the continuum, primitive narcissistic efforts at self-restoration are pervasive. These primitive narcissistic compensatory efforts rely upon the pathological defense mechanisms of projective identification, idealization, and masochistic self-depreciation.

The primitively organized patient frequently manifests her depressive–masochistic characterological core by seeking desperately after overvalued proxy objects who seem to have the preciously idealized attributes that she perceives as lacking within herself. A great deal of primitive projection and introjection is involved in this complex process of projective identification. Wangh (1962), Malin and Grotstein (1966), and Ogden (1979) have conceptually delineated and clinically described various object relational aspects of this complex process of interactional projection. What has been repeatedly noted is the fact that patients with a weakened sense of ego identity desperately rely upon external objects as containers not only for painful and unacceptable feelings and impulses, but also for treasured or idealized aspects of themselves. They repeatedly engage in interactions with narcissistically valued objects in whom they provoke feelings and behavioral tendencies unacceptable to themselves due to the largely primitive preoedipal level of their own ego and superego development. They perceive these highly significant objects in an extremely idealized way and themselves in an equally distorted and depreciated fashion.

A great deal of the structural ego and superego impairment of primitive patients tends to be expressed through these characterological and defensive maneuvers. The narcissistic level of object relations of many of these patients derives, in large part, from their heavy reliance upon such defense mechanisms. The predominantly masochistic mode of self-expression and object relatedness of these patients also can be directly related to their reliance upon these primitive defensive maneuvers. They repeatedly oscillate between a narcissistically self-protective state of self-idealization, and devaluation of significant figures in their interpersonal environment, and a more depressive and masochistic affective state in which external figures are highly idealized and the self is deflated and devalued.

Case material derived from therapeutic experience with primitively organized patients can be used to illustrate the above discussion. A predominant pattern of behavior showing preoedipal superego fixation in such patients is their tendency toward self-laceration. They frequently take masochistic delight in their various handicaps and deficiencies. One patient, in particular, spent hours deriding her physical appearance. Although relatively attractive, she insisted that she was overweight and ungainly. Her bulimic symptom was associated with an extremely poor self and body image and seemed to be a hopelessly engrained behavioral pattern. Another patient was convinced that his life had no future. He could derive no pleasure from interpersonal relationships or vocational endeavors and seemed doomed to this anhedonic mode of existence. He felt that he would never be able to marry and have children like a normal person and unrelentingly and unmercifully derided himself for this obvious flaw in his moral development and character structure.

This extreme tendency toward self-deprecation in many primitive patients is often associated with a parallel tendency to idealize some currently significant figure. Thus, the patient described in the previous section idealized in a very romantic way a man she barely knew. She compared her husband to this man incessantly in a very unfavorable manner. Her tendency to idealize this man, while deprecating her husband, suggests her heavy reliance upon splitting mechanisms. She also tended constantly to devalue herself. She idealized the other man, who was seen as possessing the phallic attributes, adventurousness, and separation–individuation capabilities that she herself lacked. Whereas she was locked into symbiotic mergers with her husband, her mother, and her son, this other man seemed free enough to pursue his life in a cavalier and independent fashion.

One basic structural factor underlying the depressive tendency in many primitive patients is their proneness toward interactional projection and proxy evocation. Their simultaneous inclination to split off affective aspects of their inner experience, leads to a tendency to cling desperately to self-devaluative perceptions and associated negative affects, and simultaneously to project more potent and maturationally higher level percepts and their associated positive affects onto and into idealized figures in their external environment. The primitive and generally preoedipal level of these patients' ego and superego structures is, in great part, responsible for these masochistic tendencies. They have not developed superego structures with the self-loving and self-esteem enhancing potential alluded to by Jacobson (1971) and Schafer (1960).

The intolerance for solitude and the unbearable loneliness, frequently noted in primitively organized patients, is linked to these structural defects. The need for proxy or selfobjects is extremely great, primarily to use as containers for unacceptable feelings of potency, self-sufficiency, and individuation. Pathological superego development is thus associated with a tendency to lacerate the self incessantly for aspirations toward potency and separateness and the positive affects associated with these aspirations. Many clinical examples indicative of this pathological form of superego structure can be offered. One patient, a chronically depressed woman, began a session by describing a very exciting and pleasurable day she had recently experienced. She noted that on that particular day, she felt alive in a way she had not felt for a long time. She ended the day by going to a movie she had been looking forward to seeing for some time. She thoroughly enjoyed the movie and was so excited when it was over that she absentmindedly stumbled on the balcony steps, severely twisting her ankle in the process. She then proceeded to shift into her more typical laments and complaints about the thoroughly intolerable and unpleasant nature of her current life situation. This particular woman's self-lacerative tendencies knew no bounds. Although never able to purchase a pretty dress or expensive decorative item for her home, she once spent $10,000 for one meeting with a gypsy fortune teller. Her exciting and positive experience at the movie theater was totally unacceptable to her primitive superego structures. She became terrified by these novel positive affects and had quickly to retreat to a more familiar mode of pessimism and dejection.

At an unconscious identificatory level, like the patient described above, she needed desperately to cling to merger objects and introjects and their associated toxic and noxious affective attributes. Positive and more benign identifications had to be projected and their self-referential potential nullified.

OBJECT RELATIONAL FACTORS UNDERLYING
DEPRESSIVE REACTIVITY IN PRIMITIVELY ORGANIZED
PATIENTS

Ultimately, many primitive patients cling desperately to severely damaged, primitive, and nonfunctional introjects. Their ego competencies, sense of self-esteem, and capacity for separation–individuation and more vibrant and alive feelings are severely marred due to these introjective tendencies. Giovacchini (1975b) has comprehensively described the severe characterological impairments and identity disturbances that stem from this pathological object relational orientation. Kernberg, too, has delineated, in a series of writings (1975b, 1976b), the impact of pathological structural development and defensive tendencies on borderline object relationships. Although Kernberg alludes to the *affective* implications of borderline defensive maneuvers and object relationships, he never fully delineates them. A primary thesis of this chapter is that depressive affects are a relatively pervasive feature of the object relations of primitive patients, as a result of the pathological identificatory and introjective–projective mechanisms so heavily utilized by such patients. There is a characterological element to these introjective processes and their associated depressive–masochistic affects which ultimately makes them ego syntonic and highly resistant to dynamic interpretive exploration and resolution during the course of therapeutic work.

The oedipal psychodynamics underlying these pathological object relations tendencies were described by Freud (1916) who spoke of patients "wrecked by success" due to the unconscious oedipal triumph associated with experiences of a potent, competent, or successful nature. These oedipal psychodynamics were even more comprehensively delineated by Nydes (1963) in a brilliant paper exploring the dread of unconscious oedipal success in patients with paranoid–masochistic character structures. Nydes emphasizes that the clinging to masochistic suffering often involves an unconscious need to camouflage and deny latent strivings toward mastery and competitive self-assertiveness.

Schafer, in a more recent paper (1984), explores some of the unconscious mental processes involved in entrenched psychic suffering. He notes two related tendencies in his clinical work with male and female patients. He finds a paradoxical tendency to pursue *failure* experiences in his male patients and an equally paradoxical tendency to *idealize* unhappy experiences in many of his female patients. The unconscious psychodynamic meanings of success for men and of happiness for women are implied by Schafer to be the primary reasons for these paradoxical tendencies to cling to neurotic suffering. At an infantile level, many patients have had to associate successful and happy experiences with disturbing and very destructive effects on emotionally significant and desperately needed parental figures. The patient ultimately begins to manifest a paradoxical need to protect the pathologically idealized parental figure from his latent strivings toward more positive affective experience.

Schafer concretized this protective tendency with case material from the treatment of a woman who manifested a pervasive depressive pattern in which she continually incorporated the unhappiness and misery of others. This Christlike, martyred role within her character structure was linked to early family dynamics in which she was consistently reinforced and valued for this capacity:

> The consequence of her incorporating the unhappiness of others in her family was that she could then more easily idealize them as secure, kind, compassionate and supportive to her as a girl and later as the woman with whom we are concerned. In her psychical reality, she gained love and importance by being unhappy and by this means, too, she added worth to her idea of herself. In line with analytic expectation, she attempted to play this role in the transference. If she could not perceive some discomfort or distress in the analyst for her to incorporate, she invented it. Thus, it was part of her transference that she was protecting or healing the suffering analyst by suffering herself and thereby reaching toward her ideal self [1984, p. 402].

Thus, Schafer adds an interesting observation to the, by now familiar, conception of pathological mourning tendencies in depressed patients alluded to by Freud in "Mourning and Melancholia" (1917). He infers that the pathological introject and consequent self-directed, masochistic inversion of rage originally felt toward the abandoning object, which is protected by a pathological idealizing tendency, also involves an attempt to protect an idealized self representation. This touches upon the *narcissistic* aspects of the masochistic character structure discussed earlier in this chapter. Depressive tendencies in both neurotic and more primitively organized patients may be linked both to rage at a protectively idealized object deflected against the self and to a paradoxical need to protect a pathologically idealized self representation.

The primitive and essentially double-binding early family dynamics underlying this irrational form of idealizing and protectiveness occurs within the family systems of patients all along the diagnostic continuum. Schafer explores these family dynamics within the neurotic range of psychopathology. Colson (1982) and Searles (1975) have explored the family dynamics underlying pathological protectiveness in borderline and profoundly psychotic patients. The common denominator in all of these clinical syndromes is the patient's need to protect idealized object and self representations via a paradoxical avoidance of more positive and maturationally higher level affects. The patient severely restricts maturational competencies and coping capacities during the course of this process of affective constriction and inhibition. The patient's superego attacks ego functions and self representations in the manner earlier alluded to by Jacobson (1971) in her description of the self-esteem disturbances of depressed patients.

The more primitive patient, due to pathological early object relationships, internalizes the nonfunctional, largely submerged and frozen introjects alluded to by Giovacchini (1975a, 1984a) and, simultaneously, becomes enmeshed in a chronically unrelenting grieving pattern. The superego and primitively idealized self representations are associated with an attack on the more realistic and potentially adaptive self representations, hence, the extremely self-critical and lacerative tendencies of these patients. This pathologically depressive mourning pattern allows for no mercy or relief from inner suffering. The protective clinging to pathological identifications rigidly walls off and isolates the patient from her more benign, loving, superego identifications and idealized self representations.

The patient discussed earlier in this chapter had to cling pathologically to a depressive self representation and identifications with her profoundly handicapped twin sister. She could not get in touch with the far more energetic and vibrant self representations that might be gleaned from identifications with her aggressively competent and assertive parents. She particularly had to dissociate herself and wall herself off from identifications with a beloved maternal grandfather who was the original wellspring and dynamic source of creative energy for both of her parents. This particular grandparent was a constant source of inspiration, tirelessly designing mechanical equipment and devices to assist the physically handicapped twin sister toward becoming more autonomous and mobile within her home environment. The patient's need to repress memories with regard to this grandparent and the more benign, coping aspects of her parents was the central dissociative mechanism that needed to be explored and eventually resolved during the course of her treatment. She desperately clung to her lack of energy and depressive identifications with her twin sister, and unconsciously resisted and dreaded any psychic connectedness to the more benign and competent ego identifications also available to her during the course of her development.

Many male patients with depressive–masochistic or paranoid character structures dissociate from the strong oedipal father figure and desperately cling to identifications with the passive, emasculated, and largely castrated father of later periods of their development. Schafer noted this in the following manner.

> Analysands tend insistently to represent only the scaled-down father of later periods of development. They hope thereby to get the analyst to accept these shrunken representations as psychically accurate and complete. These derogated representations also have their place in personal development—they, too, are psychically real but the analysis of the pursuit of failure, as of so many other problems, depends on getting beyond these limited and later representations to the early father image. The primordial father is always sexually powerful enough to overwhelm, satisfy and impregnate the mother and to castrate the oedipally rivalous son. But this primal father is not just a threatening figure, he is also a latent source of a strong and successful ideal self [1984, p. 401].

This pathological object relations tendency can be seen, of course, in both male and female patients across the diagnostic spectrum of character pathology, narcissistic, and borderline syndromes. The proneness to anxiously wall off benign, potent, and vibrantly energetic self and object representations is a central identificatory mechanism which must be transferentially explored and worked through in the analytic treatment of all patients but, particularly, those manifesting depressive character structures.

## DIAGNOSTIC DISTINCTIONS

For the purposes of this chapter, primitively organized patients are assumed to manifest forms of narcissistic character disorder with severely damaged object relations, distinctly weakened ego functioning, and identity diffusion. Weakened executive ego functions in the spheres of impulse control, synthetic capacity, and reality testing are assumed to exist but are not so pervasive that they cannot be camouflaged beneath pseudoidentity and superficially competent adaptive facade. Many patients with narcissistic personality disorders are extremely capable individuals with successful careers in areas of competency related to their narcissistic needs. They suffer decompensations, however, when their grandiose exhibitionistic strivings and needs for mirroring are no longer unconditionally and fully gratified.

The distinction between the narcissistic disorders and borderline personality pathology can and has been made by previous writers. Thus, Rinsley (1984) recently stressed the more primitive thought and personality organization of the borderline personality and contrasted this to the more internally coherent aspects of the narcissistic personality. He emphasizes, however, that the preponderance of empirical and clinical data suggests the existence of a *developmental arrest* rather than of a regression from higher maturational and object relational attainments for both types of severe character pathology.

Meissner (1983) emphasizes a similar distinction between the more primitive self-structures in the borderline patient and the relatively firmer and more cohesive self and personality organization of the narcissistic patient. Moreover, he emphasizes the fact that in both types of character pathology there are a differentiated variety of ego deficits due to pathological introjects, acute identity diffusion, and fluid shifts in self and object representations and associated affective mood states. To some degree, affective and object constancy is lacking in both types of pathology. Neither type of patient can fully empathize in a consistent and emotionally related fashion with significant others in their environment. Interpersonal relationships may be either clingy, dependent, and symbiotic in nature or emotionally detached and schizoid in nature, but they always involve a powerful and not very emotionally constant selfobject who is either excessively clung to or avoided. A distinctly narcissistic characterological orientation can be noted, to some degree, in all forms of severe character pathology.

Damaged self-esteem and body image exists in all patients manifesting severe character pathology. The self-esteem of these patients is either artificially puffed up as a result of a heavy reliance upon narcissistic defensive maneuvers, or is severely impoverished and pervaded by feelings of personal inadequacy and inferiority. Mood states are often fluidly and unpredictably changeable, oscillating between hypomanic states of self-inflation and grandiosity and extremely deflated states of hopelessness, lack of energy, and despair. In the more masochistic patients, dysphoric mood states predominate. The primary focus of this chapter has been upon the damaged self-esteem which can be noted in all forms of primitive personality organization. The depressive tendencies which stem from this damaged self-esteem has been explored from energic–narcissistic, structural, and object relational vantage points. The essential characterological and resistive features of the depressive tendency manifested by many primitive patients requires a therapeutic approach which can be consistently and systematically implemented.

## Therapeutic Considerations

The psychoanalytic model is particularly suited to the exploration and ultimate resolution of narcissistic character pathology. Many psychoanalytic writers such as Giovacchini (1975b), Kernberg (1975b, 1976b), and Kohut (1977), have evolved systematic therapeutic principles and approaches for work with more severely disturbed patients. Stolorow and Lachmann (1980) have clarified some of the significant conceptual, diagnostic, and therapeutic parameters involved in work with the developmentally arrested patient whose self-esteem is severely damaged and impoverished. They emphasize the importance of an empathic, mirroring, and largely noninterpretive therapeutic model with such patients. In a paper (1980b), the present author made a similar point with regard to the need for relatively noninterpretive *containing* experiences during the course of therapeutic work with patients manifesting primitive object relational tendencies and character structure.

The therapist must provide the mirroring and empathic containing experience that was often so lacking in the object relational histories of most developmentally arrested patients. The narcissistic tendencies of these patients create disturbing countertransference feelings and reactions in most therapists, largely due to the complex and subtle projective identificatory field that predominates in the treatment relationship.

The therapist working with more primitively organized patients gets to know them through his own emotional reactions during the course of treatment. He gets to *feel* many of the patient's primary self and object representations and associated affects. Depressive feelings of helplessness, low energy, and pessimism are constantly projected into the therapist. His containing task, in part, involves the consistent maintenance of a state of optimism, courage, and hopefulness of ultimate characterological growth and affective differentiation, in the context of these depressive projective identifications.

The depressive characterological tendency so frequently evident in developmentally arrested patients requires a particular expressive and empathic containing posture on the part of the therapist. The therapist must be constantly alert to the dissociated self and object representations and positive linking affects largely unavailable to the patient. The patient has unconsciously chosen certain pathological identifications and associated idealized self representations and has dissociated certain more positive, ego, and self-esteem enriching identifications and idealizations. She must be made gradually aware during the course of treatment of these more benign identifications, self and object representations, and affects.

This process of reownership of dissociated affects and self representations can be very slow and difficult and is impeded by seemingly intractable resistances. The depressive affects are desperately clung to, despite their largely dysphoric and unpleasant character. The therapist's patience is constantly tested, and negative countertransference affects and counterresistances are frequently present during the course of treatment. The therapist must maintain an empathic and partially noninterpretive posture, despite repeated frustrations and impulses toward a more confrontative, judgmental, and directive model. On the other hand, interpretive interventions can be helpful on occasion and ego enriching for the patient. These interpretations are particularly helpful when they clarify via genetic and object relational reconstructions the pathological identifications that underlie the patient's depressive character structure.

The primitively organized patient who is familiar with feelings of diffuse ego identity and impoverished self-esteem, needs to be made aware by interpretations of pathological identifications and largely nonfunctional introjects that underlie her self-critical and self-lacerative expressive posture. She also needs to be made aware via interpretations of the latent affects and self representations of a more positive nature that have been unconsciously dissociated. The patient who consciously fears taking risks and dreads failure due to feelings of inferiority, must be introduced to the possibility that she is unconsciously fearful of feelings of success and mastery. The patient who consciously feels energyless, helpless, and unable to cope must be introduced to the underlying unconscious dread of more positively competent, potent, and vibrant affective experience. The idealized self and object representations that underlie the depressive character structure of borderline patients must be interpretively explored and will ultimately be resolved during the course of therapy. The narcissistic and characterological nature of these depressive and masochistic defenses will require, however, a continuous oscillation by the therapist between an empathic, containing, and largely noninterpretive posture and a more interpretive posture, particularly focusing on pathological introjects, protective idealizations, and dissociated positive affectively colored identifications and idealized self representations.

The object relational therapeutic model proposed in this chapter stresses the exploration of primitive defenses, particularly those of projective identification, denial, self-depreciation, and idealization, so frequently manifested by developmentally arrested patients. These primitive defenses lead to similar feelings in the therapist which must be empathically contained and ultimately resolved by means of interpretations. A monitoring and interpretive focus upon the positive affects dissociated by these patients can lead to an ultimate process of characterological reintegration and to a diminishment of depressive reactive tendencies. The psychoanalytic model is naturally applicable to the treatment of both narcissistic and depressive characterological manifestations in primitively organized patients.

# Chapter 14

# MESHING CHARACTER STRUCTURES IN COUPLES

During the course of individual psychoanalytic psychotherapy, the therapist will, at many points, be subliminally aware of the character structure of his patient, much as Bollas (1974) has noted, as a subtle form of *semantic* self-awareness. The patient conveys an unconscious interpretation of him- or herself as well as certain distinguishable object relational memories together with their associated affects, via repetitious characterological patterns.

Freud (1912, 1914) quite early noted that the stereotypical and repetitious nature of certain pathological inhibitions, resistances, and character traits can basically be understood as the individual's way of remembering. Thus, many forms of acting out and acting in during the course of treatment can be viewed, according to Freud, as enactments which substitute for remembering.

From a more contemporary object relational perspective, we may view an individual's character structures and expressive style as reflective of inner self, object, and body image representations. A phenomenologically relevant sense of self and other is subjectively contained in the semantic notational system of an individual's repetitious characterological patterns. The therapist, thus, attempts to decipher the relatively complex forms of self-awareness and object relational memory semantically embedded within a given patient's characterological behavior and enactments.

### Projective Identification and Character Structure

The therapist has many tools with which to decipher the object relational significance of these complex character patterns. She can utilize conscious

221

interpretive tools as well as less conscious affects, fantasies, and projective counteridentificatory reactions to intuit the self and object representations and linking affects associated with these characterological modes of self-expression.

An enhanced understanding of projective identificatory processes underlying many forms of serious character pathology has recently occurred thanks to the elaborations of Klein's (1946) original contributions on this topic by theorists such as Malin and Grotstein (1966), Sandler (1987b), and Ogden (1982). Ogden, in particular, has developed the clearest and most comprehensive definition of projective identification which has broad and clarifying implications for an understanding of and productive therapeutic approach to serious forms of character pathology. His definition emphasizes both the "interactive" and the "communicative" features of projective identification. Many pathological forms of characterological enactments can be seen, therefore, as complex modes of inducing troublesome self and object representational states in another person, so that the projector can observe the other person's character structures coming to grips with them. A therapeutic metabolic process occurs when the other person (therapist) effectively contains these projections in an observable way for the projector.

## "PROXY EVOCATION" AND CHARACTEROLOGICAL MESHES IN COUPLES

Wangh (1962) has elaborated a conception of projective identification, which he calls *proxy evocation,* that has similarly interactive and communicative characteristics. This form of projective identification is particularly useful in deciphering the characterological communicative patterns of two individuals engaged in an intimate bonding and couple relationship. In this form of projective identification, one individual evokes feelings, fantasies, or impulses that are felt to be too difficult to handle in their mate. The partner who must contain the projection thereby becomes a "proxy" for the original projector.

Wangh offers an example of this process in the case of a married woman who becomes anxious over her symbiotically enmeshed son's active movements toward separation and individuation. She proceeds to provoke her husband into a rage reaction directed against the individuating son. She herself feels no rage and ends up unsuccessfully attempting to protect the son against her husband's angry outburst. She has no conscious awareness of either the psychic threat posed by the son's movement toward separation, nor of her own role as provocateur vis-à-vis her husband, in turning him angrily against the son.

Wangh explicates the proxy evocation maneuver as inherent in a broad array of dyadic interactions and couplings, including the therapeutic relationship. This subtle form of projective identificatory maneuver has particular relevance for an understanding and effective characterological intervention in a broad variety of couple relationships. The utility of this important systems construct can be generalized to individual psychoanalytic psychotherapy as well as couples and family treatment. Feldman (1982) and Scharff (1992) have explored the implications of projective identification in couples from an object relational and family systems perspective.

In the present chapter, an understanding of projective identification (particularly in the form of proxy evocation mechanisms) will be applied to a conceptual and clinical elaboration of the issues of meshing characterological structures in couples. The therapist's need to handle aspects of the couple character mesh and associated role complimentarities in patients being seen for individual treatment will be emphasized.

The therapist's capacity to contain rather than act upon certain proxy evocation demands placed upon her by individual psychoanalytic patients will be highlighted. Case material will be provided suggesting both effective and ineffective ways in which the therapist can utilize fantasies about the couple character mesh, to further the goals of individual treatment.

## "FLEXIBLE" ROLE COMPLIMENTARITIES AND CHARACTER MESHES IN COUPLE RELATIONSHIPS

Clearly, some form of mesh of character structures exists in every long-term couple relationship or marriage. This mesh tends to be taken for granted, although it has important implications for the therapy process. Every intimate couple relationship of some duration has a unique gestalt, characterological quality, and signature, which establishes it as a bounded entity that is almost defiantly separated from the external social world. The most successful couples have been able to establish relatively flexible characterological meshes of a mutually enlivening and supportive nature. The various role complimentarities underlying the character meshes of such couples are also relatively flexible and occasionally open to change.

In systems theoretical terms, mature couple relationships have less stereotypical, rigid, and closed systems boundaries. Projective identificatory interactions across these boundaries, too, are more mutually interchangeable and adaptable. A certain degree of character structure related role stereotypy does exist, but provides comforting and compatible rather than angry, regressive projective identificatory experiences and enactments.

Kernberg (1980b) notes that successful and comfortably meshed couples produce through projective identification a great deal of envy in the external group environment. Unsuccessful or pathologically enmeshed couples, on the other hand, may produce other emotions such as sympathy or even pity in others.

Comfortable characterological meshes which work well are evident to all clinical practitioners. Everyone knows a couple in which one mate enlivens, soothes, supports, or effectively integrates the other. A rather socially taciturn man may be positively stimulated and enlivened by his socially poised and active wife. A rather assertive and even aggressive woman may facilitate the expression of similarly assertive feelings in her more quiet and seemingly mellow husband. A man who is quite comfortable with his inner feelings of vulnerability may help his more emotionally constricted wife to express such inner feelings on occasion.

The warm, feeling-engaged, and practical mate may facilitate the expression of feelings in the more intellectually controlled and affectively disengaged mate. An individual comfortable with feelings of a passively dependent nature can facilitate the self-awareness and expression of such feelings in his mate who tends to be more anxious in the face of such feelings. Even more pathologically organized couples may have mutually facilitative character meshes. Nydes (1963) gives a number of pathological examples in which a masochistically organized mate enables his more paranoid partner to get in touch with passive feelings of helplessness and dependency. The sadomasochistic dimension permeates the relationships of both disturbed and well-integrated individuals (Kernberg, 1991b). Characterological modes of handling feelings of both love and aggression are an essential interactive feature of all couple systems.

Kernberg (1991a) emphasizes that for a successful, enviable, and passionately spontaneous relationship to occur in a given couple, the individuals must be relatively free of oedipal restrictions and must freely integrate aggressive feelings in a passionate and even *defiant* fashion, in their sexual interaction. In addition to a relative degree of freedom from incestually based taboos and oedipal inhibitions, two other criteria can help to assure a successful couple relationship. A broad range of affect (including both positive and negative hedonically toned feelings) of a developmentally mature nature should be available to both partners. Another essential criterion is a relatively flexible capacity for shifting role enactments and expectancies.

The freedom to provide one's mate with a flexibly differentiated range of role enactments has been noted by Kernberg (1991a) and more recently by Josephs (1991b) to be an important feature of self and ego integration relevant to effective couple interactions. A sufficient degree of emotional maturity and developmental courage is certainly related to such a capacity. Also, a relative degree of freedom from primitive, preoedipally, and oedipally based projective identificatory interactions is another relevant dimension. Rigid role enactment expectations are almost always played out through stereotyped projective identifications and proxy evocation demands in more pathological couples. The characterological mesh is consequently of a rather rigidly organized and bounded nature in such couples. Each member is forced to play out a particular array of role enactments, both due to an internal characterological defensive organization and to stereotypical expectancies emanating from the contrasting (or similar) characterological organization in the mate. More maturely organized couples have far fewer role restrictions, and make fewer rigid projective identificatory and proxy evocative demands upon each other.

## PATHOLOGICAL FORMS OF COUPLE CHARACTER ENMESHMENT

Two types of enmeshment have been underlined by Giovacchini (1984b,c) as essential for understanding pathological couple relationships. In one type of mesh, the couple unites around an unconsciously significant psychodynamic symptom or conflict. Thus, a man who had a highly unpredictable mother ended up unsuccessfully marrying a series of women, all of whom manifested this characteristic. He was never able to establish a long-term commitment, due to the lack of characterologically based symbiotic enmeshment in any of these relationships.

In the second type of pathological mesh noted by Giovacchini, a much more solidly engrained commitment occurs, due to the nature of the character structures of the two individuals. Thus, the frequently noted *obsessive–hysteric* marriage (Barnett, 1971) reflects such a rigidly engrained symbiosis and characterological enmeshment. The obsessive mate controls the hysterical partner, providing intellectual defenses and emotional distance at times of emotional turbulence and unpredictability. The hysterically organized mate, on the other hand, provides stimulating affective excitement and turbulence during more quiescent and predictable periods.

The *manic–depressive* marriage provides a similarly pathological form of characterological enmeshment. The hypomanic mate stimulates the depressive partner and provides an enlivening but potentially agitating and disruptive form of affective engagement. The latter, on the other hand, provides a proxy identificatory experience of a sad, mournful nature for the manic mate who is too threatened by such feelings to personally admit to or experience them.

In the *sado-masochistic* marriage, the sadistic mate provides a proxy experience of aggressive impulses and feelings for the masochistic mate who is too timid to directly express such feelings. The masochistic mate, on the other hand, provides an experience of suffering and self-abasement for the sadistic mate who rigidly defends against such feelings. The *paranoid–masochistic* matchups comprehensively explored by Nydes (1963), reflect a similar form of characterological enmeshment. The paranoid mate rigidly clings to fantasies, feelings, and role enactments centering about issues of power, while the masochistic mate equally rigidly clings to enactments centering about issues of love. Each thereby provides an engaging but rigidly stereotypical proxy experience of emotions defended against by their mate.

In the *narcissistic (infantile)–schizoid* couple, the narcissistic mate provides an experience of self-absorption and constant self-gratification for the more selfless and typically anhedonic schizoid partner. The schizoid mate, on the other hand, provides occasional glimpses of objectivity and the freedom from self-centered impulses and feelings for the more narcissistically organized or infantile mate.

These are merely a few of the complex range of characterological enmeshments discernible in pathologically mated couples. The issue of "object choice" (Crisp, 1988; Blum and Shadduck, 1991), although relevant to the theme of this chapter, will not be explored, other than to note the obvious fact that unconscious characterological and projective identificatory factors are intrinsic to the seemingly random couple connections made by numerous individuals. An individual discovers the unconscious basis of their particular choice of mate, frequently, only after many years of marriage or involvement in a psychoanalytic treatment intervention.

During the course of individual treatment, the characterological enmeshment underlying a particular patient's couple relationship or marriage is typically psychologically present but contextually in the background for both therapist and patient. The therapist almost always has fantasies about the mate, some of which are consciously evident and others of which are largely subliminal and unconscious.

These fantasies and characterological images of the mate are an important source of both vertical psychodynamic insights with regard to the patient and horizontal perceptions regarding systemic and projective identificatory communicative tendencies in the couple relationship of patient and mate. These fantasies can either assist the therapist in better understanding and effectively treating the patient or can lead to treatment disruptions, acting out, and potentially destructive countertransference enactments.

Occasionally, the therapist will be forced via subtle projective identification or proxy evocation on the part of the patient to directly deal with the mate, either via a telephone contact, individual consultation, or a joint consultation together with the individual patient. Such more active forms of engagement with the spouse or mate can lead either to an enhancement or disruption of the therapeutic work, depending on how they are handled.

Clinical material will next be provided to illustrate some of the issues of meshing character structures and the projective identificatory ways with which they frequently play out as a background and occasionally foreground contextual feature of individual psychoanalytic treatment.

## CASE ILLUSTRATIONS

Case material will be presented in three different contexts. In the first, the therapist has fantasies with regard to the unique characterological mesh of patient and partner which are not directly enacted but which illuminate, facilitate, and occasionally frustrate various aspects of the individual treatment. In the second context, the therapist is invited to act out role complementarity and proxy evocations with the mate and ends up doing so. In the third context, the therapist is invited to act out a proxy interaction with the mate and chooses not to go along with the request.

### Therapist Fantasies Regarding the Couple Characterological Mesh

*Case 1.* The patient was a severely agoraphobic man who relied heavily upon his wife to drive him back and forth to his place of employment and to his therapy sessions. His wife, due to her own character pathology and the traumatic nature of her early object relational experiences, outwardly resented the demands being placed upon her to be at his beck and call, but inwardly seemed to be quite comfortable with her controlling, sadistically demanding, severely anxiety-driven husband.

The therapist frequently felt frustrated and angry at the spouse whose compliance with her husband's incapacity to locomote and need for a constant companion was seen as a severe impediment to the husband's treatment. At one point, the therapist spoke of calling the spouse and (angrily) confronting her with the destructive impact upon his treatment of her passive compliance with the patient's manipulativeness. The patient did not seem comfortable with the therapist doing this and the therapist, too, had second thoughts about making the call. The call was never made.

The therapist attempted, unsuccessfully, to get the patient to encourage his wife to enter into individual treatment. He ended up having fantasies of conjoint therapeutic work with the patient and his spouse which were never to be enacted, and ultimately was forced to be satisfied with only modest therapeutic inroads into the patient's phobic symptomatology.

*Case 2.* A rather passive man had gradually and successfully been working through character resistances which had blocked his capacity to achieve at a competitive and higher level in his chosen profession. Periodically, his wife had complained about the slow nature of the treatment process and about the financial drain it had been causing. The therapist's fantasy impression of the wife was of a rather aggressive and demanding woman, quite in contrast to the patient's extremely docile characterological exterior.

Finding himself occasionally angry at the wife for her potential capacity to control the patient, and possibly to get him to quit treatment, the therapist began to wonder why he was having such strong feelings about the wife. It gradually dawned upon him that he was feeling toward the wife exactly as the patient was feeling but could never dare to admit either to himself or to his wife. Over time, the therapist was able to utilize this insight in working with him. He began to alert the patient to his dissociated angry feelings toward his wife. He also helped him become aware of his pervasive need to protect her and significant others in his life from such angry feelings. The dynamics and early object relational history underlying this protectiveness pattern could now be more productively and insightfully explored.

### The Therapist Accepts the Proxy Evocation Invitation

*Case 3.* A very capable and successful professional man entered treatment upon the prodding of his wife. His avoidant tendencies were particularly reflected in the sexual sphere via marked inhibitions and withholding behavior. Marital conflicts were initially a predominant feature of the therapy sessions, culminating in a decision to accept the wife's wish to come in for a joint session together with the patient. During the joint session, many issues were raised regarding the marital conflict and, at one point, the wife commented: "I don't have a very strong sexual drive, but would just like there to be *some* passion in our relationship."

During subsequent sessions, the therapist reminded the patient of this comment made by the wife, asking why he felt so unable to sexually enjoy the wife and gratify some of her passionate needs. The therapist's fantasies with regard to the wife were of a rather attractive and not very sexually demanding sort of woman. It was difficult to hear the patient's descriptions with regard to the wife's constant criticisms and demands.

Gradually, it dawned upon the therapist that he had become engaged in a proxy maneuver, in that he was being subtly invited to act out the patient's dissociated oedipal love feelings toward the wife (mother). The patient continued to feel the angry, criticized feelings, while the therapist got in touch with the split-off positive and loving feelings.

No subsequent joint meetings were scheduled and the therapist proceeded to work individually and more intensively with the patient on the defenses which were blocking his sexually passionate, assertive, and loving feelings from being more directly owned and ultimately expressed in an intimate fashion with the wife. Much progress was made through this renewed concentration on individual treatment.

*Case 4.* The patient came in for a couple consultation with her boyfriend (who was being seen by the therapist in individual treatment) to resolve communication difficulties in their relationship. The boyfriend was a rather sadistic and paranoid man whose severe guardedness and lack of psychological mindedness made it difficult to establish a solid therapeutic alliance. The boyfriend gradually began to pull out of treatment, and finally decided to terminate. She stopped coming in as well.

A few months later, the therapist got a call from the patient stating that she wished to come in for therapeutic consultation. Psychotherapy was begun and proceeded in a seemingly favorable and productive fashion. Her masochistic character structure was consistently explored and she seemed able to integrate and apply many of the insights obtained through treatment, in her life. Her masochism was evident in the decision to come to New York City from another city, despite the admonitions and warnings of her group therapy peers and group therapist. They repeatedly warned her about the dangers of involvement with the therapist's former patient who had visited her and been invited to sit in on her group. During that group session, he had referred to the female members as ''a bunch of bitches.''

The relationship to the former patient had rapidly deteriorated following her decision to pursue the relationship by relocating in New York City. The boyfriend repeatedly acted out by, not so secretly, becoming involved in a number of sexual liaisons with other women. She finally had sufficient strength and courage to end that relationship.

She came for individual treatment, feeling socially isolated, depressed, and rather futile about her capacity ever to have a successful relationship with a man. The therapist worked energetically toward building back her shattered self-esteem. In many ways, this treatment was successful. There were professional and financial difficulties, however, and the patient began to build up a sizable debt with the therapist, despite much discomfort. The therapist felt sufficient hope and positive regard for her so that he overlooked the resistance aspects of the debt buildup for a longer period than would typically be the case.

Finally, the patient was able to sufficiently reintegrate her emotional resources and to relocate back to her home city with a considerable degree of hope with regard to her future. A sizable debt to the therapist remained, and she promised to pay it back as quickly as she could.

A few weeks after her move, she called the therapist to reassure him of how well she was doing. She went on to note that she had put the therapist in her will. She reassured the therapist that she had no plan to harm herself and that she was feeling rather upbeat about her social and professional work possibilities.

In rethinking the proxy evocation character of this treatment which was intrinsic from its very inception, it became evident that the therapist had subtly shifted into the masochistic position, taking on a martyred role via-à-vis the patient who had become more and more idealized. The therapist, although aware of the sadistic tendencies lurking beneath the patient's masochism, often overlooked these tendencies due to a wish to idealize her. He was reenacting as her proxy the relationship to the sadistic boyfriend who was initially highly idealized by the patient. After becoming the boyfriend's proxy (by allowing the patient to substitute for him in treatment), the therapist gradually began to reenact in a reverse form the sadomasochistic features of that relationship.

Despite these severely confounding proxy evocation features, a great deal of productive therapeutic work transpired.

### The Therapist Refuses the Proxy Evocation Invitation

*Case 5.* A young woman reacted to a skin disorder by severely withdrawing from sexual contacts with men. After considerable individual treatment, she began once again to risk such relationships. She called the therapist, excitedly noting that she had initiated a sexual relationship with a man whom she would like to bring in with her for a joint session.

The therapist said that he understood how excited and anxious the patient was about having risked a sexual relationship after so many years, but emphasized that he would not see the man with her at this time. The patient gave in rather easily on this matter and came in for her therapy session by herself.

She proceeded to explore her own ambivalence about the possibilities for intimacy implied in this incipient relationship. Much of the session consisted of a detailing of her worries about the man's ambivalence and the seeming certainties that he was going to reject and, thereby, hurt her. By the end of the session, she was much more aware of her own intimacy conflicts and unconscious wishes to sabotage the budding relationship with this man.

Had the therapist agreed to see the man, there was the distinct possibility that he would have been invited to play out the proxy role for the patient's disowned and dissociated intimacy wishes. He also might have been invited to be critical of the man, reinforcing the negative side of the patient's ambivalent feelings. She might thereby build up a case for precipitously fleeing the relationship by either rejecting the man or causing him to reject her.

## Discussion and Conclusions

The last case reflects the preferred mode of handling proxy evocation expectations from a psychoanalytic perspective. The boundaries and essential framework of treatment were more steadily maintained in the previous case example. This allowed for a productive exploration of the intrapsychic dynamics in the patient, underlying the proxy demand. The first two case examples also reflect the active utilization by the analyst of countertransference fantasies associated with the character mesh between the patient and partner, while maintaining the essential frame of the treatment and not yielding to proxy expectations and role enactment demands.

Of course, under certain circumstances, the therapist is pulled into a proxy role vis-à-vis the partner. The dangers of such a role enactment pattern are most clearly illustrated in the fourth case. Although good therapeutic work can be done under such circumstances, there are subtle countertransference forces which can be disruptive to the treatment as well. The therapist becomes much more effective, as she becomes increasingly aware of the projective identificatory forces at work in the proxy role enactment.

Similarly, the patients can also profit from exposure to insights regarding the nature of the proxy evocation tendencies underlying the mesh of character structures with their partner. Thus, a man struggling to curb angry impulses associated with his sadistic character structures became aware during treatment that he was being cunningly cast as the "bad cop" within his family, particularly in relation to his children. His wife, on the other hand, who had a more dependent character structure, always seemed to be cast into the "good cop" role due to her need to be liked by everyone, especially their children. It was interesting to note the relative ease with which this pattern became reversed, as the patient gained insights into the proxy roles he and his wife were enacting.

Such flexibility, changeability, and mutuality of role enactments is characteristic of more maturely differentiated individuals and couples. More rigidly maintained projective identifications and proxy evocation patterns can be discerned in more primitively organized patients and couples. The symbiotic characterological mesh in such couples is typically characterized by rigidly stereotypical role assignments of a complementary nature. Projective identificatory interactions are pervasively evident in such relationships. The therapist treating a patient enmeshed in this primitive form of relationship needs to be constantly alert to proxy evocation patterns between patient and partner, occasionally mirrored in the relationship of patient and therapist.

The concepts of projective identification (Malin and Grotstein, 1966; Ogden, 1982), proxy evocation (Wangh, 1962), and role complementarity (Crisp, 1988), are quite complex and not clearly differentiated from each other. Nevertheless, they have extreme relevance for understanding enactments centering about the meshing character structures of couple partners as they are played out during psychoanalytic treatment. It is the systems theory implications of these constructs which allow for an ultimately more effective conceptualization and handling of pathological enactment demands involving them during individual psychoanalytic treatment.

A number of authors (Kernberg, 1975a; Ganzarain, 1977; Kissen, 1980a) have applied systems theoretical constructs to group psychotherapy interactions. There will be a greater and greater need in the future to apply the notions of boundaries in open and closed systems to couples, family, and individual psychotherapeutic processes. The interrelated issues of complimentary and meshing character structures and the clarifying constructs of projective identification (particularly in the form of proxy evocation maneuvers) will certainly need to be more systematically studied in the future, as well.

The better the individual therapist understands and conceptualizes projective identificatory and proxy evocative interactive mechanisms, the more effectively will she be able to intervene and amelioratively navigate the complex boundaries and reverberating parallel processes connecting individual, couple, family, and group systems. Almost all forms of characterological intervention may ultimately be conceived as moving a relatively closed projective identificatory system toward becoming a more open and less rigidly bounded system. A capable therapist can effectively contain and metabolize projective identifications induced during the course of work with characterologically impaired patients toward such open systems goals.

# CONCLUSION

A contemporary approach to psychoanalytic treatment requires theoretical paradigms regarding affects, object relationships, and character patterns, the three central areas covered in the present volume.

From an affect theoretical perspective, there is the need for an expansion of the continuum of differentiated affects that are the object of study. We no longer can rely upon conceptions solely centered upon negative affects such as anxiety, guilt, and anger and must increasingly shift our attention to a broad and differentiated array of positive affects and affective attitudes such as exhilaration, joy, effectiveness, hopefulness, and courage which have been much too neglected in previous psychoanalytic theorizing.

The cornerstone conceptions regarding conflict stemming from Freud's consistent reliance upon a drive model have needed to be updated both from an expanded affect theoretical and object relational perspective. Our contemporary conceptualizations regarding the complete Oedipus complex (including its preoedipal and negative oedipal manifestations) attain more specificity and clinical utility, when they are viewed from an object relational vantage point emphasizing the paradoxically loyal attachment many patients have to largely dysfunctional introjects having negative affective characteristics.

The projective identificatory and object usage patterns associated with these stubbornly loyal tendencies to cling to repetitive behavior patterns, offer plentiful opportunities for psychic pain. Almost no opportunities for maturely pleasurable ego and self gratifications, however, are offered, and these patterns are frequently at the heart of the psychopathology with which we are daily confronted. This is particularly evident when we are exposed to the repetitive patterns and tenacious resistances manifested by patients with character disorders.

The redundant and therapy-resistant aspects of character structures viewed from affect theoretical and object relational perspectives have been emphasized in the present volume. These can be seen as nostalgic and highly protective forms of object retrieval and memory which are self-perpetuating; despite their severely constricting and restricting impact upon the range of positive affects experientially available. The bulk of our psychoanalytic interventions, therefore, must be geared toward an illumination of these patterns, so that the patient can ultimately free herself of them. The therapist repetitively demonstrates his or her availability as a benignly containing and usable object who does not require the loyalties and protectiveness reactions that were felt to be so necessary in the past. This helps free the patient to tentatively risk newer and more maturationally advanced and pleasurable forms of feelingful experience.

Toxic projective identificatory and object usage patterns can gradually be relinquished, as the patient becomes more and more aware through the transference and countertransference interactions of the therapeutic relationship that the old loyalties and protectiveness reactions are no longer necessary. This, ultimately, allows for a freer experiencing and expression of the diversely differentiated range of positive affects and affective attitudes that have for so long been hidden beneath the characterological pathology manifested by the patient.

# REFERENCES

Alexander, J. M., & Isaacs, K. S. (1963), Seriousness and preconscious affective attitudes. *Internat. J. Psycho-Anal.*, 44:23–30.

——— ——— (1964), The function of affect. *Brit. J. Med. Psychol.*, 37:231–237.

Atwood, G. E., & Stolorow, R. D. (1984), *Structures of Subjectivity*. Hillsdale, NJ: Analytic Press.

Babcock, R., ed. (1976), *Webster's Third New International Dictionary of the English Language, Unabridged Edition*. Springfield, MA: G & C Merriam.

Balint, M. (1968), *The Basic Fault: Therapeutic Aspects of Regression*. New York: Brunner/Mazel.

Barnett, J. (1971), Narcissism and dependency in the obsessive–hysteric marriage. *Fam. Proc.*, 10:75–83.

Basch, M. F. (1976), The concept of affect: A reexamination. *J. Amer. Psychoanal. Assn.*, 24:759–778.

Benjamin, J. (1992), *The Bonds of Love*. New York: Pantheon Books.

Bennis, W. (1976), Defenses against "depressive anxiety" in groups: The case of the absent leader. In: *From Group Dynamics to Group Psychoanalysis*, ed. M. Kissen. New York: John Wiley, pp. 91–118.

Berliner, B. (1958), The role of object relations in moral masochism. *Psychoanal. Quart.*, 27:38–56.

Bertalanffy, L. von (1968), *General Systems Theory: Foundations, Development, Applications*. New York: George Braziller.

Blanck, G. (1984), The complete Oedipus complex. *Internat. J. Psycho-Anal.*, 65:331–339.

Blos, P. (1984), Son and father. *J. Amer. Psychoanal. Assn.*, 32:301–324.

——— (1985), *Son and Father: Before and Beyond the Oedipus Complex.* New York: Free Press.

Blum, A., & Shadduck, C. B. (1991), Object-choice revisited. *Psychoanal. Psychol.*, 8:59–68.

Blum, H. P. (1976), Masochism, the ego ideal, and the psychology of women. *J. Amer. Psychoanal. Assn.*, 24:157–191.

——— (1991), Sadomasochism in the psychoanalytic process, within and beyond the pleasure principle: Discussion. *J. Amer. Psychoanal. Assn.*, 39:431–450.

Bly, R. (1991), *Iron John.* New York: Addison-Wesley.

Bollas, C. (1974), Character: The language of the self. *Internat. J. Psycho-Anal. Psychother.*, 3:397–418.

——— (1987), *The Shadow of the Object: Psychoanalysis of the Unthought Known.* New York: Columbia University Press.

——— (1989), *Forces of Destiny.* London: Free Association Books.

——— (1992), *Being a Character.* New York: Hill & Wang.

Bowlby, J. (1969), *Attachment and Loss,* Vol. 1. New York: Basic Books.

Brenman, M. (1952), On teasing and being teased: The problem of moral masochism. *The Psychoanalytic Study of the Child,* 7:264–285. New York: International Universities Press.

Brenner, C. (1959), The masochistic character: Genesis and treatment. *J. Amer. Psychoanal. Assn.*, 7:197–226.

Brickman, A. S. (1983), Pre-oedipal development of the superego. *Internat. J. Psycho-Anal.*, 64:83–92.

Cath, S. H., Gurwitt, A. R., & Ross, J. M. (1982), *Father and Child: Developmental and Clinical Perspectives.* Boston: Little, Brown.

Chodorow, N. (1978a), *The Reproduction of Mothering. Psychoanalysis and the Sociology of Gender.* Berkeley: University of California Press.

——— (1978b), Mothering, object relations and the female oedipal configuration. *Feminist Studies,* 4:137–158.

Colson, D. (1982), Protectiveness in borderline states: A neglected object relations paradigm. *Bull. Menn. Clinic,* 46:305–319.

Courtois, C. (1987), *Healing the Incest Wound.* New York: W. W. Norton.

Crisp, P. (1988), Projective identification: A clarification in relation to object choice. *Psychoanal. Psychol.,* 5:389–402.

Davies, J., & Frawley, M. G. (1994), *The Psychodynamic Treatment of Adult Survivors of Childhood Sexual Abuse.* New York: Basic Books.

Doidge, N. (1990), Appetitive pleasure states: A biopsychoanalytic model of the pleasure threshold, mental representation, and defense. In: *Pleasure Beyond the Pleasure Principle. The Role of Affect in Motivation, Development and Adaptation,* ed. R. A. Glick & S. Bone. New Haven, CT: Yale University Press, pp. 138–173.

Dorpat, T. L. (1977), Depressive affect. *The Psychoanalytic Study of the Child*, 32:3–27. New Haven, CT: Yale University Press.

Elkind, D. (1991), Instrumental narcissism in parents. *Bull. Menn. Clinic*, 55:299–307.

Emde, R. N. (1983), The prerepresentational self and its affective core. *The Psychoanalytic Study of the Child*, 38:165–192. New Haven, CT: Yale University Press.

—— (1988), Development terminable and interminable. *Internat. J. Psycho-Anal.*, 69:23–42.

Engel, G. L. (1962), Anxiety and depression withdrawal: The primary affects of unpleasure. *Internat. J. Psycho-Anal.*, 43:89–98.

Erikson, E. H. (1950), *Childhood and Society*. New York: W. W. Norton.

—— (1959), Identity and the Life Cycle: Selected Papers. *Psychological Issues*, Monograph 1. New York: International Universities Press.

Fahrion, S. L., & Norris, P. A. (1990), Self-regulation of anxiety. *Bull. Menn. Clinic*, 54:217–231.

Fairbairn, W. R. D. (1952a), *An Object-Relations Theory of the Personality*. New York: Basic Books.

—— (1952b), *Psychoanalytic Studies of the Personality*. London: Routledge & Kegal Paul.

—— (1963), Synopsis of an object-relations theory of the personality. *Internat. J. Psycho-Anal.*, 4:224–225.

Feldman, L. B. (1982), Dysfunctional marital conflict: An integrative interpersonal intrapsychic model. *J. Marital & Fam. Ther.*, 8:417–427.

Feldman, M. (1990), Common ground: The centrality of the Oedipus complex. *Internat. J. Psycho-Anal.*, 71:37–48.

Fenichel, O. (1939), The counter-phobic attitude. *Internat. J. Psycho-Anal.*, 20:263–274.

Frank, G. (1992), Classics revisited: Wilhelm Reich's: "On Character Analysis": *Int. Rev. Psycho-Anal.*, 19:51–56.

Frankiel, R. V. (1991), A note on Freud's inattention to the negative oedipal in Little Hans. *Internat. Rev. Psycho-Anal.*, 18:181–184.

Freud, A. (1936), *The Ego and the Mechanisms of Defense*. New York: International Universities Press, 1966.

Freud, S. (1894), The neuro-psychoses of defence. *Standard Edition*, 3:43–61. London: Hogarth Press, 1962.

—— (1895), Project for a scientific psychology. *Standard Edition*, 1:283–287. London: Hogarth Press, 1966.

—— (1896), Further remarks on the neuro-psychoses of defense. *Standard Edition*, 3:159–185. London: Hogarth Press, 1962.

—— (1905a), Three essays on the theory of sexuality. *Standard Edition*, 7:125–245. London: Hogarth Press, 1957.

——— (1905b), Fragment of an analysis of a case of hysteria. *Standard Edition*, 7:7–122. London: Hogarth Press, 1953.

——— (1909), Analysis of a phobia in a five-year old boy. *Standard Edition*, 10:5–149. London: Hogarth Press, 1955.

——— (1912), The dynamics of the transference. *Standard Edition*, 12:97–108. London: Hogarth Press, 1958.

——— (1914), Remembering, repeating and working through (Further recommendations on the technique of psychoanalysis). *Standard Edition*, 12:123–144. London: Hogarth Press, 1958.

——— (1915a), Instincts and their vicissitudes. *Standard Edition*, 14:117–140. London: Hogarth Press, 1957.

——— (1915b), Repression. *Standard Edition*, 14:141–158. London: Hogarth Press, 1957.

——— (1915c), The unconscious. *Standard Edition*. 14:159–215. London: Hogarth Press, 1957.

——— (1916), Some character types met with in psychoanalytic work. *Standard Edition*, 14:309–331. London: Hogarth Press, 1957.

——— (1917), Mourning and melancholia. *Standard Edition*, 14:243–258. London: Hogarth Press, 1957.

——— (1919), A child is being beaten. *Standard Edition*, 17:179–204. London: Hogarth Press, 1955.

——— (1920), Beyond the pleasure principle. *Standard Edition*, 18:7–64. London: Hogarth Press, 1955.

——— (1921), Group psychology and the analysis of the ego. *Standard Edition*, 18:67–143. London: Hogarth Press, 1955.

——— (1923), The ego and the id. *Standard Edition*, 19:1–66. London: Hogarth Press, 1961.

——— (1924a), The dissolution of the Oedipus Complex. *Standard Edition*, 19:171–179. London: Hogarth Press, 1961.

——— (1924b), The economic problem of masochism. *Standard Edition*, 19:159–170. London: Hogarth Press, 1961.

——— (1925), Some psychical consequences of the anatomical distinction between the sexes. *Standard Edition*, 19:243–258. London: Hogarth Press, 1961.

——— (1926), Inhibitions, symptoms and anxiety. *Standard Edition*, 20:75–175. London: Hogarth Press, 1959.

——— (1931), Female sexuality. *Standard Edition*, 21:221–243. London: Hogarth Press, 1961.

——— (1933), Femininity. *Standard Edition*, 22:112–135. London: Hogarth Press, 1964.

——— (1937), Analysis terminable and interminable. *Standard Edition*, 23:211–253. London: Hogarth Press, 1964.

Galenson, E. (1988), The precursors of masochism: Protomasochism. In: *Masochism, Current Psychoanalytic Perspectives*, ed. R. A. Glick & D. I. Meyers, pp. 189–204.

Ganzarain, R. (1977), General systems theory, object relations and their usefulness in group psychotherapy. *Internat. J. Group Psychother.*, 27:441–456.

Gedo, J. E. (1979), *Beyond Interpretation: Toward a Revised Theory of Psychoanalysis*. New York: International Universities Press.

Gesell, A., & Ilg, F. L. (1943), *Infant and Child in the Culture of Today*. New York: Harper.

Giovacchini, P. (1956), Defensive meaning of a specific anxiety syndrome. *Psychoanal. Rev.*, 43:373–380.

——— (1972), *Tactics and Techniques in Psychoanalytic Therapy*. I. New York: Jason Aronson.

——— (1975a), *Psychoanalysis of Character Disorders*. New York: Jason Aronson.

——— (1975b), *Tactics and Techniques in Psychoanalytic Therapy. Countertransference*. II. New York: Jason Aronson.

——— (1979), *Treatment of Primitive Mental States*. New York: Jason Aronson.

——— (1984a), *Character Disorders and Adaptative Mechanisms*. New York: Jason Aronson.

——— (1984b), Treatment of marital disharmonies: The classical approach. In: *Character Disorders and Adaptative Mechanisms*. New York: Jason Aronson, pp. 221–252.

——— (1984c), Characterological aspects of marital interaction. In: *Character Disorders and Adaptative Mechanisms*. New York: Jason Aronson, pp. 253–260.

——— (1986), *Developmental Disorders. The Transitional Space in Mental Breakdown and Creative Integration*. Northvale, NJ: Jason Aronson.

——— Boyer, B. L. (1967), *Psychoanalytic Treatment of Schizophrenic, Borderline and Characterological Disorders*. New York: Jason Aronson, 1980.

Glick, R. A., & Meyers, D. I. (1988), *Masochism: Current Psychoanalytic Perspectives*. Hillsdale, NJ: Analytic Press.

Greenberg, J. R., & Mitchell, S. A. (1983), *Object Relations in Psychoanalytic Theory*. Cambridge, MA: Harvard University Press.

Greenson, R. R. (1968), Dis-identifying from the mother: Its special importance for the boy. *Internat. J. Psycho-Anal.*, 49:370–374.

Greenspan, S. I. (1977), The oedipal–pre-oedipal dilemma: A reformulation according to object relations theory. *Internat. Rev. Psycho-Anal.*, 4:381–391.

Grinberg, L. (1962), On a specific aspect of countertransference due to the patient's projective identification. *Internat. J. Psycho-Anal.*, 43:436–440.

Guntrip, H. (1968), *Schizoid Phenomena, Object Relations and the Self*. New York: International Universities Press.

Halpern, H. (1964), Psychodynamic and cultural determinants of work inhibition in children and adolescents. *Psychoanal. Rev.*, 53:407–417.

Hartmann, H. (1939), *Ego Psychology and the Problem of Adaptation*. New York: International Universities Press, 1958.

——— (1950), Comments on the psychoanalytic theory of the ego. In: *Essays on Ego Psychology*. New York: International Universities Press, 1964, pp. 113–141.

——— (1964), *Essays on Ego Psychology*. New York: International Universities Press.

——— Loewenstein, R. (1962), Notes on the superego. *The Psychoanalytic Study of the Child*, 17:42–81. New York: International Universities Press.

Heimann, P. (1952), Certain functions of introjection and projection in early infancy. In: *Developments in Psychoanalysis,* ed. M. Klein, P. Heimann, S. Isaacs, & J. Riviere. London: Hogarth Press, pp. 122–168.

Hendrick, I. (1942), Instinct and the ego during infancy. *Psychoanal. Quart.*, 11:33–58.

——— (1943), Work and the pleasure principle. *Psychoanal. Quart.*, 12:311–329.

Herman, J. (1992), *Trauma and Recovery*. New York: Basic Books.

Hoffert, A., & Martisen, E. W. (1990), Exposure-based integrated vs. pure psychodynamic treatment of agoraphobic inpatients. *Psychotherapy*, 27:210–218.

Horner, A. (1979), *Object Relations and the Developing Ego in Therapy*. New York: Jason Aronson.

Horner, M. S. (1970), Femininity and successful achievement: A basic inconsistency. In: *Feminine Personality and Conflict,* ed. J. Bardwick, E. M. Donovan, M. S. Horner, & D. Gutmann. Belmont, CA: Brooks-Cole, pp. 167–188.

——— Walsh, M. (1974), Psychological barriers to success in women. In: *Women and Success,* ed. R. B. Knudsin. New York: William Morrow, pp. 138–145.

Isaacs, K. S. (1980), Feeling bad and feeling badly: Implications of human emotions. Paper presented at the American Psychological Association, Division 39 meeting, Montreal, Canada.

——— (1981), Psychological theory of affect: Revisions, extension and clinical use. Paper presented at the 89th annual convention of the American Psychological Association, Los Angeles, California.

———— (1981b), Crisis intervention and affect theory. Paper presented at the American Psychological Association, Division 29 meeting, San Antonio, Texas.

———— (1982), On affect: Biographical notes on a theory. Paper presented at the 90th annual convention of the American Psychological Association, Washington, DC.

———— (1983), Affect dynamics in the genesis and cure of the classic neurosis. Paper presented at the 91st annual convention of the American Psychological Association, Anaheim, California.

———— (1984a), Affect phobia, affect blindness, and affect dynamics. Paper presented at the American Psychological Association, Division 29 and 42 meeting, San Diego, California.

———— (1984b), Feeling bad and feeling badly. *Psychoanal. Psychol.*, 1:43–60.

———— (1985), On decision making, sensation, perception, affect, and cognition. Paper presented at the 93rd annual convention of the American Psychological Association, Los Angeles, California.

———— (1987), On feeling badly: A biography of a theory. Paper presented at the Chicago School of Professional Psychology, Chicago, Illinois.

———— (1988), A reexamination of the psychoanalytic theory of affect: Implications for treatment. Paper presented at the 96th annual convention of the American Psychological Association, Atlanta, Georgia.

———— (1990), Affect and the fundamental nature of neurosis: Logic and reality. *Psychoanal. Psychol.*, 7:259–284.

———— Haggard, E. A. (1966), Some methods used in the study of affect in psychotherapy. In: *Methods of Research in Psychotherapy*, ed. L. A. Gottshalk & A. H. Auerbach. New York: Appleton-Century Crofts, pp. 226–239.

Jacobs, W. J. (1980), *Roosevelt*. Encino, CA: Glencoe.

Jacobson, E. (1950), Development of the wish for a child in boys. *The Psychoanalytic Study of the Child*, 5:139–152. New York: International Universities Press.

———— (1953), The affects and their pleasure-unpleasure quality in relation to the psychic discharge process. In: *Drives, Affects, and Behavior*, ed. R. M. Lowenstein. New York: International Universities Press.

———— (1964), *The Self and the Object World*. New York: International Universities Press.

———— (1971), *Depression: Comparative Studies of Normal, Neurotic and Psychotic Conditions*. New York: International Universities Press.

Jaffe, D. S. (1968), The masculine envy of woman's procreative function. *J. Amer. Psychoanal. Assn.*, 16:521–548.

———— (1983), Some relations between the negative Oedipus complex and aggression in the male. *J. Amer. Psychoanal. Assn.*, 31:957–984.

Joseph, B. (1982), Addiction to near-death. *Internat. J. Psycho-Anal.*, 63:449–456.

———— (1987), Projective identification: Clinical aspects. In: *Projection, Identification, Projective Identification*, ed. J. Sandler. Madison, CT: International Universities Press, pp. 65–76.

Josephs, L. (1991a), Character structure, self-esteem regulation and the principle of identity maintenance. In: *The Relational Self. Theoretical Convergences in Psychoanalysis and Social Psychology*, ed. R. D. Curtis. New York: Guilford Press, pp. 3–16.

———— (1991b), Courage, character change and the principle of identity maintenance. Paper presented at the 99th Annual Convention of the American Psychological Association, San Francisco, California.

———— (1992), *Character Structure and the Organization of the Self*. New York: Columbia University Press.

Kaftal, E. (1991), On intimacy between men. *Psychoanal. Dialogues*, 1:305–328.

Karme, L. (1979), The analysis of a male patient by a female analyst: The problem of the negative oedipal transference. *Internat. J. Psycho-Anal.*, 60:253–261.

Kaufman, R. V. (1983), Oedipal object relations and morality. *Annual of Psychoanalysis*, 11:345–356. New York: International Universities Press.

Kernberg, O. F. (1975a), A systems approach to priority setting of interventions in groups. *Internat. J. Group Psychother.*, 28:251–275.

———— (1975b), *Borderline Conditions and Pathological Narcissism*. New York: Jason Aronson.

———— (1976a), *Object Relations Theory and Clinical Psychoanalysis*. New York: Jason Aronson.

———— (1976b), Technical considerations in the treatment of borderline personality organization. *J. Amer. Psychoanal. Assn.*, 24:795–829.

———— (1980a), *Internal World and External Reality*. New York: Jason Aronson.

———— (1980b), The couple and the group. In: *Internal World and External Reality*. New York: Jason Aronson, pp. 307–331.

———— (1987), Projection and projective identification: Developmental and clinical aspects. In: *Projection, Identification, Projective Identification*, ed. J. Sandler. Madison, CT: International Universities Press, pp. 93–115.

———— (1991a), Aggression and love in the relationship of the couple. *J. Amer. Psychoanal. Assn.*, 39:45–70.

────── (1991b), Sadomasochism, sexual exitement, and perversion. *J. Amer. Psychoanal. Assn.*, 39:333–362.

Kestenberg, J. (1956), On the development of maternal feelings in early childhood. *The Psychoanalytic Study of the Child*, 11:257–291. New York: International Universities Press.

Kissen, M., ed. (1976), *From Group Dynamics to Group Psychoanalysis.* New York: John Wiley.

────── (1980a), General systems theory: Practical and theoretical implications for group intervention. *Group*, 4:29–39.

────── (1980b), Therapeutic use of self and object representations in the treatment of character disorders. Adelphi University, Garden City, New York. Typescript.

────── (1992), Essential connections between the individual and the group. Invited lecture presented at the Japanese Group Psychotherapy Association Meeting, Tokyo, Japan, April 18.

Klein, M. (1940), Mourning and its relation to manic depressive states. *Internat. J. Psycho-Anal.*, 21:125–154.

────── (1946), Notes on some schizoid mechanisms. *Internat. J. Psycho-Anal.*, 27:99–110.

Kohut, H. (1971), *The Analysis of the Self.* New York: International University Press.

────── (1977), *The Restoration of the Self.* New York: International Universities Press.

────── Wolf, E. S. (1978), The disorders of the self and their treatment. An outline. *Internat. J. Psycho-Anal.*, 59:413–425.

Krystal, H. (1974), The genetic development of affects and affect regression. *The Annual of Psychoanalysis*, 2:98–126. New York: International Universities Press.

────── (1978), Self-representation and the capacity for self-care. *The Annual of Psychoanalysis*, 6:209–247. New York: International Universities Press.

────── (1982a), Alexithymia and the effectiveness of psychoanalytic treatment. *Internat. J. Psychoanal. Psychother.*, 9:353–388.

────── (1982b), The activating aspect of emotions. *Psychoanal. & Contemp. Thought*, 5:605–642.

────── (1988), *Integration and Self-Healing. Affects, Trauma, Alexithimia.* Hillsdale, NJ: Analytic Press.

Langs, R. (1976), *The Bipersonal Field.* New York: Jason Aronson.

Loewenstein, R. (1957), A contribution to the psychoanalytic theory of masochism. *J. Amer. Psychoanal. Assn.*, 5:197–234.

Mahler, M. (1952), On child psychosis and schizophrenia: Autistic and symbiotic infantile psychoses. *The Psychoanalytic Study of the Child*, 7:286–305. New York: International Universities Press.

———— (1967), On human symbiosis and the vicissitudes of individuation. *J. Amer. Psycho-Anal. Assn.*, 15:740–763.

Malin, A., & Grotstein, J. S. (1966), Projective identification and the therapeutic process. *Internat. J. Psycho-Anal.*, 47:26–31.

Marks, I. M. (1987), *Fears, Phobias and Rituals. Panic, Anxiety and Their Disorders.* New York: Oxford University Press.

May, R. (1975), *The Courage to Create.* New York: W. W. Norton.

McBride, J. (1992), *The Catastrophe of Success.* New York: Simon & Schuster.

McDougall, J. (1982), *Theaters of the Mind: Illusion and Truth on the Psychoanalytic Stage.* New York: Basic Books, 1985.

———— (1984), The "dis-affected" patient: Reflections on affect pathology. *Psychoanal. Quart.*, 53:386–409.

———— (1989), *Theaters of the Body.* New York: W. W. Norton.

Meehl, P. E. (1975), Hedonic capacity: Some conjectures. *Bull. Menn. Clinic*, 30:295–307.

Meissner, W. W. (1983), Notes on the levels of differentiation within borderline conditions. *Psychoanal. Rev.*, 70:179–209.

Menaker, E. (1953), Masochism, a defense reaction of the ego. *Psychoanal. Quart.*, 22:205–225.

Meyers, H. (1988), A consideration of treatment techniques in relation to the functions of masochism. In: *Masochism, Current Psychoanalytic Perspectives*, ed. R. A. Glick & D. I. Meyers. Hillsdale, NJ: Analytic Press, pp. 175–188.

Mittelman, B. (1954), Motility in infants, children, and adults. *The Psychoanalytic Study of the Child*, 9:142–177. New York: International Universities Press.

Moulton, R. (1986), Professional success: A conflict for women. In: *Psychoanalysis and Women. Contemporary Reappraisals*, ed. J. L. Alpert. New York: Analytic Press, pp. 161–181.

Nelson, M. C. (1962a), *Paradigmatic Approaches to Psychoanalysis: Four Papers.* New York: Department of Psychology, Stuyvesant Polyclinic Reports in Medical and Clinical Psychology.

———— (1962b), Effect of paradigmatic techniques on the psychic economy of borderline patients. In: *Paradigmatic Approaches to Psychoanalysis: Four Papers*, ed. M. C. Nelson. New York: Department of Psychology, Stuyvesant Polyclinic Reports in Medical and Clinical Psychology, pp. 25–50.

———— (1962c), Externalization of the toxic introject: A treatment technique for borderline cases. In: *Paradigmatic Approaches to Psychoanalysis: Four Papers*, ed. M. C. Nelson. New York: Department of Psychology,

Stuyvesant Polyclinic Reports in Medical and Clinical Psychology, pp. 17–24.

—— Nelson, B. (1957), Paradigmatic psychotherapy in borderline treatment. *Psychoanalysis*, 5:28–44.

Newman, C. J., Dember, C. F., & Krug, O. (1973), "He can but he won't." A psychodynamic study of so-called "gifted underachievers." *The Psychoanalytic Study of the Child*, 28:83–129. New Haven, CT: Yale University Press.

Novey, S. (1958), Further considerations on affect theory in psychoanalysis. *Internat. J. Psycho-Anal.*, 42:21–32.

Novick, J. (1982), Termination: Themes and issues. *Psychoanal. Inqu.*, 2:329–365.

—— Novick, K. K. (1972), Beating fantasies in children. *Internat. J. Psycho-Anal.*, 53:237–242.

—— —— (1987), The essence of masochism. *The Psychoanalytic Study of the Child*, 42:353–384. New Haven, CT: International Universities Press.

—— —— (1991), Some comments on masochism and the delusion of omnipotence from a developmental perspective. *J. Amer. Psychoanal. Assn.*, 39:307–331.

Nydes, J. (1963), The paranoid-masochistic character. *Psychoanal. Rev.*, 50:215–251.

Ogden, T. S. (1979), On projective identification. *Internat. J. Psycho-Anal.*, 60:357–373.

—— (1982), *Projective Identification and Psychotherapeutic Technique*. New York: Jason Aronson.

—— (1986), *The Matrix of the Mind*. Northvale, NJ: Jason Aronson.

—— (1989), *The Primitive Edge of Experience*. Northvale, NJ: Jason Aronson.

Panken, S. (1973), *The Joy of Suffering*. New York: Jason Aronson.

Pasnau, R. O., & Bystritsky, A. (1990), An overview of anxiety disorders. *Bull. Menn. Clinic*, 54:157–170.

Piaget, J. (1936), *The Origins of Intelligence in Children*. New York: International Universities Press, 1952.

Pine, F. (1979), On the expansion of the affect array. *Bull. Menn. Clinic*, 43:79–95.

Prince, R. M. (1984), Courage and masochism in psychotherapy. *Psychoanal. Rev.*, 71:47–61.

Rapaport, D. (1953a), On the psychoanalytic theory of affects. In: *The Collected Papers of David Rapaport*, ed. M. M. Gill. New York: Basic Books, 1967, pp. 476–512.

————— (1953b), On the theory of affect. *Internat. J. Psycho-Anal.*, 34:117–198.

————— (1960), The Structure of Psychoanalytic Theory. A Systematizing Attempt. *Psychological Issues*, Monograph 6. New York: International Universities Press.

————— (1967), *The Collected Papers of David Rapaport*, ed. M. Gill. New York: Basic Books.

Reich, W. (1933), *Character Analysis*, 3rd ed. New York: Noonday Press, 1949.

Reik, T. (1941), *Masochism in Modern Man*. New York: Farrar & Strauss.

Rinsley, D. B. (1984), A comparison of borderline and narcissistic personality disorders. *Bull. Menn. Clinic*, 48:1–9.

Rosenbaum, J. F. (1990), A psychopharmacologist's perspective on panic disorder. *Bull. Menn. Clinic*, 54:184–198.

Rosenberg, E. (1949), Anxiety and the capacity to bear it. *Internat. J. Psycho-Anal.*, 30:1–12.

Rosenfeld, H. (1988), On masochism: A theoretical and clinical approach. In: *Masochism, Current Psychoanalytic Perspectives*, ed. R. A. Glick & D. I. Meyers. Hillsdale, NJ: Analytic Press, pp. 151–174.

Ruderman, E. B. (1986), Creative and reparative uses of countertransference by women psychotherapists treating women patients: A clinical research study. In: *The Psychology of Today's Woman. New Psychoanalytic Visions*, ed. T. Bernay & W. Cantor. New York: Analytic Press, pp. 339–363.

Russell, B. (1980), *Second Wind*. New York: Ballantine Books.

Sandler, J. (1960), On the concept of the superego. *The Psychoanalytic Study of the Child*, 15:128–162. New York: International Universities Press.

————— (1976), Countertransference and role-responsiveness. *Internat. Rev. Psycho-Anal.*, 3:43–47.

————— (1987a), *From Safety to Superego*. New York: Guilford Press.

————— (1987b), *Projection, Identification, Projective Identification*. Madison, CT: International Universities Press.

Schachter, J. (1992), Concepts of post-termination patient-analyst contact. *Internat. J. Psycho-Anal.*, 73:137–154.

Schafer, R. (1954), *Psychoanalytic Interpretation in Rorschach Testing*. New York: Grune & Stratton.

————— (1960), The loving and beloved superego in Freud's structural theory. *The Psychoanalytic Study of the Child*, 15:163–188. New York: International Universities Press.

————— (1964), The clinical analysis of affect. *J. Amer. Psychoanal. Assn.*, 12:275–300.

——— (1967), Ideals, the ego ideal and the ideal self. In: *Motives and Thought: Psychoanalytic Essays in Memory of David Rapaport*, ed. R. R. Holt. *Psychological Issues*, Monograph 18/19. New York: International Universities Press.

——— (1973), Termination. *Internat. J. Psychoanal. Psychother.*, 2:135–148.

——— (1976), *A New Language for Psychoanalysis*. New Haven, CT: Yale University Press.

——— (1983), The imprisoned analysand. In: *The Analytic Attitude*, ed. R. Schafer. New York: Basic Books, pp. 257–280.

——— (1984), The pursuit of failure and the idealization of unhappiness. *Amer. Psycholog.*, 39:398–405.

——— (1988), Those wrecked by success. In: *Masochism: Current Psychoanalytic Perspectives*, ed. R. A. Glick & D. I. Meyers. Hillsdale, NJ: Analytic Press, pp. 81–91.

Scharff, D. E., & Scharff, J. S. (1987), *Object Relations Family Therapy*. Northvale, NJ: Jason Aronson.

——— ——— (1991), *Object Relations Couple Therapy*. Northvale, NJ: Jason Aronson.

Scharff, J. S. (1992), *Projective and Introjective Identification and the Use of the Therapist's Self*. Northvale, NJ: Jason Aronson.

Schmale, A. H., Jr. (1964), A genetic view of affects: With special reference to the genesis of helplessness and hopelessness. *The Psychoanalytic Study of the Child*, 19:287–310. New York: International Universities Press.

Schur, M. (1953), The ego in anxiety. In: *Drives, Affects, and Behavior*, Vol. 1, ed. R. M. Lowenstein. New York: International Universities Press.

——— (1969), Affects and cognition. *Internat. J. Psycho-Anal.*, 50:647–653.

Searles, H. (1975), The patient as therapist to the analyst. In: *Tactics and Techniques in Psychoanalytic Therapy*, Vol. 2, ed. P. L. Giovacchini. New York: Jason Aronson, pp. 95–151.

——— (1979), *Countertransference and Related Subjects—Selected Papers*. New York: International Universities Press.

Shapiro, D. (1965), *Neurotic Styles*. New York: Basic Books.

——— (1989), *Psychotherapy of Neurotic Character*. New York: Basic Books.

Simon, B. (1991), Is the Oedipus complex still the cornerstone of psychoanalysis: Three obstacles to answering the question. *J. Amer. Psychoanal. Assn.*, 39:641–668.

Smith, W. H. (1990), Hypnosis in the treatment of anxiety. *Bull. Menn. Clinic*, 54:209–216.

Spotnitz, H. (1969), *Modern Psychoanalysis of the Schizophrenic Patient: Theory of the Technique*. New York: Grune & Stratton.

—— (1976), *Psychotherapy of Pre-oedipal Conditions*. New York: Jason Aronson.

Stein, J., & Urdang, L., eds. (1967), *Random House Dictionary of the English Language, Unabridged Edition*. New York: Random House.

Stern, D. N. (1985), *The Interpersonal World of the Infant*. New York: Basic Books.

Stolorow, R., & Atwood, G. E. (1979), *Faces in a Cloud: Subjectivity in Personality Theory*. New York: Jason Aronson.

—— Brandchaft, B., & Atwood, G. (1987), *Psychoanalytic Treatment: An Intersubjective Approach*. Hillsdale, NJ: Analytic Press.

—— Lachmann, R. M. (1980), *Psychoanalysis of Developmental Arrests, Theory and Treatment*. New York: International Universities Press.

Strean, H. S. (1970a), *New Approaches in Child Guidance*. Metuchen, NJ: Scarecrow Press.

—— (1970b), The use of the patient as consultant. In: *New Approaches in Child Guidance,* ed. H. S. Strean. Metuchen, NJ: Scarecrow Press, pp. 53–63.

Sugarman, A. (1991), Developmental antecedents of masochism: Vignettes from the analysis of a 3 year old girl. *Internat. J. Psycho-Anal.*, 72:107–116.

Tessman, L. H. (1983), A note on the father's contribution to the daughter's ways of loving and working. In: *Father and Child: Developmental and Clinical Perspectives,* ed. S. H. Cath, A. R. Gurwitt, & J. M. Ross. Boston: Little, Brown, pp. 219–238.

Ticho, E. E. (1972), Termination of psychoanalysis: Treatment goals, life goals. *Psychoanal. Quart.*, 41:315–333.

Tolpin, M. (1971), On the beginning of the cohesive self: An application of the concept of transmuting internalization to the study of the transitional object and signal anxiety. *The Psychoanalytic Study of the Child,* 26:316–354. New Haven, CT: Yale University Press.

Tyson, R. L. (1991), The emergence of oedipal centrality. Comments on Michael Feldman's paper 'Common ground: The centrality of the Oedipus complex.' *Internat. J. Psycho-Anal.*, 72:39–44.

Viorst, J. (1982), Experiences of loss at the end of analysis: The analyst's response to termination. *Psychoanal. Inqu.*, 2:399–418.

Wangh, N. (1962), The "Evocation of a Proxy." A psychological maneuver, its use as a defense, its purposes and genesis. *The Psychoanalytic Study of the Child,* 17:451–472. New York: International Universities Press.

Weiss, J., Sampson, H., & the Mount Zion Psychotherapy Research Group (1986), *The Psychoanalytic Process: Theory, Clinical Observation and Empirical Research.* New York: Guilford Press.

White, R. W. (1959), Motivation reconsidered: The concept of competence. *Psycholog. Rev., 66:297–333.*

———— (1960), Competence and the psychosexual stages of development. In: *Nebraska Symposium on Motivation,* ed. M. R. Jones. Lincoln, NE: University of Nebraska Press, pp. 97–141.

———— (1963), Ego and Reality in Psychoanalytic Theory. *Psychological Issues,* Monograph 3. New York: International Universities Press.

Williams, T. (1945), *The Glass Menagerie.* New York: New Directions.

Winnicott, D. W. (1947), Hate in the countertransference. In: *Collected Papers: Through Pediatrics to Psychoanalysis.* New York: Basic Books, 1958, pp. 194–203.

———— (1956), Primary maternal preoccupation. In: *Through Pediatrics to Psycho-Analysis.* London: Hogarth Press, 1958.

———— (1960), Ego distortion in terms of true and false self. In: *The Maturational Processes and the Facilitating Environment.* New York: International Universities Press, 1965, pp. 140–152.

———— (1963), The capacity for concern. In: *The Maturational Processes and the Facilitating Environment.* New York: International Universities Press, 1965, pp. 73–82.

———— (1965), *The Maturational Processes and the Facilitating Environment.* New York: International Universities Press.

———— (1968), The use of an object. In: *Playing and Reality.* New York: Basic Books, 1971, pp. 86–94.

———— (1971), *Playing and Reality.* New York: Basic Books.

Zerbe, K. J. (1990), Through the storm: Psychoanalytic theory in the psychotherapy of anxiety disorders. *Bull. Menn. Clinic, 54:171–183.*

Zetzel, E. (1949), Anxiety and the capacity to bear it. *Internat. J. Psycho-Anal., 30:1–12.*

———— (1965), Depression and the incapacity to bear it. In: *Drives, Affects, Behavior,* ed. M. Schur. New York: International Universities Press, pp. 243–274.

# NAME INDEX

251

# SUBJECT INDEX

255

194
Self-idealization, 211
Self-mastery, emerging sense of, 60–61
Self-potential
  ability to express, 134–135
  loss of, 129–130
Self-potentiating action, 18
Self-regulation, 63–64
  for phobic situations, 47
  predisposition for, 65
Self relation function, 17
Self representations, 10–12
  cluster of, 32
  dissociated, 115, 218–219
  encounters with, 114–116
  false, 129–130
  fragmenting of, 36
  negative, 32
  pathological, 146–147
  projected, 108–114
  therapeutic use of, 103–120
Self-signals, 18–19, 20
  desomatization and cognitive articulation
    of, 20
Self-soothing, 17
  development of, 18–19
  externalization of, 41
  incapacity for, 38
  internalization of, 145
  need to internalize, 39–42
  self-regulation and, 64
Self theory, 36–37
Selfobject, good and bad, 19–20
Sensorimotor learning, 59
Separation-individuation, 130, 138
  abandonment depression and, 132–133
  failure of, 188
  valuing of, 141
Sexual abuse, 117–118, 137–138
Shock theory, 73–74
Signal
  affect as, 4, 6–7, 15, 74, 91
  affective, 14–15
  assessment of, 21
  informative, 19

Signal anxiety theory, 6, 44, 98, 152, 170,
    185
Social courage, 93, 95–96
Social fittedness, 64
Social learning, 159
Sociopathic personality, 41
Splitting, 21, 33, 104–105, 126
  introversion and, 125
  masochism and, 30–32
  in narcissism and borderline disorder, 188
Static characterological patterns, 191–203
Structural constructs, 13–15
Subjective experience, 18
Sublimations, masochistic, 27–28
Success-wrecking tendencies, 27–28, 213–
    214
Suffering, entrenched psychic, 213–214. See
    also Depression; Masochism
Superego
  in affect control, 9
  evolution of, 125–126
  externalized, 210–211
  internalized monitoring and, 131
  maturation of, 210
  in oedipal developmental crisis, 187
  pathological, 12, 212–213
  protective aspects of, 127–128
  punitive, 27–28, 132
  rigid structures of, 187–188
  structural constructs of, 13
Survivor guilt, 132–133

Tension
  increment of, 57
  intra- and intersystemic, 9
  reduction of, 16–17
Termination
  decision for, 141–150
  literature on, 145
Terrible two's, 60–61
Therapeutic alliance, positive, 170–171
Therapeutic dialogue, 111
Therapeutic dyadic system, 111
Therapeutic encounters
  with object representations, 116–119